SIMILE AND IDENTITY IN OVID'S *METAMORPHOSES*

Nulli sua forma manebat. The world of Ovid's *Metamorphoses* is marked by constant flux in which nothing keeps its original form. This book argues that Ovid uses the epic simile to capture states of unresolved identity – in the transition between human, animal, and divine identity, as well as in the poem's textual ambivalence between genres and the negotiation of fiction and reality. In conjuring up a likeness, the mental image of the simile enters a dialectic of appearances in a visually complex and treacherous universe. Original and subtle close readings of episodes in the poem, from Narcissus to Adonis, from Diana's blush to the freeform dreams in the House of Sleep, trace the simile's potential for exploiting indeterminacy and immateriality. In its protean permutations the simile touches on the most profound issues of the poem – the nature of humanity and divinity and the essence of poetic creation.

MARIE LOUISE VON GLINSKI is Assistant Professor and Faculty Fellow in the Classics Department of New York University.

SIMILE AND IDENTITY IN OVID'S *METAMORPHOSES*

MARIE LOUISE VON GLINSKI

CAMBRIDGE
UNIVERSITY PRESS

CAMBRIDGE
UNIVERSITY PRESS

University Printing House, Cambridge CB2 8BS, United Kingdom

Cambridge University Press is part of the University of Cambridge.

It furthers the University's mission by disseminating knowledge in the pursuit of education, learning and research at the highest international levels of excellence.

www.cambridge.org
Information on this title: www.cambridge.org/9781316623596

First published 2012
First paperback edition 2016

A catalogue record for this publication is available from the British Library

ISBN 978-0-521-76096-6 Hardback
ISBN 978-1-316-62359-6 Paperback

Contents

Acknowledgments

This book began as a 2009 Princeton University dissertation. Thanks belong to my dissertation committee: Denis Feeney, Andrew Feldherr, and Bob Kaster.

My debt of gratitude to my advisor Denis Feeney goes back a long time; the imprinting shows everywhere. His faith in me has at times exceeded my own.

Andrew Feldherr kept his sang-froid and gave generous comments while working on his own book on Ovid.

Bob Kaster had the splendid magnanimity of becoming a converted skeptic.

Thanks to my editor Michael Sharp and the staff at Cambridge University Press, especially Liz Hanlon and Jo Lane, and to the two readers of the Press for their feedback.

Thanks also goes to Ivan Eubanks for his valuable help with the index.

Grazie to my husband Michele Cabrini for his moral support.

Introduction

HAMLET: Do you see yonder cloud that's almost in shape of a camel?
POLONIUS: By th' mass, and 'tis: like a camel, indeed.
HAMLET: Methinks it is like a weasel.
POLONIUS: It is backed like a weasel.
HAMLET: Or like a whale.
POLONIUS: Very like a whale.

Shakespeare, *Hamlet* III.ii.365–70[1]

The subject of this book is the simile in Ovid's *Metamorphoses*. For readers familiar with the epic similes of Homer, Virgil, or Milton this might seem an eccentric choice. The epic simile is defined through its grand lineage, deriving much of its force from the sweeping architecture of these epics, as it builds a superstructure of imagery that makes the cosmos reflect human fate, whether in mass scenes or in the concentrated psychology of a single hero. In comparison, Ovid's epic looks like a complicated tangle of tales that overwhelms the reader with the visual detail of mythical landscapes and bizarre transformations, threatening to render superfluous the similes' illustrating properties and drown their impact in episodes of limited reach. Parody and imitation, those banes of Ovidian scholarship, seem the only viable explanations for Ovid's use of the figure. For those not so easily satisfied, the problem may be turned on its head: how *does* the simile react with this new context? This epic which is not quite an epic, containing characters that transform into and not merely resemble animals, poses a unique challenge for the poet, as well as a chance for a reader to reflect on the essential aspect of the *Metamorphoses*: identity.

Simile and metamorphosis share obvious affinities in their preoccupation with manipulating shape, either physically or mentally. In finding similarities in disparate entities, in seeing one thing as another, both highlight the importance of surface impressions for construing identity.

[1] Wells, S. and Taylor, G. (eds.) *William Shakespeare: The Complete Works*, 2nd edn, Oxford, 2005.

Metamorphosis may even be seen as carrying simile to an extreme: if one thing can look like another, what keeps it from actually being another thing altogether, or prevents it from sliding from resemblance into sameness? While in metamorphosis the transformation is permanent and locked in the physical reality of the changed body, the suggestive power of the simile affects the perception of the thing compared without physically changing it. The relation of these two positions forms the core of this study that explores the status of the simile in Ovid's *Metamorphoses*, a poem about "forms changed into new bodies" (*In nova fert animus mutatas dicere formas/ corpora, Met.* 1.1–2).

Forms and bodies, like style and substance, make an artificial conceptual pair that suggests the desire and even the possibility of separating one from the other. However, scholars such as Pianezzola, Rosati, Barkan, Schmidt, Tissol, and Hardie [2] have drawn attention to the link between the figurative language of the poem and some of its central problems. This book follows their lead, taking as starting point the structure of the simile itself, in the connection and divide between tenor and vehicle that captures a tension based on both similarity and contrast. While the simile seems at first to be concerned with likeness, it is as vital (sometimes even more so) to see the contrast, the difference that counteracts the tendency to sameness and closure.[3] Identity emerges as the central issue, of how it is construed and undermined, and what role likeness plays in its formation and perception. While the first two chapters deal with human and divine identity, and thus deal chiefly with the characters in the poem, the last two chapters concern the form of the poem itself in discussing its genre and its fictional status. The question of identity may then be asked not only of an individual but also of a genre or a poem: what constitutes epic, and do generic markers like the simile affect more than the surface? How do we discern the illusions of the fictional world from those of our own, and how does Ovid's fiction relate to our experience of reality given the poem's aetiological claims?

Ovid's *Metamorphoses*, a poem that rejects categorization at every turn, poses the unique challenge for interpreting the simile in context, and one that has hitherto defied attempts at offering a unified theory on its role. In contrast to the epics of his predecessors, Ovid's poem does not yield, or even make desirable, a consistent pattern. Models of reading the simile

[2] Pianezzola (1979), Rosati (1983), Barkan (1986), Schmidt (1991), Tissol (1997), and Hardie (1999, 2002, 2004).

[3] Feeney (1992), 36–7.

as expression of sustained imagery, as in Homer, Virgil, and Apollonius, may not be used in the context of the *Metamorphoses*. The absence of a single hero or sustained martial action precludes associations of specific animals with an individual or group (as in Homer's lion similes),[4] while the episodic structure of the narrative, with its variety of range and tone, precludes a consistent set of imagery being used to reinforce a moral message (as in the bestialization of Turnus).[5]

It would render Ovid's multifaceted poem a disservice to conduct business as usual. Of the surprisingly few studies that have been undertaken, the earlier ones restrict themselves to classifying Ovid's similes according to his models and subject matter.[6] Even Brunner's study which attempts to find the difference between Ovid's epic and elegiac similes leans heavily on formal criteria, such as length and source material.[7] On a different plane, the idea of relating the poem's figurative language, including metaphor, to its subject, metamorphosis, led to the concept of protometamorphosis, a term coined by Barkan[8] and later developed fully in Kaufhold's study, which regards figurative language as a preliminary stage that prepares the reader for the ensuing transformation.[9] While the idea that metamorphosis is the result of reified figurative language has been accepted widely, the linearity of this argument misses the complexities and contradictions of the *Metamorphoses*. By considering metaphor, rather than simile, central to the interpretation of metamorphosis, previous scholarship has largely neglected the lack of resolution in the ambiguous nature of the transformed victim. The mismatched outside and inside of a person leads to conflicting emotions, social status, and behavior, all of them prolonged in perpetuity. The simile's openness offers a way to capture such contradictions and explore their meaning.

Instead of following more conventional treatments, it is profitable to look at simile as a key to the poem that opens new avenues of interpretation. To this end, the discussion clusters around four chapter headings, each representing a central issue in scholarship on the *Metamorphoses* today, showing how the flexibility of the figure adapts to a variety of purposes. In each, the simile functions as a point of departure for reading a particular episode in the light of wider debates. Close readings of a select

[4] Lonsdale (1990). [5] Hornsby (1970).

[6] Washietl (1883), Owen (1931), Wilkins (1932), and Richardson (1964).

[7] Brunner (1966, 1971) and von Albrecht (1999), 166–77 examine the function of the simile in its narrative context but view Ovid mostly through Homeric and Virgilian precedent.

[8] Barkan (1986), 20. [9] Kaufhold (1993, 1997).

choice of similes mark the simile as a unique place for reflecting on the issues of its immediate and wider context.

The first chapter looks at the phenomenon of metamorphosis through the lens of the simile as it brings out the lack of resolution and clarity in both the process and the end result of the transformation. Previous scholarship has linked the figurative language of the poem to its subject matter, as signaled by the considerable overlap of the vocabulary of metamorphosis with that of several rhetorical figures.[10] The privileged status of metaphor over the simile in this debate has created an imbalance that needs to be rectified. Noting the fundamental difference between metaphor and simile allows for a different perception of metamorphosis. Using metaphor as model reinforces the finality of metamorphosis, mirroring the distortion of the transformed body in the distortion of the language. Simile, by contrast, puts two shapes in relation to each other but leaves their essential identity untouched. The comparison "A (tenor) is like B (vehicle)" necessitates keeping both shapes in view. Thanks to its bipartite structure, simile captures the inherent tension in both the process of transition from one body to the other and the hybrid being that is part human, part non-human. As a result, metamorphosis may be viewed as a potentially open phenomenon that resists classification or closure.

This theoretical introduction prefaces close readings of episodes that highlight the tension inherent in metamorphosis through the use of simile. Three episodes stand out in which the perception of the body as marker of human identity for oneself and others is threatened by metamorphosis and dismemberment: Actaeon, Pentheus, and Orpheus. Actaeon undergoes metamorphosis as a deer, Pentheus is perceived as a boar by Agave, and Orpheus, despite being recognizably human, is torn apart by animal-like maenads. The dehumanizing treatment is countered by the simile, adding another visual dimension to scenes full of delusion and mental conflict as the reader recreates the scene before his inner eye. Layers of identity are equally central to the metamorphosis of Hyacinthus which refutes the theory of protometamorphosis (that is, simile as dress rehearsal for the later transformation). Rather than confirming an essential continuity between the victim and the later flower, the simile shows that the conventional markers of his person are not sufficient for establishing his individual identity. This latent instability also becomes palpable in instances in which the simile interferes at the exact moment of

[10] Ahl (1985), Hardie (2002), 228.

transformation, in which both the before and after shape are held in balance. The simile comments on three different ways (art, science, magic) to account for the mystery of metamorphosis.

The second chapter focuses on the divine in the poem and the question of both their disguise and true identity. Complementary to the first chapter, the role of appearance in construing and visualizing divine identity is explored. In particular, the collusion of divine and animal as non-human "other" forms the focus of a series of similes that have the god in the tenor of the simile. The first part of the chapter concerns the relation of gods and birds in sharing the air, an area that is taboo for humans, and in their close visual resemblance. As point of departure, the scholiasts' critique of the gods as birds in the Homeric poems marks the ambivalent status of these animals as potential manifestations of the divine which leads to a new reading of the Icarus episode. In the following section, a thematically linked series of similes about gods and bulls culminates in a discussion on the role of the god in sacrifice and the roles of man, animal, and divine in this triangle. The chapter concludes with a discussion of instances of epiphany in which the true form of the divine is approximated by the simile.

The third chapter concerns the intrinsic genre value of the epic simile. The simile as epic agent in a generically diverse poem accentuates the interaction of epic with other genres. The chapter shows the interaction of the epic simile with other genres, namely elegy and tragedy, as well its constitutive role for epic itself. The Ceyx episode examines how Ovid manipulates the form of the epic simile through exaggeration and reversal of tenor and vehicle. The Hecuba episode shows how tragic and epic elements reinforce each other as allusion through the simile works in guiding genre expectations. An examination of the episode of Apollo and Daphne shows the consequences of epicizing the erotic in the paradox of amatory epic, while Achilles' unsuccessful battle with Cycnus critically views the aesthetics of war as a key ingredient to the enjoyment of epic.

The fourth chapter examines how simile engages with the issue of fictionality. Since similes are the domain of the reader even when they are ostensibly focalized by a character inside fiction, they serve as a bridge between the inside and the outside of the poem. Similes are shown as a screen that both allows and withholds access to the image of Narcissus' subjective viewing. The mirror image poses an ekphrastic dilemma for the narrator and reader as sameness cannot be recreated by likeness. The following section on fictional belief discusses the dreams in the House of Sleep as a matter of depicting mental processes and analyses the reader's gradual engagement with the fictional world. The ephemeral nature of the simile perfectly captures the illusionist character of dreams. A final discussion on anachronism in the simile notes the disruption of the fictional illusion as it reveals the contemporary reader as a presence in the text and highlights the effects of audience manipulation.

CHAPTER I

Metamorphosis and simile

At the end of his life and far from Thebes, the hero Cadmus ponders his misfortunes. He concludes that it might all be the result of the sacred serpent he killed at the founding of the city and prays to the gods to atone for his deed (*Met.* 4.584–6):

> 'Quem si cura deum tam certa vindicat ira
> Ipse precor serpens in longam porrigar alvum!'
> Dixit et ut serpens in longam tenditur alvum ...

"If the care of the gods avenged it with such surefire wrath, I pray that I be stretched out into a long belly, a serpent!" He spoke and was stretched like a serpent into a long belly.

Cadmus' prayer is answered immediately through the near repetition in the next line as he is stretched like a serpent (*ut serpens*), beginning the gradual but unrelenting process of metamorphosis by an assimilation of form. There is a peculiar horror in witnessing this gradual takeover of the outer hide, for the bystander as well as for the victim himself. Metamorphosis plays what appears to be a cruel trick on the assured dominance of mind over body – and by extension human over animal. While Cadmus begs his wife Harmonia to touch whatever is left of him (*dumque aliquid superest de me, me tange*, 584), she protests in vain for him to shed his costume (*his exue monstris*, 591). Within a few lines, the human being Cadmus has slid from being like a serpent into actually being one and yet he/it does not behave like one, slithering into his wife's bosom as if it/he recognized her (*veluti cognosceret*, 596). Where is Cadmus, and what is he?

Ovid's choice of metamorphosis as the dominating feature of his poem may be called an inspired narratological device for organizing the heterogeneous corpus of Greek and Roman myth, with the theme of perpetual change making it possible to connect disparate subjects, perspectives, and modes. In addition, the dynamic of these continuous transformations helps to propel the narrative forward by seemingly natural association rather than a coherently constructed plot.[1] Besides its usefulness as an organizing idea, however, the ubiquitous role of metamorphosis in the poem as well as its adaptability to almost any myth poses the challenge of interpreting the phenomenon itself. Hermann Fränkel was the first to suggest that metamorphosis should be read psychologically as the expression of a "wavering identity" whose root he saw in the conflict between pagan and Christian belief,[2] and other attempts at defining the significance of metamorphosis in terms of psychology and philosophy continue to be made. Solodow for example proposed metamorphosis as the expression of inner psychological states, a position that is found in much of current literature. He writes:

> It is – and this constitutes a central paradox for the poem – a change which preserves, an alteration which maintains identity, a change of form by which content becomes represented in form.[3]

For Solodow, metamorphosis brings out the essential nature of the human being, a clarification of his or her most prominent characteristic. And yet, for every raising of content to the surface, the human identity of the victim is also erased, leading to a loss of individuality. Solodow's thesis, like the more encompassing thesis of Schmidt that sees metamorphosis as metaphor for the human psyche,[4] has the disadvantage of working mostly for established characteristics of non-human objects. Thus the characteristic nature of a wolf, a rock, a spider maps easily onto the fates of Lycaon, Niobe, and Arachne, whereas the change of shape for Daphne, Callisto, or Arethusa, for example, seems random and reveals nothing about the person underneath. The relation of content to surface remains ambiguous, as appearances can be as deceiving as they are clarifying.

The simile deals in the polyvalence of appearances, with the tension between tenor and vehicle[5] in the simile illuminating the inherently ambiguous state of metamorphosis. Simile, like metamorphosis, connects two shapes by proposing a likeness – while retaining the identity of both. Simile can thus be used as a model to investigate the central question of metamorphosis in the poem.

The idea that Ovid's use of figurative language is related to the phenomenon of metamorphosis has found growing acceptance among scholars in

[1] Wheeler (2000).
[2] Fränkel (1945), 21 and notes, 73, 79–85, 88–9, 99. For a detailed critique, see Schmidt (1991), 48–55.
[3] Solodow (1988), 174.
[4] Schmidt (1991), esp. 56–70.
[5] *Tenor* and *vehicle* refer to the thing being compared and to the thing to which it is being compared, respectively (*sic* vs. *ut*).

recent years. In talking about the way in which metamorphosis affects language, Hardie uses Ahl's work to draw attention to the overlapping Latin vocabulary for both metamorphosis and such tropes as simile, metaphor, and allegory.[6] From the opening lines the poem sets up an intricate correlation between its theme and its linguistic expression, both constantly changing. Pianezzola first proposed the idea that metamorphosis is "narrativised metaphor."[7] In a poem in which people can be literally transformed into animals, trees, or rocks, figurative and literal levels of language coincide in an ambiguity which mentally prepares the reader for the transformation. Thus Niobe's psychological state of shock at the death of her children is narrated in figurative language that anticipates her subsequent transformation into a rock (*deriguit malis, Met.* 6.303; *congelat*, 307; *intra quoque viscera saxum est*, 309).[8] Schmidt inverted these terms and proposed to see metamorphosis as metaphor for the human psyche with the result that the "whole world becomes an anthropomorphized mirror of human nature."[9] A similar argument had been made by Barkan who argued that the similes in the poem function as "protometamorphoses" anticipating in figurative language the subsequent literal transformation.[10] The idea of the reification of figurative language was further developed in Kaufhold's 1993 dissertation.[11] Following this line of interpretation metamorphosis may be construed as a kind of release, or expression of human emotion in an outward change of shape.

The building scholarly consensus around this line of interpretation is not without problems. The studies concentrate generally on metaphor and take this as the explicit or implicit model for interpretation. Simile, when examined at all, is subsumed in the argument by use of the inaccurate term "figurative language,"[12] or simply treated as interchangeable with metaphor. For example, in a discussion about the simile that introduces Hyacinthus' transformation into a flower, Sharrock's formulation reveals this underlying assumption: "The simile *is clearly a metaphor*

[6] Hardie (1999), 90.
[7] Pianezzola (1979). The exact term is "metafora narrativa."
[8] See especially Haege (1976), 85–93 for a sensitive analysis of the interplay of figurative and literal expression in this passage. The scene explicitly recalls its parallels in visual arts (*nihil est in imagine vivum*, 6.305), especially the popular groups of sculpture that depict Niobe with her children: Hardie (2002), 183.
[9] Hardie (1993), 264 in a review of Schmidt (1991).
[10] Barkan (1986), 20–1.
[11] Kaufhold (1993).
[12] Brooke-Rose (1958), 287 already calls for greater precision regarding this term, as well as the related "imagery."

for the subsequent metamorphosis."[13] In treating simile as metaphor, these studies distort our picture of the unique relationship of simile and metamorphosis.

To be fair, the notion that simile and metaphor are essentially the same reaches back to antiquity and is still the prevalent view in scholarly literature today. Beginning with Aristotle, simile and metaphor are discussed together. Even though Aristotle considers the simile to be "poetical,"[14] he does not discuss it in the *Poetics*. In his work on rhetoric, Aristotle states repeatedly that simile is a kind of metaphor:

> ἔστι γάρ ἡ εἰκών, καθάπερ εἴρηται πρότερον, μεταφορὰ διαφέρουσα προθέσει· διὸ ἧττον ἡδύ, ὅτι μακροτέρως· καὶ οὐ λέγει ὡς τοῦτο ἐκεῖνο· οὔκουν οὐδὲ ζητεῖ τοῦτο ἡ ψυχή.
>
> For the simile, as we have said, is a metaphor differing only in the addition of a word, wherefore it is less pleasant because it is longer; it does not say that this is that, so that the mind does not even examine this.[15]

Aristotle's notion of connecting the two figures, viewing simile as expanded metaphor, or as Cicero and Quintilian,[16] metaphor as condensed simile, continues to dominate the discussion today. Thus in an issue of *Poetics Today* devoted to the subject of metaphor, the editors state that "similes are metaphors."[17] Dissenting voices are few and far between.[18]

The automatic coupling of simile and metaphor blurs the profound differences between the two, viewing them as interchangeable when in fact they are not. Let us focus on the "slight" difference between the two, most notably simile's refusal to "affirm that this *is* that" and the preposition "like" on which this difference hinges. Metaphor can replace the literal meaning of a word without a change in syntax, thereby forcing an instant switch from literal to figurative. The effect of metaphor depends on mimicking literal expression. Thus "Niobe is a rock" may mean that she is petrified emotionally and therefore does not move (metaphor) or that she has changed shape. While outwardly the sentence looks the same, the semantic value of the replaced element turns the sentence into a figurative expression. The analogy of metaphor and metamorphosis is exceptionally close. Metaphor distorts the literal meaning of language, while

13 Sharrock (1996), 127 (emphasis mine). For my own interpretation, see below.

14 Arist. *Rh.* III.4.1406b7.

15 Arist. *Rh.* III.10.1410b21–4, translation Freese (1994). Cf. *Rh.* III.4; III.11.11. See Kirby (1997) for a detailed discussion of Aristotle's views and the enormous literature on this subject.

16 Cic. *De or.* 3.39.157; Quint. *Inst.* VIII.6.8. According to McCall (1969), 229–36, Latin writers seem to privilege comparison over metaphor.

17 Fludernik *et al.* (1997), 385.

18 Brooke-Rose (1958), Hornsby (1970), Brogan (1986), Ben-Porat (1992), Bethlehem (1996).

metamorphosis distorts reality to such a degree that it brings literal language to a breaking point in reflecting the change. Either phenomenon provokes a need for explanation since it challenges conventional usage and experience. Content and form are bound up with each other as can be seen as well in Ovid's frequent use of syllepsis,[19] a pattern within the poem which, as Tissol has pointed out, reinforces the reader's ability to switch constantly between the literal and figurative modes.[20]

As a result, metaphor can easily be assimilated to narrativization in the poem. The ease with which metaphor fits into existing linguistic structures allows Ovid to play with the bleeding or ambiguity of literal and figurative expression. In the description of Niobe in shock after the death of her children, the linguistic ambiguity of petrification is exploited to create uncertainty on when her metamorphosis begins. To say that Niobe is a rock requires no shift in the syntax to go from literal to figurative. The phrase *intra quoque viscera saxum est* (*Met.* 6.309) can be read figuratively at first, before one comprehends that it is meant literally. The second, literal reading is only available in the context of metamorphosis which makes credible the idea that humans may turn into stone.

The exclusive focus on metaphor as a model for metamorphosis leads to an interpretation in which the human being is seen solely in terms of the end result, the transformed body. This static view of metamorphosis denies the ongoing tension and lack of resolution between the human and non-human elements of the victim, and especially that of the human mind trapped in the animal body. By interpreting the body as an expression of an inner emotional state this kind of argument literally goes only skin deep. Transposed to the notion of metamorphosis, the tendency of metaphor to replace one thing with another essentially cancels out the identity of that which was there before. The very neatness which makes this solution so attractive should make the reader suspicious. The pattern is suggested by the first metamorphosis of the poem, that of Lycaon, whose figurative bestiality finds its literal expression in his transformation: *fit lupus et veteris servat vestigia formae:/ canities eadem est, eadem violentia vultus,/ idem oculi lucent, eadem feritatis imago est* (*Met.* 1.237–9).[21] The fact that the story is related by Jupiter, with the simultaneous assurance that the problem has already been taken care of offstage makes alternative interpretations of this

[19] A classic example is Jupiter's action against Phaethon*: pariterque animaque rotisque/ expulit, Met.* 2.312–13.

[20] Tissol (1997), 18.

[21] The exemplum of Lycaon figures prominently in the discussions of Pianezzola (1979), 86–8 and Schmidt (1991).

event impossible.[22] Lycaon's transformation achieves iconic status (*feritatis imago*). Yet this reference to the visual creates another problem, namely of interpretation, as Ginsberg points out: "But how can the anti-type be distinguished from the type? Can the wolf that is Lycaon really be told apart from the wolf that is Rome?"[23] Lycaon's metaphorical bestiality that exiles him from humankind appears at odds with the legendary humanity of the she-wolf that is the symbol of Rome's foundation. In fact, Jupiter's insistence on the sameness of the before and after reinforces the need to interpret this hybrid creature. The wolf's wild mind reveals itself as a retrojection of anthropomorphism on the animal world. Yet by crossing the physical and not just figurative boundary of human and animal, ambiguity rather than certainty about the status of the transformed creature results. Is a wolf that goes after sheep the same as a human who challenges Jupiter's divinity by violating both the rules of hospitality and the taboo of cannibalism, of not eating one's own kind? Lycaon's delight in slaughter that is natural for an animal but unnatural for a human recalls the delusions of Ajax slaughtering his comrades mistaking them for sheep in his temporary insanity.

The tendency to read metamorphosis solely in terms of clarification or closure needs to be countered by emphasizing the inherent instability of metamorphosis as a phenomenon that undermines classification. Similarity and contrast, rather than sameness, are the poles of the simile. Instead of replacing one element with another, simile necessitates keeping both tenor and vehicle in plain view. Without such a simultaneous presence of both objects, comparison would be impossible. Transferred onto the subject of metamorphosis, this double vision allows the reader to see both elements and to retain the tension between the outer and inner, or former and present, self of the victim. The presence of both elements means that while appearance may be compromised (vehicle), the integrity of the self (tenor) is not. The simile may thus be seen as a means of capturing the dynamic tension as well as the process of metamorphosis.

In the scholarly literature on simile and metaphor, Brogan's study of Wallace Stevens' use of simile is one of the few studies that maintain the essential difference of metaphor and simile. In her interpretation of Stevens' poem "Prologues to what is possible"[24] she writes:

22 Feldherr (2002), 171.

23 Ginsberg (1989), 229. On Lycaon as "deceptive paradigm" see Anderson (1989). On Niobe's ambiguous status see Feldherr (2004).

24 Wallace Stevens (1974), 515: "There was an ease of mind that was like being alone in a boat at sea..."

This poem is particularly interesting because it explores what is often ignored in the discussions of metaphor – the frightening potential of the impulse toward unity: annihilation of individuality in the "one-ness." The "metaphor" is frightening because such unity or "one-ness" would be more than human speech, even more than human: as the poem says, if the "point of central arrival," the place where meaning and syllable could unite, were attained, the entrance into it must "shatter the boat and leave the oarsmen quiet". In other words, if the impulse toward unity were realized, we would no longer have the "diff[é]rance" Derrida explains is requisite for the play of language: instead we would have only "quiet," the unspoken where being and essence are joined, that which is "more than human" and cannot be said "with human voice."[25]

As Brogan observes, Stevens disrupts the tendency toward unity by his use of simile "which deliberately withholds the 'one-ness' that the poem posits: it never *is* the 'ease of mind'; it is only 'like' that."[26]

My application of simile as model for metamorphosis makes a similar claim. The transformed victim both is and is not his new form. Simile is thus able to capture the paradox of likeness and identity which is central to metamorphosis. The victim has ceased to be human from the perspective of his environment; nonetheless, his human identity lies dormant in the transformed body. When Myrrha gives birth to Adonis, for example, her transformation into a tree has been completed, but Ovid makes her come alive, that is human again, through anthropomorphizing language: *nitenti tamen est similis curvataque crebros/ dat gemitus arbor lacrimisque cedentibus umet* (*Met.* 10.508–9).

Metamorphosis contains a puzzle. On the one hand, the change is permanent, since the finality of the metamorphosis cannot be reversed.[27] On the other hand, metamorphosis also preserves in perpetuity a marker of human nature, such as the tears of Niobe and Myrrha.[28] This double nature is constantly present and gets reactivated or reawakened at the moment that the story gets retold. In the case of the *Metamorphoses* this retelling is activated by rereading, so that the reader replicates the creation process.[29] While the result of metamorphosis may be permanent for the character, the retelling of the story counteracts that sense of closure.

The distinction between metaphor and simile makes an enormous difference when applied to the phenomenon of metamorphosis, since the

[25] Brogan (1986), 16–17. [26] Brogan (1986), 18.

[27] Io and Callisto are notable exceptions, in that they undergo two changes. For multiple metamorphoses of the same person see Fantham (1993).

[28] Niobe (*Met.* 6.310–2): *flet tamen / … / et lacrimas etiamnum marmora manant*; Myrrha (*Met.* 10.500): *flet tamen, et tepidae manant ex arbore guttae.*

[29] Feldherr (2002), 176–7.

model on which an analogy is being based is obviously crucially important for the end result. By preserving the semantic gap between tenor and vehicle, the simile alerts the reader to the dangers of a unified vision and allows for an alternative view. This model of metamorphosis comes out in three stories of dismemberment, those of Actaeon, Pentheus, and Orpheus. The episodes are clearly meant to echo and reinforce each other. In fact, Pentheus invokes his cousin Actaeon's fate in vain to appeal to his aunt Autonoe, and the two stories form a ring composition within the structure of book 3. At the beginning of book 11, Orpheus gets ripped apart by a band of maenads, repeating Pentheus' fate. Each episode builds on the association of the earlier examples with intensifying force.

Central to all three episodes is the theme of perception, specifically the human being perceived as animal. Actaeon is the only one who undergoes actual metamorphosis. In Pentheus' case, the metamorphosis is 'mental,' as Agave's distorted vision perceives him as an animal. By contrast, Orpheus suffers dismemberment even though the maenads clearly recognize him as human. The three cases show the simile counteracting metamorphosis to a certain degree: where the body is metamorphosed, the challenge is to show its human reactions; where the body is recognizably human, the simile maps animal behavior onto human cruelty. The following examples then present metamorphosis as destabilizing the absolute boundary between human and animal body, as a mental distortion with physical consequences. The anguish of the "mind in exile"[30] is acted out on the level of language in which the simile, not the metaphor, is capable of distancing one semblance from another and thus presents an acute double perception.

Dismemberment in itself is an extreme fate and may be seen as an intensification of metamorphosis. If metamorphosis signifies the loss of human form and identity through transformation into a non-human body, dismemberment signifies the loss of the body itself, and therefore the most complete loss of self. The alienation from the body as it is transformed limb by limb until the alien shape takes over the victim's metamorphosis completely has undeniable affinities with the experience of being plucked apart limb by limb, with physical separation making one's own body appear strange. Thus when Philomela is mutilated by Tereus, her tongue, now separate from her, is likened to a snake: *radix micat ultima linguae/ ipsa iacet terraeque tremens immurmurat atrae/ utque salire solet mutilatae cauda colubrae/ palpitat et moriens dominae vestigia quaerit*

[30] Skulsky (1981).

(*Met.* 6.557–60). The tongue becomes an alien animal, trying to rejoin its mistress. Its symbolism as externalized self which continues the faculty its mistress has lost anticipates Philomela's later, silent speech through communication through the tapestry. The gruesome way of killing another human being by dismemberment seems to necessitate seeing the victim as other than human; hence the maenads' distorted vision. By contrast, seeing both human and animal, as in metamorphosis, makes empathy possible.

ACTAEON

As punishment for accidentally seeing Diana naked while bathing, she changes him into a stag, from hunter to prey (*Met.* 3.193–9):

> nec plura minata
> dat sparso capiti uiuacis cornua cerui
> dat spatium collo summasque cacuminat aures
> cum pedibusque manus, cum longis bracchia mutat
> cruribus et uelat maculoso uellere corpus;
> additus et pauor est. fugit Autonoeius heros
> et se tam celerem cursu miratur in ipso.

Done with her threats, she sprinkles his head on which she puts the horns of a lively deer, stretches out his neck and sharpens the tips of his ears, switches hands for feet and arms for long limbs and shrouds his body in a spotted hide; fear is added, too. Autonoe's son, the hero, flees and marvels at himself, so fast at running.

While Actaeon's body changes, his human identity as "Autoneius heros" remains clearly separate. His marvel at his own speed (*se celerem miratur … in ipso*, 199) brings out the mental detachment from his transformed body, his inner and outer self. The change in focalization from the outside (in the description of the body), to Actaeon's inner thoughts further emphasizes the divide. As a result of the transformation, Actaeon is caught between civilization and wilderness with his animal instinct competing against his human consciousness. This animal instinct for flight is not natural but external (*additus … est*, 198), a consequence of the transformation, which conflicts with the culturally imposed heroic code that makes such flight shameful to humans.

As his own dogs chase him, the mock-epic catalogue of their names (a full nineteen lines, *Met.* 3.206–25) humanizes the dogs as individuals. The narrator here takes over Actaeon's usual task of calling them to order, emphasizing Actaeon's own inability to speak. Ironically, when his companions call out Actaeon's name he responds by turning his head like a dog (*Actaeona clamant/ (ad nomen caput ille refert)*, *Met.* 3.244–5). Metamorphosis destroys Actaeon's human ability to communicate because his animal body distorts the signs (*Met.* 3.237–41):[31]

> iam loca uulneribus desunt; gemit ille sonumque
> etsi non hominis, *quem non tamen edere possit*
> *ceruus*, habet maestisque replet iuga nota querelis
> et genibus pronis supplex similisque roganti
> circumfert tacitos *tamquam sua bracchia* uultus.

Already there are no more places for wounds; he groans and makes a sound if not a man's, not one that a deer could pronounce, either, and fills the familiar ridges with his sad laments, and on his bent knees, suppliant, like one who begs, casts around his silent looks as if they were his arms.

The simile reflects the cognitive dissonance between Actaeon and his companions. Although Actaeon bends his animal limbs in a suppliant's gesture (*et genibus pronis supplex similisque roganti*, 240), this move eludes interpretation because he is an animal: no longer human, he is but like a human being. In his own mind, Actaeon *is* a suppliant, yet his animal body causes him only to *look like* a suppliant. The simile conveys an entirely mental image which does not correspond to the actual image of the deer: lacking arms, it cannot even take up the position of the suppliant.[32] The overly precise use of *similis* thus emphasizes the failed communication. Actaeon's animal form also destroys the only available path of communication through his eyes (*circumfert tacitos … vultus*, 241). Whereas the human gaze is powerful in invoking pity, an animal's gaze does so only if it undergoes anthropomorphization through a sympathetic onlooker.[33]

[31] Italics mine.

[32] The issue of focalization is crucial – he *looks like* a suppliant only to those who know how to *look* which in the scene itself could only apply to the goddess herself. This visual detail calls attention to the reader's implicit involvement in the scene. How would he be able to judge the image otherwise? One might even speak of a parallel narrative at this point as Ovid relates the words that Actaeon might have uttered (*clamare libebat:/ 'Actaeon ego sum: dominum cognoscere vestrum!'/ verba animo desunt, Met.* 3.230–1). (The oddity of communication from human to dog is brought out in Actaeon's inability to speak now that he is an animal himself.) The reader's education in looking through appearances has begun with Callisto. Note the many parallels, including her invocations of divine pity (*qualescumque manus ad caelum et sidera tollit/ ingratumque Iovem, nequeat cum dicere, sentit, Met.* 2.487). When she sees Arcas, her own semblance of recognition (*incidit in matrem, quae restitit Arcade viso/ et* ***cognoscenti similis*** *fuit …, Met.* 2.500–1) contrasts forcefully with her son's ignorance of metamorphosis (*ecce Lycaoniae proles ignara parentis, Met.* 2.496). See also Fränkel (1945) 79–81 on the reader's empathy that restores the humanity of the victim.

[33] Cf. the description of Ocyrhoe's voice: *mox nec verba quidem nec ecquae sonus ille videtur,/ sed simulantis ecquam, parvoque in tempore certos/ edidit hinnitus et bracchia movit in herbas, Met.* 2.667–69. Cf. Chapter 2 for a simile that captures Apollo's divine voice.

Actaeon's alienation from his new body and inability to overcome its limits shows in the confusion of body parts. He uses his eyes to replace the impossible suppliant gesture of his arms (*tamquam sua bracchia*, 241) thus replacing body language for verbal communication, but his eyes are called silent (*tacitos ... vultus*, 241) as if they were meant to speak like his mouth. The tragedy of metamorphosis lies less in the animal body than in the continuation of human awareness, that opens a gap between one's own perception and that of others.

When Actaeon's companions call him 'as if' he were absent (*et velut absentem certatim Actaeona clamant/ .../ vellet abesse quidem*), the near assonance of *velut* and *vellet* reinforces the gap between appearance and reality. For Actaeon, his companions' behavior stands for a reality that is only accessible through magical thinking (*vellet*), while they act in a manner that is at odds with the 'reality' of the scene (*velut*). We can see from these examples that the non-identity between tenor and vehicle in the simile, signaled by the seemingly insignificant semantic marker *like* or *as*, has the potential of allowing us to see double, thus recognizing the human being inside the stag.

We may compare Ovid's Actaeon to another victim of Diana that was turned into a stag, Iphigenia. Ovid mentions her only in passing at *Met.* 12.27–38, where he seems to imply that she was transformed into, not replaced by, a stag (*supposita fertur mutasse Mycenida cerva, Met.* 12.31).[34] However, he does not aim to retell the story but bows to tradition (*fertur*). Of the various versions of the sacrifice scene, the one told by the chorus in the beginning of Aeschylus' *Agamemnon* shows a remarkable coincidence in the treatment of simile to render Iphigenia's ambiguous status as human victim of sacrifice (Aesch. *Ag.* 231–47).

Iphigenia's humanity is compromised as she is treated like an animal. The men lift her up like a goat (δίκαν χιμαίρας ὕπερθε βωμοῦ, 232) and her mouth is gagged with a horse's bridle (βίαι χαλινῶν τ᾽ἀναύδωι μένει, 238). Even the simile that describes her as though in a painting turns her into an aesthetic object of art at one remove (241–3). At the same time she fixes each one of her killers with her eyes (240–1) in an attempt to break down this artificial barrier. The gesture signals her revolt as much as a plea for mercy: the sacrificial victim was supposed to direct his gaze downward in assent.[35] Iphigenia has the courage to meet their gaze and asserts herself as an equal human being.

[34] Cf. *Met.* 13.181–8 where Odysseus speaks of the sacrifice but gives no indication at what happened to her.

[35] Holoka (1985), 229. For a reading of Artemis' gaze see also Sharrock (2002a).

In Ovid, the boundaries between the human and non-human state are even more tenuous, since humans do get transformed into animals. Nonetheless, in both cases the dissonance of human and animal nature achieved through the use of simile provokes empathy in the reader for their cruel deaths. 'Seeing as other' can thus work in both ways: seeing the human as animal, or seeing the animal as human.[36]

PENTHEUS

The Pentheus episode stands out in the poem because the myth does not contain a true metamorphosis. Ovid justifies its inclusion in the poem instead by means of an inset narrative by Pentheus' prisoner Acoetes (arguably Bacchus himself) who tells the cautionary tale of the Tyrrhenian sailors transformed into dolphins by Bacchus. In the context of the Pentheus episode, the theme of metamorphosis is thus used as a diversionary tactic that delays and thereby heightens the expected climax of Pentheus' dismemberment.[37] Pentheus himself never undergoes any physical transformation through either metamorphosis or disguise. In this Dionysiac context, the simile offers an additional point of view that cuts through the subjectivity of the characters and shows the reader's own involvement in visualizing the scene.

Ovid makes a point of not following Euripides' model, in which Dionysus gets Pentheus dressed up as a bacchante. Instead, Pentheus is at all times visibly human and recognizably himself, even capable of speech, in contrast to his cousin Actaeon, whose fate he fruitlessly invokes as an exemplum. Of course what does happen is a "mental" metamorphosis in the eyes of Agave, who sees a boar instead of Pentheus. As James writes in a study of the scene:

> Pentheus' physical metamorphosis takes place only in the eyes of the beholders. Perception not reality is transformed but the result is equally terrible and the line between subjective and objective transformation must be deliberately tenuous.[38]

James is right to point out that the end result for both Actaeon and Pentheus is the same, in that physical and mental metamorphosis are

[36] For an example of the latter see Pythagoras' use of simile to deter humans from animal sacrifice: *aut qui vagitus similes puerilibus haedum/ edentem iugulare potest aut alite vesci/ cui dedit ipse cibos?* (*Met.* 15.466–8). For the sacrifice connection see Feldherr (1997). Only the rigid demarcation of animal and human roles upholds the legitimate use of violence (46–9).

[37] Feldherr (1997), 33–6 shows how this diversionary tactic is actually a sleight-of-hand that intensifies rather than distracts from the themes of the ensuing narrative.

[38] James (1991–3).

virtually interchangeable. However, it is possible to go even further and argue that the Pentheus episode is an escalation of the story of Actaeon. Not only is Pentheus objectively still human at the moment of dismemberment (even if an animal in Agave's eyes), Agave herself in tearing him apart is acting in a non-human way in her Dionysiac frenzy, while Actaeon's dogs act out of animal instinct alone.

Moreover, Ovid shows Agave's "mental" metamorphosis of Pentheus into a boar as complete. Unlike her Euripidean counterpart, she never leaves her distorted frame of mind and regains her senses. In a reworking of the recognition scene of Euripides' *Bacchae*, Agave looks Pentheus in the face before she rips his head off as he implores her pity (*Met.* 3.725–8):

> 'aspice, mater!' ait; uisis ululauit Agaue
> collaque iactauit mouitque per aera crinem,
> auulsumque caput digitis complexa cruentis
> clamat 'io comites, opus hoc uictoria nostra est!'

"Look at me, mother!", he says. At the sight Agave howls and tosses her neck and whips her hair through the air, and cries out, clasping the head she wrenched off in her bloody fingers: "Io, comrades, this deed is our victory!"

The exhortation to look at his face not only tries to penetrate her blindness but also emphasizes the mother–son bond between them.[39] While she responds to his plea for looking at his face, her distorted vision protects her from the moral obligation that comes with looking at another human being directly in the eye. As she rips Pentheus' body apart, mother and son are perversely united: she rips off his right arm (721) which he then lacks for his supplication.

Pentheus' plea to Autonoe to remember Actaeon's fate (*Met.* 3.719–20) is only 'heard' by the reader. Unlike Actaeon, who cannot speak, Pentheus does speak but cannot be heard. While tragic characters are notorious for not learning from the example of those before them, the reader has been trained in seeing twofold. Agave's mono-vision provides a negative example for seeing only the animal in metamorphosis. In the poem's wider context this story provides a meta-poetic reflection on what happens to the reader's mind, and the process of visualization that is involved in picturing metamorphosis. Unlike Agave, however, the reader is privileged to

[39] An obvious parallel is the failed recognition scene between Arcas and Callisto. His mother recognizes him but he does not recognize her, and tries to attack her (*Met.* 2.496–507).

Compare also Pentheus' own uncompromising gaze at his divine prisoner: *Aspicit hunc Pentheus oculis quos ira tremendos/ fecerat et, quamquam poenae vix tempora differt/, 'o periture, tuaque aliis documenta dature/ morte' ait* ... (*Met* 3.577–80).

see "double" as it were, to see both the human and the animal part in metamorphosis.

As noted above, Pentheus does not undergo physical transformation through either metamorphosis or disguise. However, we have seen that "mental" metamorphosis can be just as real. Let us now focus on the "mental" costuming achieved by the simile that describes Pentheus' entrance. Pentheus' perception of himself and his delusion that he can beat the women back by martial force are central to the interpretation of the story. Pentheus is characterized in two similes, the first at the end of his speech to his fellow countrymen, to a torrent (*Met.* 3.568–71), the second at the beginning of the final scene (*Met.* 3.704–7):[40]

> ut fremit acer equus, cum bellicus aere canoro
> signa dedit tubicen, pugnaeque adsumit amorem,
> Penthea sic ictus longis ululatibus aether
> mouit et audito clamore recanduit ira.

Like an eager horse neighs, when the war-trumpet with its resounding blast gives the signal, and takes on a lust for battle, so does the aether, struck by long howls, urge on Pentheus, and his wrath grows white hot as he hears the noise.

The simile picks up the martial spirit that Pentheus had invoked earlier (*pugnaeque adsumit amorem*, 705). James claims that in contrast to the Euripidean dress-up, in Ovid "the Theban king is given more dignity, retains more of his rashness (*ut fremit acer equus*, 740) and goes as a warrior to the mountain."[41] However, when one looks at the simile more closely, Pentheus does not go as a warrior, but as a war-horse to the mountain. In comparing Pentheus to an animal, Ovid suggests that his rage is fueled by animal instinct not human free will – the horse image suggests that somebody else (Dionysus) is "riding" Pentheus. The notion that he is no longer master of himself comes out also in the formulation of the apodosis *Penthea sic ... aether / movit* (706). Thus the simile mimics Pentheus' own distorted sense of self, on the one hand replicating his martial fantasy but on the other hand subjugating it under the Bacchic power. The battle-horse reacts with excitement to the sound of the war-trumpet (*fremit*), just as the landscape resounds at Bacchus' first triumphal entrance (*Liber adest festisque fremunt ululatibus agri*, 3.528). Pentheus is figuratively swept up in the Bacchic frenzy. He had earlier ridiculed the effect in his speech to the soldiers (*Met.* 3.532–7):

[40] The river and the horse are elements of an intriguing exemplum at Lucretius 4.420 where he discusses optical illusion in language reminiscent of Dionysiac mania.

[41] James (1986), 24 n.19. See also James (1991–3), 88.

> aerane tantum
> aere repulsa ualent et adunco tibia cornu
> et magicae fraudes, ut quos non bellicus ensis,
> non tuba terruerit, non strictis agmina telis,
> feminea uoces et mota insania uino
> obscenique greges et inania tympana vincant?

Is such the power of air clashing with air, of the pipe with its crooked horn and magic tricks over men whom neither the battle-sword nor the trumpet nor the lines of outstretched bows has frightened, that women's voices, wine-induced insanity, filthy herds and hollow cymbals defeat them?

The simile which associates Bacchic noise (*longis ululatibus*, 706) with the war-trumpet (*bellicus tubicen*, 704–5) causes a collapse of Pentheus' strict contrast between the male world of martial power and the female world of irrational hysterics.

More effective than outright costume, the similes emphasize the divergent perspectives of Pentheus, Agave, and the omniscient narrator. The reader is made aware of his privileged vision as spectator in this tragedy.[42] This distance from the compromised vision of the characters should make us more aware of our own participation in imagining a human being as non-human. Ovid takes great pains to point out the absence of "true" metamorphosis in the story by providing the alibi story of the Tyrrhenian sailors. The Pentheus story by contrast gives us a meta-poetic view on the workings of metamorphosis, emphasizing perception as the only truth. By carefully delineating the real from the imagined, Ovid gives the reader a triple perspective on the scene, and shows how objective and subjective visions collide.

ORPHEUS

The story of Orpheus' dismemberment deliberately echoes the Pentheus episode as it shows maenads attacking and killing the singer, provoked by his renunciation of women. Under the pretense of Bacchic madness, the women take revenge on Orpheus. The battle cry of the first maenad (*'en', ait, 'en, hic est nostri contemptor'* …, *Met.* 11.7) echoes Agave's own discovery of Pentheus (*Met.* 3.713–15). However, their later punishment by Baccchus shows that they were not divinely inspired but acted out of their

[42] Feldherr (1997), 32 delineates the shift in the roles for the reader, from spectator to participant, that this recognition entails.

own motives. The contrast between animal and human behavior comes out in a series of similes that call into question human moral superiority.

After losing Eurydice for the second time, Orpheus turns his back on human society, especially on women, and exiles himself to the countryside. Through his singing he creates an alternative society in which wild beasts and the landscape in general act in human ways. The civilizing effect of his singing on wild beasts and the rest of nature makes them form a quasi-human audience.[43] The harmony among the wild beasts evokes a Golden Age without natural violence.

Intruding on this bucolic idyll are the maenads, deliberately rejecting human civilization. They dress in fawn skins, thus masquerading as animals, and their human language regresses to grunts and shrieks which ultimately overpower the civilizing influence of Orpheus' voice. Nonetheless, they are not in a state of manic rapture, since they clearly recognize Orpheus as a human being. Unlike Agave who sees a boar instead of Pentheus (*ille mihi feriendus aper*, *Met.* 3.715), the maenads clearly recognize Orpheus as the man who rejected heterosexual love (*en, hic est nostri contemptor*, 11.7). Since they are interested not in Bacchus' glory but their own, the dress-up is really just 'costume' without sacred context or motivation.

Despite his objective isolation, Orpheus is surrounded by anthropomorphized nature that keeps him company. The human maenads are paradoxically a wild intrusion into the civilized world of Orpheus' creation. The sympathetic union between Orpheus and the surrounding landscape comes out in the first simile of this passage which describes a stone cast against Orpheus by the maenads (*Met.* 11.10–13):

> alterius telum lapis est, qui missus in ipso
> aere concentu uictus uocisque lyraeque est
> ac ueluti supplex pro tam furialibus ausis
> ante pedes iacuit.

Another's weapon is a stone. As it is hurled, it is overcome by the air itself through the harmony of voice and lyre, and like a suppliant for such frenzied daring falls down before his feet.

While human suppliant gestures in general abound, the phrase *veluti supplex* only occurs twice in the poem, where it is used only of non-human actors. The first instance, discussed previously, illustrates the human self of

[43] Their behavior may seem less odd if we remember that some of them were human at one time. Wheeler (1999), 94.

the transformed Actaeon. When applied to a rock, the simile appears even more exaggerated. While an animal has limbs and eyes to mimic the gesture of a human suppliant, stones are notoriously inanimate and unfeeling. Even without the line of the simile the description would already be a testament to Orpheus' magical powers. The addition of the simile imbues the stone with religious feeling and thereby suggests the blasphemous nature of the maenads' actions.

If nature becomes anthropomorphized where does this leave humans? In the double simile that describes the maenads' successful attack on Orpheus, the human actors are likened to animals (*Met.* 11.20–8):

> ac primum attonitas etiamnum uoce canentis
> innumeras uolucres anguesque agmenque ferarum
> Maenades Orphei titulum rapuere theatri
> inde cruentatis uertuntur in Orphea dextris
> et coeunt ut aues, si quando luce uagantem
> noctis auem cernunt, structoque utrimque theatro
> ceu matutina ceruus periturus harena
> praeda canum est; uatemque petunt et fronde uirentes
> coniciunt thyrsos non haec in munera factos.

And at first the maenads snatch the playbill of Orpheus' theater, the innumerable birds and snakes and the whole line of beasts, still struck by the voice of the singer. Then they turn their bloody hands against Orpheus and come together like birds that chance to spot the bird of night erring in the light, or as in a round theater a deer about to die in the morning becomes the prey of the dogs in the arena; they aim at the bard and hurl their thyrsi, still green in leaf and not made for this purpose.

John Miller has made the convincing argument that the simile cruelly parodies Orpheus' animal audience.[44] The simile of birds crowding around an owl has precedence in a Hellenistic description of an audience surrounding the singer. Now, Orpheus' little *bande de théâtre* finds itself in a different amphitheater setting with a different program. It should not be forgotten, either, that behind the internal animal audience stands yet another audience – the reader who, by reading Orpheus' songs, has identified vicariously with his actual animal audience. Human and animal world, and their respective allegiances, can be seen as thoroughly confused.

Let us now turn our attention to the traditional nature of this predator–prey simile. Epic poetry abounds in such similes, with the *Metamorphoses* being no exception. Moreover, the image of the poet as victim of his

[44] Miller (1990).

detractors in ornithological terms goes back to Hesiod's self-portrait as a nightingale fleeing from a hawk.[45] Yet the traditional content of the simile is radically at odds with the Golden Age setting of the context. Orpheus' singing had united nature in harmony and eliminated the sorts of scenes represented in the simile. The use of a predator–prey simile at this point thus turns on its head the notion of natural violence among animals. The human actors, isolated in the simile, are the odd ones out, whereas nature itself gives the opposite picture. Given that there are no human witnesses to this event, one may even imagine the simile as being focalized through an animal audience.

From Homer onwards, the predator–prey simile is not merely illustrative but normative, by viewing the relationship of one human and another as predator and prey. The observed animal behavior becomes a naturally derived norm for culturally imposed human behavior.[46] The roles of the simile thus justify the violence employed. Achilles, without doubt the most meta-poetically aware character of the *Iliad*, tells Hector that just as there cannot be peace between wolves and lambs so Trojans and Greeks must kill each other in war.[47] However, in the context of the Golden Age setting that is created by Orpheus, in which such peace is possible, the use of the simile turns such rationalization for human violence on its head.

Moreover, both settings of the double simile suggest artificial displacement. The owl is out of its element in the daytime, which makes it vulnerable to attack. Not only are the numbers uneven, the inversion of gender expectations in the application of the simile underlines the maenads' role as sexual aggressor. Ovid had similarly marked out the transgressive nature of Salmacis (*Met.* 4.361–7). Similarly, the artificial setting of the enclosed amphitheater precludes the stag's flight *(periturus*, 26). The choice of a staged hunting scene (itself redolent of Actaeon's fate) calls into question the human audience's morbid fascination with this kind of 'natural' violence. The insertion of the anachronism in the simile points to the reader's own involvement in the tale. While the maenads' actions are despicable and blasphemous, the tale of Orpheus' dismemberment also gives vicarious aesthetic pleasure to the reader.

In response to their behavior, Dionysus asserts his godhead and restores the lost balance in nature. The maenads' punishment by metamorphosis into trees is told via another bird simile (*Met.* 11.73–8):

[45] Hesiod *Op.* 202–12.

[46] For the pitfalls of this logic see Myrrha's speech at *Met.* 10.324–31.

[47] *Il.* 22.325–34. The preceding predator–prey similes force this conclusion (*Il.* 22.175–80, mountain falcon–dove; *Il.* 22. 234–40, dog–deer).

utque suum laqueis, quos callidus abdidit auceps
crus ubi commisit uolucris sensitque teneri,
plangitur ac trepidans astringit uincula motu
sic, ut quaeque solo defixa cohaeserat harum,
exsternata fugam frustra temptabat; at illam
lenta tenet radix exsultantemque coercet.

As when a bird puts its leg into a trap that a clever bird-catcher has hidden, and feels itself being held, and beats itself and in fluttering draws tighter its bonds by movement, so, each of them was stuck, fixed to the ground, and, terrified, was trying uselessly her escape, but the tenacious root holds her and restrains her as she leaps.

This simile is modeled on one used by Homer to describe the punishment of the maids, a reassertion of Odysseus' power in his household.[48] Ovid continues the bird imagery from the earlier scene, mocking the maenads' characterization in the first simile as birds of prey.

Ovid captures the unconscious beginning of metamorphosis by locating the moment within the simile. From the Homeric model we may expect that the women will still be women as the simile ends, that they are only likened to birds. Ovid instead literally entraps the maenads in the simile, not allowing them to get out of the altered form. Thus the figure of the simile can be employed to enact the mechanics of metamorphosis.

The punishment also recalls the crime. Whereas the predator–prey simile shows animals hunting other animals, the trap in this simile stands as a symbol for human (or in this case divine) domination over nature through the use of intelligence. Bacchus' punishment redresses the balance between wilderness and civilization. The irony of Bacchus' name Lyaeus (*Met.* 11.67) in applying a punishment that is the opposite of his usual "loosening" also reasserts his dominion over the sacred ritual which the maenads have abused.

The metamorphosis of the maenads into trees is deliberately at odds with the expectations raised by the bird imagery of the previous similes. Their inability to move is a direct consequence of the deed for which they are punished. Only Orpheus' voice could move trees, for example the recently metamorphosed Cyparissus (*Adfuit huic turbae metas imitata cupressus/ nunc arbor, puer ante deo dilectus ab illo*, 10.106–7). In killing the bard, the maenads have condemned themselves to perpetual immobility. Orpheus, like other artist figures in the *Metamorphoses*, stands in for the poet's alter ego. The episode illustrates the poetic power of

48 *Od.* 22.468–72.

anthropomorphizing nature which counteracts the deadening power of metamorphosis. While metamorphosis is final and permanent, the retelling of the stories of metamorphosis reanimates the transformed being and gives it back its individuality. The absence of the poet's voice signals the finality of metamorphosis.

HYACINTHUS

In the previous examples, the simile counteracted the finality of metamorphosis to some degree, calling into question the absolute division between humans and the natural world around them. Another aspect of human identity that gets compromised by metamorphosis is individuality. Victims of metamorphosis are no longer one particular person but represent a given species. Hyacinthus' speaking name foreshadows his later transformation into the flower, an association that is strengthened further by a flower simile that precedes the transformation. This simile is routinely used as evidence for the symbiotic relationship between simile and metamorphosis. Barkan proposed that the simile acts as a kind of protometamorphosis, anticipating the subsequent metamorphosis in figurative language.[49] A similar idea was developed by Kaufhold, who argued in her dissertation that metamorphosis constitutes the reification of figurative language.[50] The argument of the literalization of the figurative has proved persuasive to many scholars, perhaps because it suggests the power of poetic imagination (figurative) in creating its own (literal) world.

While such a reading might seem intuitively attractive, it poses the danger of a reductive simplification. The idea of the simile as a mental rehearsal for the metamorphosis does not go beyond the surface of the image proffered, avoiding the more difficult question of the identity of this changed shape, which is at stake in both simile and metamorphosis. In the *Metamorphoses* in general, A turning into B is hardly an uncomplicated affair. Ovid repeatedly emphasizes this in narrating the struggle of the human individual in its non-human changed body. It is perhaps telling that Haege, in his careful study of the transformation process in the *Metamorphoses*, did not find the pattern of figurative into literal consistent enough.[51]

Quite to the contrary of received wisdom, the simile complicates rather than simplifies an inquiry into the nature of metamorphosis. As test case

[49] Barkan (1986), 20–1. [50] Kaufhold (1993). [51] Haege (1976), 85–93.

may serve the story of Hyacinthus, as it is used by several scholars[52] to illustrate the idea of reification. Accidentally killed by his lover, Apollo, Hyacinthus is transformed into a flower. As he lies dying his drooping head is compared to a flower (*Met.* 10.190–5):

> ut, si quis uiolas riguoque papauera in horto
> liliaque infringat fuluis horrentia linguis
> marcida demittant subito caput illa grauatum
> nec se sustineant spectentque cacumine terram,
> sic uultus moriens iacet, et defecta vigore
> ipsa sibi est oneri ceruix umeroque recumbit.

As when somebody breaks off violets or a poppy in a dewy garden and lilies bristling with their yellow tongues; withered, they let drop immediately their heavy head and cannot hold themselves up and look with their top to the ground, so does his dying face lie, and as his strength departed, his neck is a burden for itself and rests on his shoulder.

The simile recalls well-known models from both epic and erotic poetry, most prominently Homer (*Il.* 8.306–8, on the death of Gorgythion), Catullus (11.22–4), and Virgil (*Aen.* 9.435–7, death of Euryalus; 11.68–71, death of Pallas).[53] Ovid's use of the simile thus appears traditional and appropriate in pathos for the death of the youth, simultaneously alluding to the erotic relationship of Hyacinthus and Apollo as well as elevating Hyacinthus to a status equivalent to an epic hero because of it.

What comes next can only happen in the *Metamorphoses*. The simile finds its literal expression as Hyacinthus is transformed into a flower (*Met.* 10.209–13):

> talia dum uero memorantur Apollinis ore,
> ecce cruor, qui fusus humo signauerat herbas,
> desinit esse cruor, Tyrioque nitentior ostro
> flos oritur formamque capit quam lilia, si non
> purpureus color his, argenteus esset in illis.

And while such things were proclaimed from the true mouth of Apollo, look, the blood that, spilt on the ground, had marked the grass ceases to be blood, and a flower arises, more shining than Tyrian purple, and takes the shape of a lily, if not these had a purple color, and those a silvery.

The case for reification seems obvious, even inevitable, as the traditional simile on the death of a young man finds a satisfying resolution in his

[52] Hardie (1999), 91; Hardie (2002), 65, 230; Dyson (1999), 283; Kaufhold (1993).
[53] Cf. Bömer (1969–86) ad loc.

transformation as part of the natural landscape. While Apollo cannot rescue Hyacinthus from death, metamorphosis offers a compromise between life and death that allows Hyacinthus to live on in altered form.[54]

Another strong pull towards reification is inherent in the story itself. Hyacinthus' name determines his destiny as the myth exists solely because of the flower, one name deriving from the other. Thus his name, like that of Daphne, Arachne, Cyparissus, and others prefigures their eventual metamorphosis with inescapable logic.[55] For the reader, familiar with both the flower and the myth, the metamorphosis of the boy into the flower is no surprise.

All the more surprising, then, is the variety of images proffered. The simile that is said to anticipate the eventual metamorphosis gives three flowers, not just one. Violet, poppy, and lily are presented in an ascending tricolon, as if Ovid were gradually homing in on the most fitting comparison. The triple image in the simile thus conveys a moment of wavering uncertainty on how to represent Hyacinthus' dying body. The sense of aesthetic detachment at the moment of death is enhanced by the fact that the point of comparison is Hyacinthus' *vultus moriens* (not *morientis*), as if he had already ceased to be anything but the parts of his body in anticipation of the metamorphosis. Hyacinthus' loss of a defining, exclusive identity is already anticipated at the moment of Apollo's accidental killing.[56] The discus hits Hyacinthus in the face (*vultus*), and thus erases the prime signifier of his human identity (*Met.* 10.183–5):

at illum
dura repercusso subiecit pondere tellus
in uultus, Hyacinthe, tuos.

But the hard earth cast it up with rebounding weight in your face, Hyacinthus.

The very same *vultus* is used as the tenor for the first flower simile anticipating the loss of his human shape through metamorphosis (*Met.* 10.194).

The triple image also calls attention to the fact that none of the flowers fits perfectly. Only the hyacinth which is present in Virgil's simile (*qualem virgineo demessum pollice florem/ seu mollis violae seu languentis hyacinthi*, *Aen.* 11.68–9) would achieve that. Ovid's replacement of the hyacinth with the lily is a reminder of the necessary difference between tenor and vehicle in the simile. To compare the body of the dying Hyacinthus to a hyacinth

[54] Solodow (1988), 172–4. [55] Hardie (2002), 239–57.
[56] Cf. the displacement of the killing agent to the earth with the hammer in the Apollo simile discussed in Chapter 2.

would be a tautological absurdity that would lead to the collapse of the simile.

It is therefore not enough to say that Hyacinthus is compared to a flower and then is transformed into a flower, even though such a statement on one level may be read as obviously true. The precise terms of violet, poppy, lily, and hyacinth are of paramount importance to Ovid as shown at the moment of metamorphosis itself.[57]

The sense that Ovid is gradually homing in on the most appropriate image in the first simile is confirmed by the following simile at the moment of metamorphosis that picks out the last element, the lily, to describe the new flower. This simile tends to be overlooked, with two notable exceptions, Solodow and, more extensively, Hardie.[58] It belongs to Hardie's category of "approximative similes," defined as "similes which consider, or invite the reader to consider, how the approximation of *comparans* and *comparandum* might be completed …"

Instead of a linear trajectory from figurative into literal, with the flower of the simile dissolving into the real presence of a new flower, the description of this metamorphosis never leaves the realm of the figurative. Even at the moment of his metamorphosis Hyacinthus is likened to the lily, not identified with the hyacinth. However, even the image of lily does not fit perfectly since only its shape but not its color resembles the hyacinth, an overly precise correction of Virgil's purple lilies (*Aen.* 6.882–6), as Hardie points out:

> As with the wider contexts of the conditional qualifications in the approximate similes applied to Syrinx and Philomela, the wish to draw a clear distinction, here about the colour of flowers, occurs in the context of a narrative of confused and merged identities.[59]

While the tradition of the myth clearly identifies the youth with the flower, Ovid's use of the simile at this particular moment suspends the full realization of the metamorphosis in order to retain the ambiguity of who the flower represents, Hyacinthus – or Ajax.

But even then the transformation is not complete. Apollo's inscription of his mourning sighs on the leaves of the flower adds another layer. In the *Fasti*'s version of the myth, told by Flora/Chloris as the author of the transformation,[60] the AI AI on the petals were the sigh of the victim as

[57] See also Dyson (1999) on the significance of the Virgilian allusion in the choice of flowers.

[58] Solodow (1988), 57; Hardie (2004), 84.

[59] Hardie (2004), 100.

[60] Flora's claim that she is the first (***prima … feci***) to transform Hyacinthus adds another dimension of complexity to this metamorphosis. Clearly, there can only be one author of the transformation

he died: *prima Therapneo feci de sanguine florem,/ et manet in folio scripta querela suo* (*Fast.* 5.223–4). The writing on the leaves was thus connected organically with the transformed body as a kind of silent speech, frozen at the moment of Hyacinthus' death and externalized on the body of the flower.

The *Metamorphoses* version of the myth focuses instead on Apollo's grief, not Hyacinthus' pain. Ovid alludes to this inverted relationship between mourner and mourned when Apollo claims that Hyacinthus will imitate his sighs (*flosque novus scripto* ***gemitus*** *imitabere* ***nostros***, *Met.* 10.206).[61] However, their roles are sharply divided only eight lines later, with Apollo the focus of attention, Hyacinthus serving merely as a passive writing surface (*Met.* 10.215–16):

> **ipse suos gemitus** foliis **inscribit** et AI AI
> **flos habet inscriptum** funestaque littera ducta est.

And he inscribes his groans on the leaves and the flower has the inscription AI AI and shows the mournful letters.

As Janan points out: "Hyacinthus-as-text has not really won an immortal identity: rather he points beyond himself to his creator."[62] Apollo honors Hyacinthus by turning the flower as a monument to his grief, allowing Apollo possession of his beloved even as his human shape has vanished.[63] Apollo's self-centeredness recalls Ovid's own persona in the *Amores* promising immortality to his beloved through his writing – only to differentiate the *nos* into its separate compartments (*Am.* 1.3.25–6):

> Nos quoque per totum pariter cantabimur orbem
> iunctaque semper erunt nomina nostra tuis.

We too will be the subject of song throughout the whole world, and forever will my name be linked to yours.

just as there can really be only one victim of it, despite claims of priority (*purpureum viridi genuit de caespite florem, qui prius Oebalio de vulnere fuerat natus, Met.* 13. 395–6). In order to reconcile the two authors, one has to split Hyacinthus into (Flora's) flower (*feci de sanguine florem*), and (Apollo's) flower-text (*ipse suos gemitus … inscribit*).

61 The jarring *pluralis maiestatis* at this point mocks the collaborative effort of Hyacinthus in Apollo's mourning. Paradoxically, Hyacinthus is mourned by Apollo only by mourning for himself. Contrast Apollo's consolation for Cyparissus that emphasizes reciprocity (*lugebere nobis/ lugebisque alios .., Met.* 10.141–2).

62 Janan (1988), 124.

63 Daphne is an obvious parallel, except for the fact that she aims to escape Apollo through metamorphosis. See Feeney (1999c), 72–3 for the self-centeredness of Apollo's pursuit and appropriation of her as his symbol.

In both cases the monument that is meant to recall the beloved in reality eradicates the memory by not naming him or her. Corinna's name is absent from the poem, just as Hyacinthus' name is absent from the flower-text.

Hyacinthus' changed body alone does not suffice to identify him. The accumulation of similes thus can be seen as anticipating the ambiguity of the flower's shape. The imposition of Apollo's writing on the leaves makes the hyacinth a generic *flos* whose true identity depends on the correct reading of the inscription. The focus on the inscription rather than the shape of the flower itself turns Hyacinth into "the flower of Apollo's lament" and denies the realization of Hyacinthus' speaking name. The obliteration of Hyacinthus' identity forms a curious undercurrent in the story that is meant to preserve the memory of him.

Hyacinthus' identity as expressed through his face gets erased by Apollo's throw of the discus. Face and name as signifiers of identity are contrasted at this point as the words *vultus … tuos* form a frame around the pronounced pathos of Orpheus' address of Hyacinthus by his name. Orpheus' use of Hyacinthus' name stands in deliberate contrast to Apollo's roundabout and more generic apostrophe *Oebalide* in his speech of lament (*Met.* 10.196), an ethnic assignation rather than a personal name. The same term is repeated at the moment of Ajax's transformation, only obliquely recalling Hyacinthus' claim to the flower (*Oebalio vulnere, Met.* 13.396). Apollo had prophesied this second metamorphosis at the moment of Hyacinthus' transformation. His prophetic words do not bring about the change but rather seem to upstage it in favor of the future transformation of Ajax. His choice of address thus anticipates the comparative insignificance of Hyacinthus as opposed to Ajax and detracts from a clear identification of Hyacinthus with the homonymous flower. Apollo's aesthetic choice of addressing Hyacinthus may be a preference for Alexandrian obscurity. However, it reveals itself at this point as a political strategy to relegate Hyacinthus to the obscure, the second row behind the more famous epic heroes. The competition between artist figure and god in Hyacinthus' memorialization recalls similar struggles for narratorial control in the *Metamorphoses*.

Hyacinthus' identity can thus be seen to be compromised on a variety of levels: in the denial of true reification through the simile, the obliteration of his face and name, and the dissociation of his body as exclusive signifier in becoming the passive surface for Apollo's inscription. The split between flower and flower-text means that the same flower can be reused at Ajax's death (*Met.* 13.394–8):

> expulit ipse cruor, rubefactaque sanguine tellus
> purpureum uiridi genuit de caespite florem,
> qui prius Oebalio fuerat de uulnere natus.
> littera communis mediis pueroque uiroque
> inscripta est foliis, haec nominis, illa querelae.

The blood itself pushed it out, and, reddened by the blood, the earth brought forth from its green turf a purple flower, which before had been born from the Oebalian's wound. A shared word is inscribed in the middle of its petals for boy and man, this for his name and that for the lament.

This double claim to the same form constitutes a unique exception to the overall pattern of metamorphosis according to which a victim is always changed into a specific bird, flower, tree, etc. often retaining or mimicking a chief characteristic of the victim. Tereus, Procne, and Philomela are not just changed into birds but into a hoopoe, nightingale, and swallow, respectively.[64] Their transformed selves still retain a measure of human individuality.

The paradox that Hyacinthus and Ajax share the same flower is only possible through the addition of writing (*littera communis*), open to divergent interpretation. Hardie points out that Ovid's painstaking differentiation in the etymology of Apollo's lament and Ajax's name is unnecessary, as they both derive from the same root.[65] His deliberate combination of two incompatible myths[66] answers Menalcas' riddle in Virgil's third eclogue: *Dic, quibus in terris inscripti nomina regum/ nascantur flores …* (*Ecl.* 3.105–6). The myth's divergent origin has geographical roots in oral versions, which are here obliterated by the use of writing. The double riddle is a product of the literary compilation of myths, independent of locality.

What gets lost in the appropriation of the flower through writing, first through Apollo's flower-text and then through Ajax's name as a kind of palimpsest, is the intimate connection of Hyacinthus' name and the flower he turns into. When we see Hyacinthus' drooping head looking like a flower in the preceding similes, we anticipate the transformation of his body into the form of a flower, as if Hyacinthus at last found the true meaning of his name in literally embodying the hyacinth. However, as shown above, that stage of realization is never reached, as the new

64 Solodow (1988), 176–83. 65 Hardie (2004), 100. 66 Bömer (1969–86) on *Met.* 10.162.

flower takes its form from other objects in the comparison (*nitentior … ostro, formamque capit quam lilia, Met.* 10.211–12). And just as the hyacinth is described as imitating the form of another flower (the lily), so Ajax can re-enact and reincarnate Hyacinthus' metamorphosis into the same flower in this semiotic niche (*florem/ qui prius Oebalio de vulnere fuerat natus, Met.* 13.396). Appearance fails to function in determining individuality. Hyacinthus' likeness to a flower, as well as the duplication of the flower metamorphosis, appears as a mirroring trick that prevents the reader from seeing past the surface.

For both Hyacinthus and Ajax their names predetermine the outcome of their metamorphoses, but the presence of two versions of the myth confounds the assumption of name as definitive signifier of identity. While Ajax is not named in Apollo's prophesy either, only described as *fortissimus heros* (*Met.* 10.207), this reticence hurts Ajax less since his name is treated as a detachable attribute, or abstract idea of his self as character that surpasses his mortal body.[67] He talks of himself in the third person to Odysseus (*atque Aiax armis, non Aiaci arma petuntur, Met.* 13.97), who then picks upon this by the rhetorical question (*fortis ubi est Aiax, Met.* 13.340). In his final tragic act, the repetition of his name splits him into both perpetrator and victim of the same act, creating an artificial distance between himself and his name (*ne quisquam Aiacem possit superare Aiax, Met.* 13.390).[68] By contrast, the shared name of Hyacinthus and the flower would seem to guarantee, but ultimately does not, his survival in the vegetable kingdom.

DEUCALION AND PYRRHA

While simile, then, does not prefigure the metamorphosis, one may be tempted to read simile as an explanation of the process. When confronted with something outside of our understanding it is common to link it with something that is part of our existing world. The following discussion looks at simile as a means of explaining the mysterious moment of transition. Thus the process of metamorphosis may be compared to the act of creation, to art, or to science. In using references to these ways of understanding our world, Ovid seems to challenge his reader to judge their applicability in his own creation of a fictional world. Once more,

[67] Cf. the narrator's comment on Achilles' fate: *et de tam magno restat Achille/ nescio quid parvum, quod non bene conpleat urnam./ at vivit totum quae gloria conpleat orbem* (*Met.* 12. 615–17).

[68] Hardie (2002), 251.

the insertion of the connective particle "like" should alert us that we are in fact crossing a divide.

As a rule, Ovid does not use simile to illustrate the process of metamorphosis. After all, as Sharrock demonstrated, plain narrative lends itself astonishingly well to the gradual change of one form into the other.[69] As a diachronic medium, narrative can show metamorphosis in the sequence of time in which it occurs. The reader is made to follow along as the alien shape progressively takes over the human body, with the face or mouth being the last vestige of humanity to be erased.[70] The technique resembles ekphrasis in that it gradually completes the mental image of the object depicted.[71] Ovid's language in relating the actual transformation is intentionally blunt with the new reality of the changed body simply being asserted as reality. This matter-of-fact way of describing metamorphosis only increases the mystery of what happens during metamorphosis.

In a select few cases, however, which are presented here, Ovid inserts a simile at the exact moment of transformation. These similes do not show the change from one to the other as before/after but rather convey the ephemeral moment in the middle: detached from either side, they focus on the mysterious nature of the process itself. The purpose of this technique therefore should not be seen as a mental rehearsal of the change to come.[72] The image in the simile rarely corresponds to the actual transformation – as we have seen, the immediacy with which the metamorphosis is related as fact is an effective technique to surprise the reader. It appears that the reason for inserting a simile at this point lies in the artificial distance which is created allowing for reflection and amplification on the process.

A poignant example comes from the first book of the *Metamorphoses* when the stones thrown by Deucalion and Pyrrha are transformed into human bodies (*Met.* 1.400–6):

> saxa (quis hoc credat nisi sit pro teste uetustas?)
> ponere duritiam coepere suumque rigorem
> mollirique mora mollitaque ducere formam.
> mox ubi creuerunt naturaque mitior illis

[69] Sharrock (1996), 106–7.

[70] See in particular the transformation of the Heliades (*Met.* 2.345–63), Cadmus (*Met.* 4.576–603), Philemon and Baucis (*Met.* 8.712–19).

[71] Hardie (2002), 174.

[72] Lyne's observation on the function of simile seems apposite here: "The main function of a simile is not to illustrate something already mentioned in the narrative but to add things which are not mentioned, in a different medium: imagery" Lyne (1989), 86.

> contigit, ut quaedam, sic non manifesta, uideri
> forma potest hominis, sed uti de marmore coepta,
> non exacta satis rudibusque simillima signis.

The stones (who would believe it if not antiquity itself were witness?) began to cast off their hardness and to soften in a while and trace a shape once softened. And as soon as they began to grow and their softer nature touched them just as some certain, if not manifest, form of a man can be seen just as if begun in marble, not yet defined enough but very like it in its rough traces.

At first sight, the simile may strike the reader as anachronistic. The reference to sculpture made out of marble clearly belongs closer to the world of Ovid's contemporary reader than to the beginning of human history.[73] The simile reverses the conventional roles of the theory of mimesis, in which art is thought to imitate nature. The uncanny creation of the human shape out of stone is such a common experience for the reader that it can be used as subject in the simile as easily as examples from nature may be used in a more conventional epic simile. Added to that, there seems to be almost no contrast between tenor and vehicle as if to confuse further the priority of art over nature.[74]

The simile accurately reflects the imitative nature of this second generation of men created from earth. Prometheus, the quasi-divine demiurge, had created humankind from earth by imitating the shape of the gods (*in effigiem … deorum, Met.* 1.83). In this re-creation of humankind, Deucalion and Pyrrha serve as the only remaining *exempla* of the original race (*Met.* 1.366).[75] As living statues to be imitated, they are at the same time human and artifact. The imitative nature of this second creation can be seen in the absence of a clear artist figure as creation is displaced to the simile and the focus falls on the artifact rather than the artist. Metamorphosis just happens miraculously as if it were in the nature of the stone to find human form. Deucalion and Pyrrha have no creative ability themselves; their only agency seems to lie in the determination of sex in the resulting figure. This second transformation, of one form into the other, contrasts with the artistic ability to invent *forma* in the first place. This signals the end of the creation phase and thus the first metamorphosis in the poem.

[73] See Solodow (1988), ch.6 for a discussion of the role of art in the poem, including a reading of the simile, 203–4. Barchiesi (2005b) ad loc. suggests that the marble might signify moral degradation from the earlier terracotta generation.

[74] Wheeler (1995) argues that Ovid's cosmogony already constitutes ekphrasis. This would increase the problem of priority that plagues the beginning(s) (*coepta*) of the poem as a whole.

[75] Solodow (1988), 204.

The apparent conflict of nature versus art in the simile conceals an even more interesting contest between visual and narrative art. Barchiesi comments that Ovid's narrative art is the implied *tertium comparationis* in this simile.[76] Words such as *coepta* (404) and *signis* (405) could be applied to narrative art as well, and it has often been remarked that the artist figures in the poem may stand in as a proxy for the poet himself.[77] However, the connection of visual and narrative art goes even deeper than that.

Comparisons of humans to sculpture are extraordinarily common in the *Metamorphoses*, and in particular are used often in the description of the final stage of metamorphosis, for example in the case of Niobe whose petrifaction renders her into an *imago* of herself (*nihil est in imagine vivum, Met.* 6.305). Similarly, Andromeda appears as a piece of art to Perseus for the absolute stillness of her body except for her tears and hair that animate the picture (*Met.* 4.672–7).[78] The description of the human as a piece of art in the manner of ekphrasis reinforces the notion that what is left is only the empty outer frame of the body, with life, indicated through motion, being absent.

Ovid's use of ekphrases at the end of metamorphosis points to an inherent paradox of their presence in narrative art. Feldherr points out the interplay between static and dynamic representation in these instances:

> It thus seems better to speak of an oscillation between two processes: the distant and other becomes 'real' through translation into an artistic product, which in turn becomes 'real' in the opposite sense, in the sense that its illusion works, that it ceases to be a representation and gives the viewer/reader access to what it represents.[79]

While the highest achievement of a sculptor was thought to be the ability to suggest motion, Ovid points out how sculpture freezes motion, for example in the tableau scene of Niobe's children that captures the victims in the middle of the action (***stabant ...*** *sorores*, 6.288; *e quibus una* ***trahens*** *haerentia viscere tela ... relanguit*, 6.290). Narrative and sculpture mirror one another when one of Perseus' own men marvels at the lifelike image of the Gorgon's victim (*Met.* 5.203–6):[80]

> quem ratus Astyages etiamnum uiuere, longo
> ense ferit; sonuit tinnitibus ensis acutis.
> dum stupet Astyages, naturam traxit eandem
> marmoreoque manet uultus mirantis in ore.

[76] Barchiesi (2005b) ad loc. [77] See in particular Leach (1974) and Lateiner (1984).
[78] Hardie (2002), 183. [79] Feldherr (2002), 176–7. [80] Hardie (2002), 180.

Astyages struck him with his long sword, thinking him still alive: the sword sounds with shrill ringing. While Astyages marvels, he takes on the same nature, his puzzled expression remains in the marble face.

By contrast, the simile of Deucalion and Pyrrha's stones is truly ekphrastic in the sense that it dynamically appropriates a work of static art. In contrast to a complete, static piece of sculpture the simile shows a half-finished form as still in the making. Sharrock sees the simile as temporarily suspending the metamorphosis, freezing it in the moment.[81] However, this freezing effect, in contrast to the sculpture similes mentioned above, in which it signals a complete loss of movement as in death, only reinforces the inherent dynamism of the image. The focalizer of this simile strains to mark out and complete the form that inspires the imagination by virtue of its fragmented nature (*non manifesta, … non exacta satis*, 404, 406).[82]

The half-finished state of the image undercuts the main difference between verbal and visual art, the factor of chronicity. Visual arts are not dynamic but static, synchronic rather than diachronic. The ekphrastic technique of the simile highlights in fact the superior art of the poet. In ekphrasis, the shield of Achilles is not really out there, despite the conceit that it is a concrete, real piece of art. It has no reality beyond the text in which it is described and thus is rather and primarily a literary artifact impersonating visual art. This is of course the conceit behind Ovid's description of metamorphosis itself, as Hardie points out:

The ultimate test of Ovid's ecphrastic powers in the *Metamorphoses* is to secure assent to the visible presence of a world that is not there to be seen because it does not really exist, because it is the product of a narrative of what Ovid will later define as 'bodies transformed in unbelievable ways' (*Trist.* 2. 64 *in non credendos corpora versa modos*).[83]

[81] Sharrock (1996), 123: "the simile 'like an unfinished statue' turns the evolving stone-bodies *into* unfinished statues. The linear progression of the narrative has been arrested with the metamorphosis incomplete by the interruption of the simile. The result is something very like the visual representation of metamorphosis. All similes, all metaphors even, in verbal and visual art are potential metamorphoses." Sharrock's reifying reading (the simile … turns the bodies *into* statues) unfortunately makes her gloss over the conflict between the two modes of representation.

[82] Anderson (1997) ad loc. refers to Rodin's habit of leaving his sculptures unfinished "in order to achieve the effect of an emerging form that the viewer's imagination could complete." Cf. Pliny *HN* 35.145 on the superiority of unfinished pictures: *illud vero perquam rarum ac memoria dignum est, suprema opera artificum imperfectasque tabulas, sicut Irmi Aristidis, Tyndaridias Nicomachi, Mediam Timomachi et quam diximus Venerem Apellis, in maiore admiratione esse quam perfecta, quippe in iis liniamenta reliqua ipsaeque cogitationes artificum spectantur, atque in lenocinio commendationis dolor est manus, cum id ageret, exstinctae.*

[83] Hardie (2002), 178.

As if caught in the act of writing ekphrasis, Ovid shows how his words literally build the artifact diachronically, and do not merely replicate it mimetically. To complicate matters, neither tenor nor vehicle have as yet any ontological status since they are both in the process of being created. Verbal and visual suggestiveness are perfectly matched.

LICHAS

The memory of this stony genesis remains in the collective memory of humankind (*inde genus durum sumus experiensque laborum/ et documenta damus qua simus origine nati, Met.* 1.414–15). Despite the artificial beginnings of this connection, in the many subsequent metamorphoses of human beings into stones the transformation will appear as an almost natural return to this original form.[84] One of the numerous examples of this process throughout the poem, the story of Lichas, seems to follow this pattern as it employs a scientific simile to explain the metamorphosis. Hurled through the air by Hercules, Lichas' body shrivels up and turns into stone. Lichas' death and the imagery of hail and snow that accompanies it stand in pointed contrast to the fiery apotheosis of Hercules. While Lichas' mortal frame condenses, Hercules expands and leaves his shape as a snake sheds its skin (*Met.* 9.266–70). Lichas' mortality, bound to his material body, is forcefully contrasted with Hercules' immortality and transcendence of the constraints of his mortal shape (*quodcumque fuit populabile flammae/ Mulciber abstulerat, Met.* 9.262; *ubi mortales Tirynthius exuit artus, Met.* 9.269). While Hercules' apotheosis is described as a mythical, supernatural event, Lichas' metamorphosis into stone is couched in the language of science, with reference to Lucretius, in particular (*Met.* 9.219–25):

> ille per aerias pendens induruit auras,
> utque ferunt imbres gelidis concrescere uentis,
> inde niues fieri, niuibus quoque molle rotatis
> adstringi et spissa glomerari grandine corpus,
> sic illum ualidis iactum per inane lacertis
> exsanguemque metu nec quicquam umoris habentem
> in rigidos uersum silices prior edidit aetas.

[84] The Greek origin of this metamorphosis emphasizes the etymologizing connection between Greek λᾶας (stone) and λαός (people), Anderson (1997) ad loc. Since Ovid cannot imitate this in Latin, the connection between humans and stones appears even more artificial.

Aloft he hardens through the airy breezes, as they say that rain condenses through icy winds and whence becomes snow, and as the snow spins its softness, too, is frozen and gathers into a body of dense hail, so Lichas, tradition claimed, hurled through the void by strong limbs, bloodless with fear and no longer having any moisture was turned into rigid stone.

Myers sees in the jolting incongruity of scientific language and mythical event a humorous contrast between Lucretius' and Ovid's explanatory mode of physical change.[85] The joke may go even deeper than the playful appropriation of language that she suggests. According to Epicurean thought, all matter is interrelated, and invisible phenomena can be rationally deduced by analogy with close observation of the visible world.[86] In the Lucretian argument about meteorological phenomena that Ovid invokes, the human body is seen as analogous to the cosmos (Lucretius 6.497–502). The physical phenomena of the sky can be understood through observation of one's own body (*ut pariter nobis cum corpore sanguine crescit/ sudor item atque umor quicumque est denique membris*, Lucretius 6.501–2).

Ovid inverts these terms by showing the metamorphosis of Lichas' body as akin to precipitation, even though the likeness is purely visual, not grounded in atomic theory. Since Lichas travels through the air like a piece of hail, it follows that he should undergo the same physical changes. The visual impression of Lichas' body in the distance collapses the Lucretian model of analogy in a single image that emphasizes the distance of both the body and the sky from the observer. Anderson draws attention to the sudden shift in the reader's perspective.[87] Lichas' transformation happens out of the range of close observation. This contrasts with the usual observation of the physical change of metamorphosis at close range – by either the victim himself or his environment. There is nobody in the sky to observe the transformation; the focalizer is rooted to the earth.[88] Ovid's pseudo-scientific stance mocks the delusion that attentive observation of metamorphosis will serve to explain it. The urge to absorb the inexplicable

85 Myers (1994), 47–8.

86 Schiesaro (1990), 31: "Questo procedimento d'indagine nasce all'interno della dottrina fisica epicureo-lucreziana. La realtà visibile è composta di *concilia*: gli atomi, e alcuni *concilia* di limitate dimensione restono al di sotto della soglia di percezione. I *concilia*, però, sono formati da atomi (e accolgono al loro interno del vuoto), e ne derivano quindi alcune caratteristiche. Per questo motivo l'indagine riferita ai *primordia* non può prescindere dall osservazione dei *concilia* visibili, e quindi dall' esistenza di un rapporto di causa ed effetto che collega le due sfere. L'immagine della realtà che è sottintesa a questo procedimento è quella di un *continuum* fra atomi, *concilia* invisibili e – finalmente – *concilia* visibili in grado di superare la soglia della percezione umana."

87 Anderson (1972) ad loc.

88 Similar observations of celestial phenomena have proven false before: Phaethon appears to be a falling star (*Met.* 2.319–22); Daedalus and Icarus are mistaken for gods (*Met.* 8.219–22).

into our frame of reference should be resisted. Metamorphosis is not made 'natural' simply by being presented as such – the two modes of aetiology are polar opposites. By using scientific language in this inappropriate context Ovid makes us doubt the validity of science itself.[89] The fact that Lichas' body has actually been transformed into a stone Ovid only reports from hearsay (*Met.* 9.224–5):

> exsanguemque metu nec quicquam umoris habentem
> in rigidos uersum silices prior edidit aetas.

Lichas, bloodless from fear and no longer having any moisture, was turned into a rigid rock, tradition claimed.

Ovid may ridicule our credulity in quasi-scientific explanation, as we willingly accept that a dried-up body changes into stone because of the loss of moisture. However, myth does not necessarily trump science. As with other transformations, including the first transformation of stones into human beings, Ovid forestalls our incredulity by reference to authority.[90] Even so, the sailors in the story half-believe, half-disbelieve that rock and body are one (*scopulus brevis …, quem quasi sensurum, nautae calcare verentur,/ appellantque Lichan, Met.* 9. 226–8). Ovid's phrase *prior aetas* self-referentially recalls our human origins in stone from book 1, a pattern that gets reactivated with every tale of a human being transformed into stone. The continuous exposure to stories of metamorphosis has changed the reader's mind in the direction of accepting the miraculous. Thus the sailors treat the stone as if it were sentient (*quasi sensurum*),[91] an oxymoron if ever there was one, since stones are precisely lacking in sentiency; they, not the poet, equate the stone with the human being by calling it "Lichas."[92] It is important to note this slight gap in continuity, first in the conditional endorsement of the scientific account of transformation and then in the aetiological act performed by the sailors who give "it" a name. It is precisely this gray area of non-identification that makes metamorphosis such a fascinating subject for mythological narrative in that it leaves room for mystery and disbelief. In Lichas' story we see the metamorphosis as myth in the making.

89 Myers (1994), 49–60. 90 Cf. *Met.* 1.400: *quis hoc credat, nisi sit pro teste vetustas?*

91 Their caution in stepping on the rock contrasts ironically with the phrase *humanae … vestigia formae*; they do not wish to disrupt the "footprint" (s.v. *vestigium* (1a) OLD) of Lichas' prior shape.

92 This contrasts with the logical continuity of a speaking name such as Daphne, Myrrha, Arethusa which preserves the individual while the body changes. See Hardie (2002), 239–57.

ADONIS

Lichas' metamorphosis happens at great distance and leaves open to doubt the reliability of such observations. Inference from empirical observation refers the reader back to the original problem of interpreting images. In the following example Ovid uses simile at the point of transformation shows metamorphosis at extremely close range. Venus' beloved Adonis has been killed by a boar, and Venus declares that his blood will be transformed into a flower (*Met.* 10.728). We are invited to observe the transformation with scientific precision (*Met.* 10.731–7):

> sic fata cruorem
> nectare odorato sparsit, qui tactus ab illo
> intumuit sic, ut fuluo perlucida caeno
> surgere bulla solet; nec plena longior hora
> facta mora est, cum flos de sanguine concolor ortus,
> qualem quae lento celant sub cortice granum
> punica ferre solent.

Speaking thus, she sprinkled the blood with perfumed nectar; touched by it, it swelled up like a translucent bubble does from yellow mud, and after a delay that took no more than an hour, a flower was born, the same color as the blood, such as the seed of pomegranates that hides under the unyielding rind.

Whereas Ovid had elided the precise moment of transformation in the Hyacinthus story by simply stating "*ecce cruor/ … desinit esse cruor*" (*Met.* 10.210–11), here we are made to witness metamorphosis as a science experiment with precise instructions, with the incongruous ingredients of human blood and divine nectar. Even the time it takes, quantified precisely as one hour (*nec plena longior hora/ facta mora est, Met.* 10.734–5) contrasts with more subjective impressions of time in all other metamorphoses.

Ovid's pseudo-scientific detachment in relating this bizarre sight contrasts forcefully with the symbolic resonance of this event. Not only does Venus cite the (odd) precedent of Persephone turning Mentha into a plant to forestall invidia,[93] but the flower's red color recalls both Adonis' blood and the kernels of the symbolic fruit of eros and death, the pomegranate. The flower itself, of course, serves also as a reminder of the brevity of life, not so much a reminder of Adonis as an image of death itself, a *mortis imago*.

[93] Persephone punished Mentha out of jealousy, not love. Note also the hypothetical presence of Livor at Adonis' birth (*laudaret faciem Livor quoque, Met.* 10.515).

Despite these resonances, Ovid seems to go out of his way to show that all meaning shows on the surface. The oddity of this privileged view comes out if one contrasts the usual glossing over of such moments of transubstantiation of tears or blood in other stories. There is something unsettling, revolting even, in witnessing this event at such close range. The image of a bubble arising from mud in describing the mixture of human blood and the 'stuff of immortality' proves so lacking in decorum to Anderson that he resists Merkel's widely accepted emendation "*caeno*" for "*caelo*," and offers a more sanitized version of transparent bubbles floating towards the sky.[94] While Bömer has vindicated *caeno* since, the challenge to interpret this strange sight remains.[95]

What sets this metamorphosis apart is Venus' perfumed nectar as catalyst for the transformation. That this mingling of divine and human fluids is Ovid's invention becomes clear when one compares this version to the one told in Bion's *Lament of Adonis*, where, separately, Adonis' blood creates the rose and Venus' tears bring forth the anemone.[96] Ovid uses Bion's poem as model for his lament for Tibullus where he makes Venus almost shed tears for her beloved vates *(avertit vultus, Erycis quae possidet arces;/ sunt quoque, qui lacrimas continuisse negant, Am.* 3.9.45). The delicacy with which Ovid describes Venus' grief respects the etiquette that forbids gods to come in touch with human death.

Ovid's restraint in his earlier poem renders even more spectacular the mingling of divine and human, at least in the abstract sense, at Adonis' death. Instead of keeping human and divine apart, Ovid insists on the mixture of the two. The image of the bubbling mud[97] giving birth to new forms recalls the genesis of the rest of creation after that of mankind from stones (*Met.* 1.416–21):

> cetera diuersis tellus animalia formis
> sponte sua peperit, postquam uetus umor ab igne
> percaluit solis **caenumque** udaeque paludes
> **intumuere** aestu, fecundaque semina rerum,
> uiuaci nutrita solo ceu matris in aluo[98]
> creuerunt faciemque aliquam cepere **morando**.

94 Anderson (1972) ad loc. 95 Bömer (1969–86) ad loc.

96 Bion 1.64–7, Reed (1997), 128: δάκρυον ἁ Παφία τόσον ἐκχέει ὅσσον Ἄδωνις/ αἷμα χέει, τὰ δὲ πάντα ποτὶ χθονὶ γίνεται ἄνθη/ αἷμα ῥόδον τίκτει, τὰ δὲ δάκρυα τὰν ἀνεμώναν.

97 *caenum* is used only in these two instances in the *Metamorphoses*. It is not a frequent word in Ovid; the other places are *Pont.* 4.3.47 and *Ib.* 443.

98 As Deucalion says at *Met.* 1.393, *magna parens terra est*. Note the importance of this allegorical reading for the subsequent discussion on displaced motherhood.

The rest of the animals in diverse forms the earth brought forth of its own accord, after the old humidity had been warmed through by the sun and the swamps and the mud swelled up with the heat, and the fertile seeds of things had grown in the life giving ground nourished as in a mother's womb, and took another likeness in the delay.

The image of the fertile mud that has the potential to produce monsters (*Met.* 1.438–40) points to the problematic sexual attraction of Venus and Adonis. Hardie has pointed out the implication of incest when Venus falls in love with the spitting image of her son.[99] Her infatuation with Adonis is instigated by Cupid himself and is said to be a revenge for Myrrha's fate (*Met.* 10.524–8).

Myrrha's incestuous relationship with her father is made all the worse because of her conception of Adonis (*plena patris thalamis excedit impia diro/ semina fert utero conceptaque crimina portat*, *Met.* 10.469–70). In fact, Orpheus had begun the story with the pronouncement that Cinyras would have been better off without any offspring (*editus hac ille est, qui si sine prole fuisset,/ inter felices Cinyras potuisset haberi, Met.* 10.298–9). That Adonis is the product of this incest is not omitted; he is called by his patronymic *Cinyreius heros* by the narrator (*Met.* 10.712) and by Venus herself (*Met.* 10.730).

Unlike Myrrha, Venus is not shown crossing the threshold of sexual contact and thus narrowly avoids the messy implications of a potential pregnancy. The tale of her love for Adonis stops short of showing her as his lover despite the fact that she shows all the symptoms of physical desire (*Met.* 10.529–32). However, at the very moment of greatest seduction, as she lies down with Adonis under a tree (*Met.* 10.553–89), her telling of the cautionary tale of Hippomenes and Atalanta replaces the lovemaking. This delicate veiling of the goddess' sex life on part of the internal narrator Orpheus is made even more impressive as the goddess herself covers with talk the lacuna in her own love story. Venus leaves immediately after the telling of the story (*Met.* 10.708–9), and we are never sure whether she has made love to Adonis or not.

At the moment of metamorphosis, however, the mingling of human blood and perfumed nectar has deliberate sexual overtones. Adonis' blood comes from his groin (*sub inguine*, 715). It swells up at the touch of Venus' sensually perfumed nectar (*sic fata cruorem/ nectare odorato sparsit; qui tactus ab illo/ intumuit*, 731–3).[100] Instead of human and divine sex, Venus' creation of the flower sublimates her desire through a harmless addition

[99] Hardie (2004), 102. [100] Adams (1982) s.v. *inguen, tango, tumor.*

to the vegetable kingdom, while Myrrha's earlier transformation into a tree did not succeed in dehumanizing her offspring. Adonis' death extinguishes at last the unfortunate bloodline of Cinyras and bans both mother and son from the human race.[101] At the same time, the flower that results from the metamorphosis continuously replays the issue of mortality and immortality in its seasonal rebirth and death.

Ovid's use of simile in these examples of metamorphosis does not seem to resolve the mystery surrounding the event. Rather than giving the reader an explanation, the simile seems to introduce another layer of confusion. Is metamorphosis natural or artificial? Does it represent a regression to an earlier form of life, affinity or alienation of the human race from its other in nature? The questions have only multiplied with the images proffered. Ovid's world is a world of constant surface delusion where simply looking is not enough. The simile thus complicates rather than simplifies the process by suggesting that likeness might reveal the truth or just prove to be an illusion. Metamorphosis is and is not like the world we know, both a part of and apart from the universe the reader inhabits.

101 Such was Myrrha's prayer (*Met.* 10.483–7). Cf. also Detienne's theory (1972) of the Adonia as a festival that stresses sterility, not fertility.

CHAPTER 2

The gods and the simile

The control over form marks the crucial divide between gods and mortals in the *Metamorphoses*. As we have seen, for mortals the loss of the human form comes with the loss of their human identity and individuality. The gods, by contrast, as agents of metamorphosis, are master manipulators of form, from the beginning of the poem (*nam vos mutastis et illa, Met.* 1.2). Apart from inflicting metamorphosis on humans, the gods also change their own shape through disguise, although their transformation is both temporary and voluntary. The gods' habit of disguise therefore forms a logical counterpart to human metamorphosis.[1] Feeney notes that the gods' privileged position as exempt from ultimate change means that they "always become again themselves."[2] This divine ability to return to its former shape foregrounds the question of the representation and identity of the divine in this poem. The gods are involved in the puzzle of appearances, that is the contradiction of being and seeming, as much as any other character in the poem. Even when the gods are "themselves," they are pictured according to the anthropomorphic convention of the visual arts, a convention that emphasizes the mutual dependence of mortals and immortals.[3]

In the poetic tradition of ancient epic, humans are regularly compared to the divine in similes that focus on the mortal's beauty (*forma*). The relative position of the human as the tenor and the divine as the vehicle reflects the aspirational nature of the comparison, in which the mortal is augmented and brought into association with the immortals

[1] Zgoll (2004), 157–204 differentiates the gods' change of form from human metamorphosis by using the term *Allophanie*.

[2] Feeney (1991), 202.

[3] Cicero's *De natura deorum* explores the issue of the gods' physical shape, and the tradition of their anthropomorphic representation. Cotta's critique of Epicurean doctrine contains this pertinent statement (*Nat. D.* 1.90): *Nec vero intellego cur maluerit Epicurus deos hominum similes dicere quam homines deorum. Quaeres quid intersit; si enim hoc illi simile sit, esse illud huic. Video, sed hoc dico, non an hominibus formae figuram venisse ad deos; di enim semper fuerunt … non ergo illorum humana forma sed nostra divina dicenda est.*

while not quite reaching divine status. While these similes do exist in the *Metamorphoses*, a more intriguing group of similes reverses the positions and makes the god the tenor of the vehicle. The inversion shifts the traditional focus on beauty to the more fundamental one of shape – what do the gods look like? As a result the poem offers two likenesses of the gods: the disguise they choose for themselves and the likeness they are given by the poet through the use of simile. By introducing an extraneous image in the simile Ovid compromises the gods' ability to control their appearance. His visual manipulation of the gods' likeness highlights the challenge of both imagining and representing the divine.

The necessity for the gods to disguise themselves when encountering mortals goes back to the Homeric poems, yet the need becomes more acute in the world of the *Metamorphoses* which, as Bernbeck observed, has gods and mortals interacting on a central plane.[4] Rather than darting in and out of the action, the gods in the *Metamorphoses* are constantly present, and their encounters with the mortals form the story not the backdrop of the poem. The gods' ability to disguise themselves means that they can be present at any moment, unobserved by the characters in the scene. The latent consciousness of their existence oddly applies also to some human victims of metamorphosis. From a mortal's perspective, an animal might be a god in disguise, a transformed human, or simply its animal self.

Borrowing a natural shape, the gods become part of the human world and blend into the landscape.[5] When assimilating themselves to the human form, they often choose unremarkable characters, such as an old woman or a traveler,[6] characters that are commonplace to the point of being invisible. Unlike the privileged communication of Homeric or Virgilian heroes where the gods step into the "character" of a hero's friend, in the *Metamorphoses* mortals encounter the gods seemingly at random.[7] While

4 Bernbeck (1967), 88.

5 The exceptions to this are gods that are literally part of the landscape, such as the river god Acheloos who nonetheless brags about his shape-shifting abilities (*Met.* 8.879–84).

6 Zgoll's (2004), 353–4 (incomplete) list of gods disguised as humans shows the prevalence of gods disguising themselves as friends or family in deceiving mortals in Homer and Virgil.

For the gods in unassuming disguise in the *Metamorphoses*, see for example Jupiter's test of Lycaon's piety, which becomes Lycaon's test of Jupiter divinity (*Met.* 1.209–43), Jupiter and Mercury as travelers received by Baucis and Philemon (*Met.* 8.618–724). Minerva's disguise as an old woman (*Met.* 6.26–7), the same as Vertumnus' (*Met.* 14.654–7), does not inspire reverence. Salzman-Mitchell (2005b) 205–6, notes that old women are practically invisible by lack of attracting anybody's attention.

7 Privileged relationships between gods and humans in which they appear without disguise do exist, e.g. Callisto and Diana (book 2), Apollo and Hyacinthus (book 10), Cyparissus (book 10), Coronis (book 2), Venus and Adonis (book 10), and Hippolytus and Diana (book 15). However, the essence

the gods are disguised as they enter the human world, they always reveal their divinity after the fact in order to inspire fear and devotion from the mortals.[8] Involuntary detection of their identity is punished severely.

Bömer noted that the divine entrances in the poem are emphasized by a pattern of similes.[9] Rather than letting the gods slip into the action unnoticed, the narrator makes a point of highlighting the divine presence. The simile thus indicates the gods' liminal state as they cross from the divine into the human sphere. Using the form of the simile, the immortal is assimilated to the natural world of which he becomes a part. Let us observe such an entrance.

As the messenger god, Mercury acts as a go-between between the human and divine realm. He is thus eminently suited for a discussion of the gods' traversing this boundary and its visual representation. In the second book of the *Metamorphoses*, Mercury happens to fly over Attica as the inhabitants celebrate the Panathenaea. He notices Herse and decides to take a closer look. In flight, he is compared to a kite (*Met.* 2.714–21):

> inde reuertentes deus aspicit ales iterque
> non agit in rectum, sed in orbem curuat eundem.
> ut uolucris visis rapidissima miluus extis,
> dum timet et densi circumstant sacra ministri,
> flectitur in gyrum nec longius audet abire
> spemque suam motis auidus circumuolat alis,
> sic super Actaeas agilis Cyllenius arces
> inclinat cursus et easdem circinat auras.

As they come back, the god spies them, and turns his winged flight not straight back but circles in the same arc. Like a kite, swiftest of birds, on seeing the entrails, though it fears the attendants standing packed around the sacrifice, turns in a spiral and does not dare to go farther away and greedily hovers around the object of its hope with beaten wings, so the nimble Cyllenian turns his path over the Actaean citadel and circles on the same breezes.

The comparison can be perceived as perfectly appropriate as it logically associates the appearance of two winged creatures. Gods and birds share their otherness in their ability to move through the air. The simile functions in an almost literal way in answering the question of how to

of these stories is the expulsion of the mortal from the shared space with the divine. I will discuss some of these episodes below.

8 Zgoll (2004), 165–74 for a very detailed discussion of the terms used to indicate the gods' disguise and revelation.

9 Bömer (1969) at *Met.* 1. 200 refers to similes marking the gods' entrance at 1.533–9, 2.623, 716, 726; 3.183.

represent the gods' passage through air – since only birds can fly the gods must look like birds (*ales iterque/ non agit in rectum, sed in orbem curvat eundem*, 714–15; *motis ... circumvolat alis*, 722). Mercury's impromptu decision to turn around is compared and explained by the typical flying gesture of the kite.

The bird's presence might be interpreted as a good omen for sacrifice. The sacrificial context provides a plausible (if wrong) reason for the god's presence. Mercury is an interloper at another god's festival, a detail present in the scavenger motif (*avidus*, 719). The simile also plays up, ironically, the religious significance of this vision by combining the two most important ritual aspects of Roman sacrifice (augury and inspection of the entrails) in the incongruous context of Athenian ritual. The focalization of the simile from the ground perspective implies that Mercury is being noticed at his entrance in the mortal sphere.

Ovid's simile alludes to its model in Virgil's *Aeneid* which marks the only instance of a god being compared to a bird. Virgil's simile furthermore comes at a crucial juncture of the plot in the *Aeneid*. Mercury comes to Carthage in order to admonish Aeneas to leave Dido (*Aen.* 4.251–8), and pauses dramatically on Mount Atlas before making his way to Carthage (*Aen.* 4.252–6):

> hic primum paribus nitens Cyllenius alis
> constitit: hinc toto praeceps se corpore ad undas
> misit avi similis, quae circum litora, circum
> piscosos scopulos humilis volat aequora iuxta.
> haud aliter terras inter caelumque volabat ...

Here first did the Cyllenian land, shining on even wings: hence did he throw himself headlong with all his body towards the waves, like a bird, which flies low, right next to the sea's surface around the shore and the crags teeming with fish. No different was he flying between the lands and the sky...

By implying that Mercury could be seen flying towards Carthage, Aeneas' claim that he has seen the god (*ipse deum manifesto in lumine vidi, Aen.* 4.358) receives outside proof from the focalizer of the simile. By using the Virgilian model, Ovid creates an exaggerated sense of suspense that contradicts the casualness of the god's motivation. Ovid's use of the phrase *illa forte die* in conjunction with sacrifice recalls and parodies the highly charged significance of such "coincidences" in the *Aeneid*, for example the meeting of Aeneas and Evander.[10]

[10] *Aen.* 8.102–4: *Forte die sollemnem illo rex Arcas honorem/ Amphitryoniadae magno divisque ferebat/ ante urbem in luco.*

The fact that the bird is a scavenger, and his imagined motive, namely snatching meat from the altar (716), neatly aligns Mercury with the other gods coming to earth in order to rape a girl.[11] The simile sets up the by now familiar story of divine rape, but does so misleadingly. Mercury will in fact formally court Herse as a suitor, and makes a point of not tricking the mortal by disguise.

The text continues unbroken with another simile in which the unclear subject at last turns out to be Herse (724). Ovid's technique of clustering similes thus brings together the mortal and the immortal as close as possible (*Met.* 2.722–5).

> quanto splendidior quam cetera sidera fulget
> Lucifer et quanto quam Lucifer aurea Phoebe,
> tanto virginibus praestantior omnibus Herse
> ibat eratque decus pompae comitumque suarum.

By as much as Lucifer shines more brightly than the other stars and by as much as golden Phoebe more brightly than Lucifer, so much more prominent was Herse walking among all the maidens, the glory of the train and her companions.

Barchiesi recognized Bion's cletic hymn to Hesperus as the source of this simile, in which a lover asks Hesperus to light his way to his lover.[12] In using the address to a god for a mortal, Ovid might be seen as divinizing Herse by association. Moreover, Lucifer's association with Venus, and Phoebe's with the goddess Diana, conjure up Herse's sexual innocence and attraction simultaneously. The point of comparison, however, is not the divinity but the degree or distance by which Herse outshines her company. The unusual construction of this simile with the two comparatives building on each other emphasizes her increasing distance from the other mortals. The first image, the star, literally pales in contrast with the second, the moon, as if to render the effort made to match her splendor.[13]

In contrast with other encounters of gods and mortal women in the *Metamorphoses*, Herse is not compared to a goddess to make up for the "subhuman debasement of Mercury's appetites."[14] The simile refers instead

[11] The best example for this association is the story of Apollo and Daphne in which Apollo protests that he is not the enemy (*Met.* 1.505–7), only to be overruled by the narrator (*Met.* 1.533–9).

[12] Barchiesi (2005b) on *Met.* 2.722–3, Bion 11.1–5. Reed (1997), 170–2. Hesperus and Lucifer refer to the same planet, Venus: the substitution of one name for the other marks the allusion.

[13] The evening star in Bion's simile shows the progression in the evening sky: the evening star is the first to appear, then the moon becomes the brightest object.

[14] Galinsky (1975), 165.

to the planets, the evening star (Hesperus),[15] and the moon (Phoebe) and the abstract quality of their radiance. Since Mercury can also be thought of as a planet, the simile describing Herse's radiance lifts her off the ground and includes her in the attraction of the two constellations in the high air (*easdem auras*, 721; *aethere*, 726; *sub nubibus*, 729). The transition between the two similes appears all the more natural as all eyes are on the sky already, watching Mercury.

A third simile switches the perspective back to Mercury, as his burning passion is compared to a lead bullet shot from a sling (*Met.* 2.726–9):

> obstipuit forma Iove natus et aethere pendens
> non secus exarsit quam cum Balearica plumbum
> funda iacit; uolat illud et incandescit eundo,
> et quos non habuit sub nubibus inuenit ignis.

The son of Jupiter was struck by her beauty and hovering in the aether caught fire, not unlike when a Balearic sling hurls a leaden bullet; it flies and grows white hot as it goes and finds under the clouds the fire it did not have before.

In addition to using a passive image for the god's passion, the simile adds the technical detail of heat through friction. As Mercury makes his way to earth, he gradually becomes more human in his amorous passion (*quos non habuit … invenit ignis*, 729). The simile thus signals the change in identity from god to lover.[16]

The significance of this last simile in describing the god's transition between divine and human sphere comes out in its repetition in describing the apotheosis of Romulus where it is used to indicate the opposite direction, from mortal to god.[17] As Romulus makes his way towards heaven he loses his mortal body (*Met.* 14.824–6):

> corpus mortale per auras
> dilapsum tenues, ceu lata plumbea funda
> missa solet medio glans intabescere caelo

His mortal body dropped behind through the thin airs, like a leaden bullet, shot by a far-reaching sling, begins to melt in the middle of the sky.

With this doubling Ovid calls attention to the corporeality of the gods. If Romulus has to lose his mortal body to become a god, one has to assume

[15] Barchiesi (2005b) ad loc. The fact that the evening star is male would make the substitution awkward.

[16] In his speech to Aglauros, Mercury makes the same transition from god to lover (*Met.* 2.742–7).

[17] Ovid uses the motif of the sling in a third instance in describing Lichas being hurled through the air by Hercules (*Met.* 9.217–25), which I discuss in the first chapter.

that the gods are likewise bound to become more human when they meet mortals. The simile thus prepares the reader for the extended description of Mercury's anthropomorphic appearance.

This piling up of similes at this critical stage then attracts attention to the blurring of boundaries between human and divine. By remaining inside the world of simile for four consecutive images, Ovid emphasizes the liminal nature of the encounter between mortal and divine. The progression and alternation of focus in this sequence from Mercury's outward appearance (*volucris miluus*, 716) to Herse's appearance (Lucifer, Phoebe) and then back to Mercury's human-like feelings of love (*exarsit*, 727) give an almost universal view on this scene with an implied mortal perspective on Mercury disrupted by the simile that describes Herse from Mercury's point of view.

As Mercury changes course towards earth, the reader is made aware of the simile's retarding effect on the narrative. The hovering in the air that marks the simile sequence, the undecided state of human and divine categories and space, is replicated on the level of narrative as the attention returns to the action. Even this is anticipated in the image of the lead shot as the arc towards the earth finds its parallel in Mercury's own landing.

Mercury now prepares himself for a meeting with Herse. While the poet disguises the god through the simile, the god himself, breaching divine etiquette, does not.[18] He makes a point of it in deciding to dress as himself, complete with his divine regalia. In fact, the description of his toilette is detailed to the point of being ekphrasis, so that the grooming seems excessive and faintly comical (*Met.* 2.731–6):[19]

> nec se dissimulat; tanta est fiducia formae.
> quae quamquam iusta est, cura tamen adiuvat illam
> permulcetque comas chlamydenque ut pendeat apte
> conlocat, ut limbus totumque appareat aurum,
> ut teres in dextra quae somnos ducit et arcet
> uirga sit, ut tersis niteant talaria plantis.

Nor does he disguise himself; so much confidence has he in his beauty. Although it is perfect, he still sets it off with special care; he smooths down his hair and

[18] Barkan (1986), 90 points Mercury's *fiducia formae* as an example for the gods' ability to return to their own self. His honesty costs him, however: Aglauros makes him leave (751).

[19] Galinsky (1975), 166–7 notes the contradiction between Mercury's human behavior in grooming and his divine confidence in his beauty. The irony might lie rather in his effeminate behavior that is represented by the act of grooming as Barchiesi (2005b) ad loc. points out: "Tutta la preparazione del dio è in conflitto con le concezioni tradizionali della mascolinità romana …" Aiming to seduce Herse, not rape her, Mercury follows elegiac, rather than epic etiquette. For the genre implications, see Chapter 3 on Apollo and Daphne.

arranges his cloak to fall properly and makes sure that its fringe looks golden and that the wand that he has in his right hand which brings and protects the dreams is polished and that his winged sandals shine with clean soles.

Mercury's grooming emphasizes the traditional accessories that make him look like a work of art. Mercury's decision to come as himself actually provides a puzzle of representation. He is already wearing costume that is the costume of standard iconography that identifies him by his regalia – the sandals, and the staff. The repeated purpose clauses show artistic care for detail, in the attention to the folds of cloth (*ut pendeat apte*), smoothness and shine (*teres, niteant*), and the impression of precious material (*ut limbus totumque appareat aurum*) which would be criteria for appraising a statue.[20]

While Mercury rejects disguise and thus a change in identity, he nonetheless is concerned with adjusting the surface to reflect an ideal image of himself. Mercury's preparations ironically mirror the beautifying of Aeneas by Venus before meeting Dido, his mortal form augmented to reflect his divine mission. Mercury's splendid appearance prevents an unobserved entrance in the human realm as Herse's sister Aglauros notices him. It might even have been his shiny golden appearance that puts the thought of golden ransom in Aglauros' head (*Met.* 2.750–1). Aglauros' skill in detecting the divine in the world marks her impudence (*Met.* 2.748–9):

aspicit hunc oculis isdem quibus abdita nuper
uiderat Aglauros flauae secreta Mineruae.

She looks at him with the same eyes with which Aglauros had recently seen the hidden secret of blonde Minerva.

Ironically, the god's body will be one of the images that torture her in her sleep as a punishment (804). Ovid's use of the simile in this passage highlights the difficulty of imagining the shape of the divine. In crossing towards the human realm the shape of the god becomes open to manipulation and interpretation. Even Mercury's rejection of disguise necessitates that he literally step into a conventional, anthropomorphic image of himself.

Ovid explores the relation of divine shape and identity also in the story of Battus (*Met.* 2.680–707) immediately preceding this episode. Mercury tests Battus by twice changing his disguise and voice. Battus fails the test

[20] Cf. Propertius 2.31.5 in which Ovid praises a statue of Apollo Palatinus as being more beautiful than the god himself. Barchiesi (2005a), 284 suggests that this might be because of the implied resemblance to Augustus.

of loyalty by going for the larger bribe and is punished by being changed into a rock on which he perjured himself (oath, 696–7; *saxo*, 707), an almost exact double of Aglauros (oath, 816–17; *saxum*, 830). Mercury finds the joke in this game of mistaken identities (*Met.* 2.704–5):

> risit Atlantiades et 'me mihi, perfide, prodis?
> me mihi prodis?' ait

Mercury laughs and says: "Traitor, are you betraying me to myself? Myself to my own self?"

Ovid's use of the personal pronouns in this seemingly paradoxical fashion underlines the god's mastery over his sense of self. The phrase echoes Marsyas' plaint when skinned alive as punishment for challenging Apollo: *Quid me mihi detrahis?* (*Met.* 6.385). For the mortal Marsyas, the skin, the carrier of his identity, cannot be separated from a separate "inner" self without death as a consequence.[21]

It is no coincidence that Ovid chooses Mercury for this role. In the opening scene of Plautus' *Amphitruo*, Mercury engages Sosia in a battle of wits by persistently confusing the personal pronouns as marker of identity (e.g. *ego sum Sosia ille quem tu dudum esse aiebas mihi, Amph.* 387). Defeated, Sosia is forced to give up his identity. In his plea to the gods as he leaves the scene, he reminds one of a victim of metamorphosis (*Amph.* 455–7):

> Di immortales, obsecro vostram fidem.
> ubi ego perii? ubi immutatus sum? ubi ego formam perdidi?
> an egomet me illic reliqui, si forte oblitus fui?

Immortal gods, I implore your protection. When did I die, change, lose my shape? Or maybe I forgot and left myself behind back there?

Thus the gods' change of shape marks a true divide between them and the mortal victims of metamorphosis. The gods, simply put, are never "themselves" but are seen as constantly adopting or borrowing shapes. This habit in turn only serves to enhance the mystery of their true identity. The profound difference from mortals lies in the gods' innate disregard for letting their identity become attached to their likeness.

The image of Mercury as a kite in the simile above captures the god at a transitional moment and illustrates his ambivalent state, and calls

[21] The stripping of Marsyas' outer skin cruelly parodies the ease with which the gods can dispose of their disguise as if it were a garment. See Feldherr and James (2004) for complementary readings of this episode.

attention to the special significance of using the bird image. Since birds are seen as communicating the will of the gods, their appearance and movement through the air in a particular situation challenges the observer to interpret what he sees. A bird is not just a bird, it is always potentially charged with meaning.

In the context of the *Metamorphoses*, these similes are charged moreover with an implied violation of category and the hierarchy of beings. Both the god and the bird are "other" on opposite sides of the spectrum from a mortal perspective, yet they also are seen as exceptionally close.[22] Here, a brief excursion on the history of the problem will be necessary before we proceed with a simile that directly engages with controversy of depicting gods as birds, that of Daedalus and Icarus as birds (*Met.* 8.211–16).

Virgil, with one exception, appears to avoid such similes. The reason for this may be seen in criticism of similes likening a god to a bird in the Homeric poems,[23] a subject of great debate in the Homeric scholia. The issue in particular seems to be whether the gods are actually changing their shape to that of a bird or whether the likeness is limited to their ability to move quickly and vertically. The latter view in particular is often accompanied with a strong disclaimer that the god has not changed shape.[24] West sees in this a possible bias against the idea of theriomorphic gods.[25]

The debate has carried over into modern studies, notably by Dirlmeier who proposed that all instances of a god being likened to a bird should be read as similes.[26] In separate articles Bannert and Erbse have since refuted this argument and shown that the Homeric poems show the gods disguised as birds as well as being compared to birds.[27]

It is difficult to distinguish semantically between simile and disguise in the Homeric poems since the same equivalent of "like" may be used for either one. For example εἰδομένη should be taken as "likening/disguising

[22] Aristophanes *Birds* reveals the comic potential of their liminal status. See in particular the promise that the 'birds' will always be present, contrasting with the stately remoteness of the Olympians: *Av.* 723–36.

[23] The comparison of gods to birds lies principally in motion. See Janko (1992) on *Il.* 13.62–5, Kirk (1990) on *Il.* 7.59–60. For the gods' bird-like movement cf. *Il.* 5.778, 13.62–5, 19.350. Moulton (1977), 138 draws attention to the gods' own preference to disguise themselves in bird form, e.g. Athena *Od.* 1.320, 3.37; *Il.* 7.59, 14.268; Hermes *Od.* 5.51; Leucothea *Od.* 5.337, 353.

[24] The problem with reading all instances as similes comes out in the tortured explanation of one scholiast (T *Il.* 7.59) of Athena and Apollo sitting on a tree and watching the battle "like vultures." He explains that they are not birds but that they are sitting in the manner of birds, lightly.

[25] West (1988), on *Od.* 3.371–2. On *Od.* 5.337 she suggests that "the 'scientific' MSS that omitted the line conceivably misunderstood the comparison and took offense at a theriomorphic goddess."

[26] Dirlmeier (1967). [27] Bannert (1978), Erbse (1980).

herself," therefore a change of shape,[28] whereas εἰκυῖα suggests a comparison.[29] In the first instance, the god is determining his appearance through disguise, in the second instance the bird-like quality of his movement is a subjective impression.

However, the continuity in bird imagery for the gods in the Homeric poems allows for slippage between the god as bird and the god moving like a bird. On leaving their human interlocutor the gods often reveal themselves through their unusual, sudden movement that is similar to that of birds.[30] Yet at *Odyssey* 3.371–2 Athena literally changes her disguise from Mentor to that of a sea-eagle and thus signals an omen to Telemachus, promptly interpreted by Nestor (*Od.* 3.375–84). Athena thus can be said physically to incorporate her own omen in the disguise of a bird.

In his study of the Homeric simile, Moulton shows a poignant example of such interplay of bird imagery in the *Odyssey* that highlights the closeness of simile and disguise.[31] At the beginning of Odysseus' fight with the suitors the narrator depicts Athena sitting on one of the rafters. She is disguised as a swallow.[32] While the suitors do not notice her because they see a bird (they might overlook it/her altogether), Odysseus notices her support because he is able to recognize Athena's presence as the divine omen it represents. This connection between the hero and his patron goddess is deepened, as Moulton observes, by the echo of an earlier simile that likens the sound of Odysseus' bow to the sound of a swallow.[33] Thus omen, simile, and the god transformed into a bird coalesce in one continuous set of imagery for the character (Odysseus) and the reader who are able to interpret the connection between the impression of the bird simile and the bird disguise.

The pervasiveness and difficulty of interpreting bird signs in the Homeric poems serve as a constant reminder of the divine will for both experts and non-experts in the Homeric poems which govern their actions. Bushnell points out the possible misreadings of these appearances, not only for the characters but also for the reader.[34] She argues that the different figures of bird imagery can effectively represent a sign of divine intent to both, citing Austin's insight in the similarity between omen and similes. According to Austin, omens are "similes that are the property of the characters in

[28] West (1988) on *Od.* 3.371–2 εἰδομένη with parallels for the use of the word indicating disguise.

[29] Hainsworth (1988) on *Od.* 5.337; "εἰκυῖα: of manner not appearance" (Leucothea appearing to Odysseus). For an example of εἰκυῖα combining both simile and appearance see Kirk (1985) on *Il.* 4.75–84 and Edwards (1991) on *Il.* 17.547–52.

[30] Bannert (1978), 39–41. [31] Moulton (1977), 137–8. [32] *Od.* 22.239–40.

[33] *Od.* 21.410–11. [34] Bushnell (1982).

the poetry rather than of the poet."[35] Omens are produced by the gods, who are of course themselves characters in the poem, leading to a self-contained circle of interpretation. Thus similes are markers for the reader with which the poet conveys his authorial intent, while omens are markers for the human characters that convey the divine will. Pointing to the inherent challenge of the bird sign, and the difficulty of neat classification, Bushnell writes:

> Not only do bird signs have the same form and similar function as similes, but further, bird similes are often linguistically indistinguishable from epiphanies of gods in bird form, and epiphanies themselves resemble bird signs in both form and function.[36]

The likeness between gods and birds thus underlines the limits of communication between human and divine, a line of communication that can be blocked on either side. The divine sign depends on the human's ability to interpret it correctly.

Returning to Ovid, we can see that the debate over the likeness of gods to birds in Homer has special significance for such representations in the *Metamorphoses*. Both the theme of human metamorphosis and the customary disguise by the gods when confronting mortals put the emphasis on outward shape as the prime signifier of identity.

The potential relevance of the Homeric scholia for Roman poets has been explored by Schlunk in his study of their influence on Virgil in composing the *Aeneid*.[37] Schlunk shows in detail how criticism in the Homeric scholia was used by Virgil in his stylistic choices. We may assume that Ovid, both as *poeta doctus* in his own right and as successor to Virgil, might have consulted them as well.[38] The debate should be read as backdrop to the myth of Daedalus and Icarus.

The myth of Daedalus and Icarus who escape Crete by the means of wings shows humans transgressing into a space that is the privilege of birds on the one hand and gods on the other.[39] Their flight has often been interpreted as mortal aspiration and failure to reach the divine. In addition,

[35] Bushnell (1982), 3; Austin (1975), 118. [36] Bushnell (1982), 9. [37] Schlunk (1974).

[38] On Virgil's use of Homeric scholarship since Schlunk see Lausberg (1989), Schmit-Neuerberg (1999). Feeney (1991), 237 n.188 cites some instances of Homeric exegesis (AbT *Il.* 15.668; AT 16.432; bT 16.666; AT 18.356) that seem to have inspired Ovid's treatment of the gods' action in his own epic. See also McKeown (1979) on Ovid responding to early criticism of Virgil. On Ovid and ancient literary history see Tarrant (2002).

[39] The passage is set up earlier in the book when Scylla wishes for the wings of a bird to make her way *into* Minos' camp in order to become his voluntary hostage (*Met.* 8.50–1): *o ego ter felix, si pennas lapsa per auras/ Gnosiaci castris possem insistere regis.*

the myth has special significance for poets who have identified with this aspiration to immortality through poetry.[40] Within his work Ovid has two prominent versions of the myth, an earlier version in the *Ars amatoria* (2.17–98) as well as the one in the *Metamorphoses* (8.183–253). Ovid's treatment of the myth has been subject of much scholarly attention, mostly in comparing the two passages in terms of genre.[41] This interpretation of the *Metamorphoses* passage makes use of the *Ars* version principally where the former deviates in giving divine or animal attributes to Daedalus and Icarus, focusing on the way in which the transformation of Daedalus and Icarus into birds affects the idea of divine iconography.

Two problems with this myth make it stand out in the narrative of the *Metamorphoses* as a whole: there seems to be neither a metamorphosis nor a god to inflict it. Attempts to find either must therefore resort to the figurative level. Thus Daedalus is said to be like a god in that he is able to inflict metamorphosis; alternatively, both Icarus and Daedalus are seen as undergoing metamorphosis in 'becoming' birds.[42]

We should retain the sense of incongruity and focus on the false metamorphosis and the false gods in this episode. Daedalus and Icarus can be said to be "like" gods or "like" birds in flying, but neither the metamorphosis nor their divine or human nature is unequivocal. Ovid's language makes them approximate, rather than complete an altered state of identity. Let us start with the transformation of Daedalus and Icarus into birds.

After Daedalus has decided to escape by air, he gets to work on the wings (*Met.* 8.186–7). In the ekphrasis that follows, art oscillates between imitating nature and improving it (*ignotas … in artes/ naturamque novat*, 188–9). On the one hand Daedalus uses the natural idea of bird wings; on the other hand his technical use of them is new and unsettling. Daedalus' use of birds' wings for human purposes, and thus the crossing of species boundaries, is carried over in the narrator's view of the wings (animal) as reeds (plants) in a simile (*Met.* 8.189–92):

> nam ponit in ordine pennas,
> [a minima coeptas, longam breuiore sequente,]
> ut cliuo creuisse putes; sic rustica quondam
> fistula disparibus paulatim surgit auenis

40 See Sharrock (1994), 96–126 for a discussion of this topos in Greek and Latin literature.

41 See for example von Albrecht (1977). Sharrock (1994), 87–195 offers a comparison of the two passages that also puts the *Ars* version in its own context.

42 See Hoefmans (1998), 137–40 for a detailed critique of the relevant criticism. Hoefmans argues for a Lucretian reading to explain the absence of the gods in this passage.

He puts the wings in order, [beginning with the smallest; the shorter aside the long]. You would think they had grown on a slope: just so once the rustic pipe rose little by little from uneven reeds.

The simile alludes to the story of the nymph Syrinx,[43] told earlier in the poem (*Met.* 1.705–12). Pursued by the god Pan, she escapes by being suddenly transformed into a reed. In addition to being a plant, she also becomes a 'natural' instrument through the wind that makes her resound (also called a technical innovation: *arte nova, Met.* 1.709). The allusion to this story signals the fluid boundaries between nature and art in this critical passage.

The ekphrasis of Daedalus' work ends with his stated purpose: *ut veras imitetur aves* (*Met.* 8.195). In describing the fitting of the wings and the advice, Ovid gradually moves the characters towards their bird identity which finally culminates in a simile describing the two as birds (*Met.* 8.211–16):

dedit oscula nato
non iterum repetenda suo pennisque leuatus
ante uolat comitique timet, uelut ales ab alto
quae teneram prolem produxit in aera nido,
hortaturque sequi damnosasque erudit artes
[et mouet ipse suas et nati respicit alas.]

He gave kisses to his son, no more to be repeated, and, balanced on the wings, flies in front and fears for his companion, like a bird that leads its tender young from the high nest into the air and urges it to follow and teaches the ruinous arts [and moves its own wings and looks back on those of its young].

The simile is unusual in that it describes rather than compares what is really happening. The simile begins as Daedalus is already in the air (*pennisque levatus*, 212), acting like a bird. In using a bird simile to picture the bird-men Ovid moves the simile as close as possible to the narrative.[44] Segal also points out the lack of a clear subject in line 215:

'and urges it (him) to follow and teaches it (him) the destructive arts' ... The simile is so placed that it can describe either the mother-bird or Daedalus, and so skillfully suggests the ambiguous unnaturalness of the situation. [45]

43 Bömer (1969–86) on *Met.* 8.192. One should note that the reeds get their order from Pan himself, not from nature: *atque ita* ***disparibus calamis*** *conpagine cerae/* ***inter se iunctis*** *nomen tenuisse puellae* (emphasis mine).

44 von Albrecht (1999), 175: " Since Ovid tries to adapt the simile as far as possible to the main action, sometimes, except for the characters and the place of the action, there seems to be no noticeable difference between narrative and simile ..."

45 Segal (1998), 16.

The much shorter *Ars* version of this simile focuses primarily on the bird teaching its young, appropriate to the didactic nature of that poem: *Dum monet, aptat opus puero monstratque moveri,/ erudit infirmas ut sua mater aves*. Both are still on the ground and thus cannot be mistaken for birds in flying. This "dry run" as well corresponds to the theoretical nature of the *Ars* in which learning the arts of love by reading precedes practice. By contrast, the simile in the *Metamorphoses* compares the feelings of the bird (*comitique timet*, 213) in addition to the act of flying. Likewise the ominous phrase *damnosas artes* can only refer to Daedalus' unnatural use of technology. It is typical for the epic simile to anthropomorphize animals to illustrate human feelings.[46] By reflecting this technique back onto Daedalus and Icarus the narrator highlights their unresolved status of animal and human.

To all appearances Icarus and Daedalus then look like and behave like birds, and yet it is significant that the simile functions on the same level as the wings that Daedalus fits on Icarus, namely as an addition and not a change of identity. By using a simile to describe their flight, Ovid signals that this is not a complete metamorphosis. Daedalus and Icarus are "like" birds, but they are not identical with them.[47] In this they resemble the gods who can take up or leave off their disguise and, more to the point, their wings.[48] Virgil makes this connection in the *Aeneid* when he calls Daedalus' wings *remigium alarum*, the same phrase he later uses for Mercury's mode of transport.[49] Thus, although the material comes from the animal, the use of it and the ability to detach from it is god-like – rather than bird-like. In this the myth differs pointedly from the number of bird metamorphoses that immediately precede and follow it. Unlike the complete transformation of metamorphosis that leaves the victim no outer sign of his former identity, this partial transformation challenges the reader's visual imagination. Do Daedalus and Icarus look like birds to the

[46] Cf. *Od*. 16.216–18, for an especially pertinent simile that is used in the recognition scene between Odysseus and Telemachus. Their voices are likened to the shrieks of birds, preserving their unfathomable feelings while offering room for projection to the reader. See Feeney (1992), 37.

[47] See Haege (1976), 55 on the distance created by using *ipse* in line 202. Also note the separation of body and wings in lines 202, *libravit in alas/ipse suum corpus*, and 233–4 *pennas ... in undis/ ... corpusque sepulcro*. Metamorphosis typically happens limb by limb.

[48] *Met*. 1.670–4 (Mercury): *parva mora est alas pedibus virgamque potenti/ somniferam sumpsisse manu tegumenque capillis;/ haec ubi disposuit, patria Iove natus ab arce/ desilit in terras.* ***illic*** *tegumenque removit/* ***et posuit pennas****; tantummodo virga retenta est* (emphasis mine). See also *Met*. 8.627 where Ovid contrasts Mercury's divine epithet with his unassuming disguise: *venit Atlantiades positis caducifer alis*. Cf. Virgil *Aen*. 4.239–41.

[49] Virgil *Aen*. 1.301 (Mercury); 6.19 (Daedalus). By contrast, the *Ars am*. 2.45 *remigium volucrum* stresses their bird origin.

point of being mistaken for them?[50] The power of the simile is such that it conditions the reader's point of view and pretends that a metamorphosis has in fact happened.

At this point of maximum approximation, even fusion of bird and human in the simile, Ovid introduces a dramatic shift of perspective. He describes the reaction of some human onlookers (*Met.* 8.217–20):

> hos aliquis tremula dum captat harundine pisces
> aut pastor baculo stiuaue innixus arator
> uidit et obstipuit, quique aethera carpere possent
> credidit esse deos.

Somebody saw them while catching fish with a quivering line, or a herdsman bent on his staff, or a ploughman on his plough-handle, saw them and was struck, and believed them, who could seize the air, to be gods.

The three represent a generic "anybody" (*aliquis*) in the figures of a fisher, a shepherd, and a farmer who look up at the figures in the sky. As they do not share the reader's knowledge that humans can fly they reach the only possible explanation, that the creatures they are seeing are gods.[51] This conclusion comes not as a vague guess but through reasoned deduction (*quique aethera carpere possent*, 219).

In contrast to the earlier version of the *Ars* where a lonely figure has a subjective, mystical experience,[52] here the figure of three denotes their universality, and thus lends an air of objectivity to their interpretation. Their occupations have also been interpreted as marking them out as belonging to the Silver Age, in possibly ascending order of complexity in their tools.[53] They contrast with Daedalus' more transgressive use of technical innovation.

Bömer[54] observes that their activities would normally necessitate their looking downwards and remarks on the lack of verisimilitude of this situation ("Unwirklichkeit"). Yet the fact that they must have raised their

[50] A figurative interpretation of the story in the later writer Giovanni del Virgilio sounds like an echo of the Homeric scholiasts: "*quia navigio* ***veloci ut aves*** *abiere, ideo fictum est quod alis sibi factis fugerunt. Forte autem filius e puppi excidit*" (emphasis mine). Quoted by Rudd (1988), 37.

[51] Hoefmans (1998), 151 and n.51 points out the allusion to Lucretius' critique of religion at Lucr. 6.60–4.

[52] *Hos aliquis, tremula dum captat harundine pisces,/ vidit et inceptum dextra reliquit opus, Ars am.* 2.77–8. Sharrock (1994), 193–4 makes the attractive suggestion that this figure represents the poet, captured by his own digression and dropping the "*harundo*"/ writing reed.

[53] Davisson (1997), 271.

[54] Bömer (1969–86) on *Met.* 8.217: "Im allgemeinen schaut ein Angler nicht in den Himmel (ein Hirte und ein Pflüger, zumal *stiva innixus*, auch nicht)."

heads is highly significant. As Ovid tells us, following the anatomical theory on the origin of religion in the upright posture of man: *os homini sublime dedit caelumque videre/ iussit et erectos ad sidera tollere vultus* (*Met.* 1.86–7). Thus the onlookers' unusual upright posture serves to underline their witnessing of men as gods. Whereas the later fall of Icarus, the proof of human mortality, remains unobserved, even by Daedalus himself,[55] the moment of flight, and thus their proximity to the immortals, does not.

The claim of truth of this incredible story is underscored by the three eyewitnesses. The onlookers' certainty in a divine presence is expressed in the phrase *credidit esse deos. Credidit,* as perfect indicative, states the fact, while the more cautious imperfect subjunctive used by Ovid in the *Ars* version leaves the ground open to speculation. To speak of Daedalus and Icarus as "being" rather than "seeming" gods affirms their divinity at this point unapologetically, albeit mistakenly. Unlike the earlier simile that compares Daedalus and Icarus to birds, the language here positively affirms not their likeness but their identity (*esse deos* not *aves videri*). Through the act of flying they are no longer completely comprehensible as human. By contrast the *Ars* passage stays within the boundaries of a rhetorical question and does not change the narratorial perspective: *quis crederet umquam/ aerias hominem carpere posse vias?* (*Ars am.* 2.43–4).

The false epiphany of the three onlookers fits in with the many stories in the *Metamorphoses* of a lack of recognition of the divine by humans or, in the case of Niobe, false divine honors given to a human.[56] That Ovid means to evoke a moment of epiphany comes out in the verbal parallel with the encounter of Telemachus and Athena at *Odyssey* 1.102–324, which anticipates the later public epiphany interpreted by Nestor mentioned earlier. Athena, in the guise of Mentes, encourages Telemachus to look for his father. She assures him of the gods' good will, even though she is no soothsayer or interpreter of bird signs (!) (*Od.* 1.200–2). She then takes her leave in the form of a bird, and the narrator describes Telemachus' reaction (*Od.* 1.323):

[55] Note that Daedalus also uses deduction to understand that Icarus has drowned: "*'Icare' dixit,/ 'Icare' dixit, 'ubi es? qua te regione requiram?'/'Icare', dicebat: pennas adspexit in undis*" (8.233). Ironically, he does not recognize Icarus' body but his wings. The change in tense from perfect to imperfect (*dixit/ dicebat*) reflects the moment of his realization. Bömer (1969–86) at *Met.* 8.233 sees an allusion to the Roman funeral tradition of *conclamatio,* calling out the name of the dead three times.

[56] Davisson (1997), 272–3. The general absence of the gods in this passage is merely temporary; however, the hemistich that completes line 220 hints at the potential for the gods' anger (*et iam Iunonia laeva/ ...*) In the *Ars* version, the sun that melts Icarus' wings is seen as divine (*cera deo propiore liquescit, Ars. am.* 2.85), the only geographical indication is by association Apollo's Delos (*Ars. am.* 2.80), not Juno's Samos.

θάμβησεν κατὰ θυμόν· οἴσατο γὰρ θεὸν εἶναι

He was struck in his soul for he knew it was a god.

vidit et obstipuit … / credidit esse deos. (*Met.* 8.219–20)

He saw [them] and was struck … he believed them to be gods.

Ovid's linking of *vidit* with *obstipuit* underlines once more the importance of shape as an immediate, if wrong, signifier of identity. Seeing and believing is one. In Homer, it is Telemachus' privileged relationship to Athena that allows for true recognition of the divine, in singling out the soul (κατὰ θυμόν) as the basis of epiphany.

In the *Metamorphoses'* puzzle of images, Icarus and Daedalus represent the triple potential of species inherent in any shape. They are human in that they use technology and have the hybris to attempt flight that is unnatural to their species; they are birds in that they use the same plumage and have the same care for their young; and they are gods in that they are marveled at in their flight, and identified as gods by the anonymous onlookers. Ovid plays on the limits of perception by offering a simile that pictures them as birds, thus transformed into animal shape, and then contrasting it with their 'real' appearance, that is the human shape augmented by wings, a common image of the divine. They are at the same time birds, gods, and humans – winged creatures of a kind.

The comparison of gods to birds, based on their common ability to travel through the air, retains the ambivalence of omens as manifestation of the divine in the world. The even more problematic case of representing the god as animals other than birds also deserves consideration. While birds share the air with the gods, the other animals share the land and sea with humans. In representing the gods in this way, Ovid makes them literally touch ground.[57] The thematic link of bovine imagery shows how the animal other is used to investigate the connection between human and divine, beginning with the disparate experiences of Io and Jupiter in bovine form. The triangle of human, divine, and animal forms the basis of my interpretation for a highly intricate simile which renders Apollo's grief at the death of Coronis (*Met.* 2.619–25).

[57] Animals other than birds may of course be used for *prodigia* as well, such as the white bull that shows Cadmus where to settle, immediately after Jupiter has relinquished his disguise after the rape of Europa (*Met.* 3.1–23). The cow is sacrificed by the new settlers; see Feldherr (1997), 47 n.41.
Jupiter's manipulation of his shape for his own ends undermines the religious contract between human and divine (*quis enim deprendere possit/ furta Iovis?, Met.* 3.6–7).

The myths of gods in animal disguise are a well-known staple in the repertoire of stories about the gods. However, in the *Metamorphoses* the telling of these stories is presented as a challenge to the gods' dignity. Thus in book 5 of the *Metamorphoses* Minerva is told a summary of the song with which one of the Pierides challenged the Muses (*Met.* 5.326–31). The Muse's summary breaks off after that in order to let Calliope recite her hymn-like version of the rape of Proserpina.[58] The main subject of the mortal's song was the battle of the giants to whom the Pierid had given too much attention, while downplaying the gods (*bella canit superum falsoque in honore Gigantas/ ponit et extenuat magnorum facta deorum*, *Met.* 5.319–20). The gods are shown disguised as animals on their flight from the monster Typhoeus.[59] The Pierides episode functions as the prelude to Arachne's contest with Minerva in which Arachne shows the gods in various disguises (*Met.* 6.103–28) instead of their conventional divine representation.[60] In both cases the stories of the gods as animals are shown to be a challenge to the gods' authority, and a deviation from the norm in genre, aesthetics, and respect for the divine.

These myths seem at odds with the majesty and seriousness that is required of gods in epic. Ovid's choice of subject matter compromises therefore not only the genre itself but also the genre adherence of the divine machinery. In telling the stories of divine rapes or love stories Ovid stands accused of "humanizing" the divine. Bernbeck discusses the tradition of anthropomorphizing the gods in respect to their emotions, starting with the Homeric poems. He sees Ovid's innovation in abolishing the boundary between the world of the mortals and immortals. He observes that the gods no longer merely *act like humans* in a separate divine realm

58 See Hinds (1987) for the allusion to the Homeric hymn to Demeter. Calliope's song seeks to cancel out the challenger's view of the divine, in the same way that Arachne's tapestry is destroyed by Minerva. Yet by telling the story Ovid preserves physically as well as conceptually both views in his own poem. Leach (1974), 104: "As the creator of the poem, Ovid maintains a vision embracing both points of view."

59 Ovid's probable source for this story is Nicander book 4, summarized by Antoninus Liberalis 28.1–4. In Nicander's story Zeus and Athena remain without disguise. In Ovid, Jupiter as *dux gregis* in the Pierides' song cuts a pathetic figure (Papathomopoulos [1968], 132: "une addition d'Ovide à son modèle: elle rend plus aggressive encore l'impiété des Piérides") In the same manner the division of the original story in the shameful flight by the gods told by Pierides and the triumphant part (Jupiter crushing Typhoeus with Mount Etna) told in the hymn to Ceres (*Met.* 5.346–61) underlines the deep division between the human and the divine view.

60 Ovid chooses animals connected to the gods' cult figures, at least in more exotic locales like Egypt (such as Jupiter Ammon, Juno as a cow, Artemis as a cat). The Muse's whitewashing of these foreign associations can thus be seen as an equally aggressive move, insisting on one sanctioned view of the divine in Greco-Roman terms.

but even *as humans* among them.[61] In contrast to earlier epic, much of the action of the *Metamorphoses* takes place on a central plane where humans, animals, and gods intermingle in a variety of shapes which makes it hard to tell which is which.

The purpose of this human treatment of the gods has generally been thought to elicit humor. Galinsky's treatment of the divine in the *Metamorphoses* comes under that chapter heading.[62] Yet Ovid's trademark humor often conceals more serious observations, and it will prove worthwhile to dig beneath the surface. His treatment of the divine does not stem from a lack of respect for the divine or a gratuitous tearing down of their epic grandeur. Rather, the issue is one of a more encompassing vision of the divine that subsumes their epic nature under the same category as their amorous escapades and parallels his treatment of the epic as a whole. His epic is an epic that subsumes traditional epic material and treatment under the greater design of telling the universal tale of the *Metamorphoses.* The gods' erotic adventures are a vital part of conceptualizing the divine and establishing a connection to the mortals through aetiology and genealogy.

Ovid does not stop at humanizing the gods; he even goes so far as to treat them on the even lower level of animals.[63] A prime example is the undignified conduct of Jupiter as a bull in seducing Europa. The passage is regularly cited as an example of Ovid's iconoclastic treatment of divine majesty (*Met.* 2.846–51):

> non bene conueniunt nec in una sede morantur
> maiestas et amor: sceptri grauitate relicta
> ille pater rectorque deum, cui dextra trisulcis
> ignibus armata est, qui nutu concutit orbem,
> induitur faciem tauri mixtusque iuuencis
> mugit et in teneris formosus obambulat herbis.

Majesty and love do not go well together or linger in one place. Leaving behind his scepter and his dignity, that father and ruler of gods, whose right hand is armed with three-pronged fire, who shakes the world with his nod, puts on the mask of a bull and mingling with heifers he moos and roams across the soft grass in his beauty.

[61] "Die Götter handeln nicht mehr nur *wie* Menschen in einer abgeschlossenen Himmelswelt, sondern *als* Menschen unter ihnen." Bernbeck (1967), 88 (italics mine).

[62] Galinsky (1975), 162–72. While I do not agree with his interpretation, Galinsky's focus on similes in this section affirms my own conviction that they are a central part of the construction of the divine in the poem.

[63] Galinsky (1975), 162.

Ovid's explicit avowal of destroying Jupiter's epic persona should give the reader pause. The split in Jupiter's persona (*nec in una sede morantur/ maiestas et amor*) into the imperial Jupiter on the one hand and the erotic Jupiter on the other is signaled by a loss of his divine insignia. It is important to note that Jupiter does not lose but actively relinquishes his gravitas for the moment (847). The contrast is heightened by the incongruity of Jupiter's divine epic persona that is left behind, told in the first two and a half lines and the ensuing disguise in the following two lines, all in one sentence. The elevated diction of the epic formula *ille pater rectorque deum* is replaced by the comically grotesque vision of Jupiter as he gets into his animal act (*mugit, obambulat*). Ovid's treatment of Jupiter's transformation recalls the act of human metamorphosis in its insistence on retaining the before and after of the transformation.

The description becomes even more surreal in the following images that render his bovine exterior (*Met.* 2.852–6):

> quippe color niuis est, quam nec uestigia duri
> calcauere pedis nec soluit aquaticus Auster;
> colla toris exstant, armis palearia pendent
> cornua parua quidem, sed quae contendere possis
> facta manu, puraque magis perlucida gemma.

Sure enough, it is the color of snow which has not been trampled by heavy footprints or melted by the rain-bringing Auster. Its neck stands out with muscles, and the dewlap hangs as protection, its horns are small but such that you could claim they were made by hand, and more clear and transparent than gemstones.

Jupiter's hide is as white as snow, its perfection a pointer to the animal's divine associations. Despite the use of a natural substance for comparison, the fact that the snow does not melt or get dingy alludes to the gods' immunity from change. The reference to footsteps in particular gives away the bull's sacred identity as it cynically exploits the virginal associations of the untrodden meadow, while the *cornua parva* suggest that the bull is just beginning to mate.[64]

His horns are not menacing but rather beautiful works of art. Ovid's game of illusion, as shown by Hardie,[65] here involves Jupiter's superior art of disguise. It also hints at Europa's own corruptibility, as all girls are supposed to be seduced by jewels.[66] What is more, Ovid invites the reader's

[64] Jupiter is a Callimachean dream in his pristine perfection (*quam nec vestigia duri/ calcavere pedis*).

[65] Hardie (2002), 163 on the illusion of the looking-glass of the text for the reader. Note also the literal transparency of Jupiter's disguise (*magis perlucida*).

[66] Cf. *Am.* 1.10.

scrutiny of this image. His use of the second person singular, *sed quae contendere possis*, invites the reader to almost physically enter his imaginary world to ascertain the verisimilitude of the comparison, and thus makes him partner in the seduction. Ovid's comparison of the bull's horns thus highlights the difficulty of telling real from fake and makes the reader empathize with Europa's fascination with this toy bull. Barkan draws attention to the ambivalence of Jupiter's disguise:

> The *imago tauri* may be dazzlingly true to life but the very fact that he is not real, that he is a representation, makes him transcend the real at the same time.[67]

The description thus contains three competing images: Jupiter as the *rector paterque deum* complete with divine insignia of which he is stripped in his transformation, the image of Jupiter completely transformed into a bull to the point of animal behavior, and finally Ovid's comparisons to snow and the jewel-like horns that oscillate between real and fake, reality and illusion, the reader's superior knowledge and Europa's visual experience.[68] It is only in the following book that this illusion is pierced (*iamque deus posita fallacis imagine tauri/ se confessus erat, Met.* 3.1–2). The telling of the myth thus rests on the illusion of Jupiter as a bull and at the same time on the reader's implicit acceptance that such deception is possible. As Europa believes the reality of the bull so the reader believes its fictionality. Thus the competition of images in describing Jupiter makes the reader aware of both the gods' own vacillating, changeable nature and the illusion of creating a divine persona in poetry.

Ovid's humorous description of Jupiter as a bull that turns him into a beautiful artifact lulls the reader into Europa's own fallacy that the bull cannot do any harm (*nullae in fronte minae, nec formidable lumen:/ pacem vultus habet, Met.* 2.857–8)[69]. Ovid presents Jupiter as a lover who feels human emotions: *gaudet amans et dum veniat sperata voluptas,/ oscula dat manibus*, 862–3). It is precisely the lessening of the god's majesty that makes this scene so effective. The disguise and the description of the god in humanizing terms gradually lower Europa's sense of caution at the same time heightening the reader's sense of suspense (*nunc adludit …, nunc deponit …; paulatim …, modo … / modo …*, 864–7) until Europa sits down on his back and Jupiter immediately returns to his identity, if not yet shape, as *deus* (870). The god's erotic urges and ridiculous costume

[67] Barkan (1986), 11.
[68] Contrast the representation of the bull on Arachne's tapestry; the bull is so fake that he must be real (*Maeonis elusam designat imagine tauri/ Europen; verum taurum, freta vera putares*, 6.103–4).
[69] The reverse of Jupiter's standard iconography. Cf. *Met.* 1.177–80.

might make him less majestic in an epic sense but they do not take away from his real power. Ovid's humanizing or subhumanizing treatment thus brings out in concrete visual terms the profound power imbalance between mortal and immortal.

The story of Io (*Met.* 1.588–624) provides a powerful contrast to the frivolous mood of the Europa episode. Jupiter first chases and then rapes Io.[70] When Juno senses Jupiter's adultery and confronts him, he has already changed Io into a cow. The horror that she feels at her changed form stands in marked contrast to Jupiter's disguise as a bull. Where he sounds like a bull to lend verisimilitude to his disguise (*mugit*), Io's attempts at human speech get twisted beyond recognition into animal sound (*Met.* 1.637–8):[71] *et conata queri mugitus edidit ore/ [pertimuitque sonos propriaque exterrita voce est].*

Similarly, when she tries to express her affection for her father, her human emotions are twisted into animal behavior (*Met.* 1.643–6):

> at illa patrem sequitur sequiturque sorores
> **et patitur tangi seque admirantibus offert.**
> **decerptas** senior **porrexerat** Inachus **herbas;**
> illa manus lambit patriisque **dat oscula palmis**, …

… but she follows her father, and follows her sisters and lets herself be touched and offers herself to her admirers. Old Inachus had extended some grass he plucked, and she licks his hands and gives kisses to her father's palms …

The same diction applied to Jupiter instead emphasizes the cuteness of the tame bull (*Met.* 2.861–8):

> mox adit et flores **ad candida porrigit ora**./ … /
> **oscula dat manibus**/ … /
> … **pectora praebet/**
> **virginea plaudenda manu**, modo cornua sertis
> impedienda novis …

… soon she comes near and extends flowers to the white mouth … he kisses her hands … he offers his chest to be stroked by the virgin hand, and now his horns must be decorated by new garlands.

Ovid's treatment of the gods in human or animal terms thus goes beyond a humorous destruction of the conventional epic image of the gods. It lets

[70] The scene is a replay (this time successful) of Daphne's flight from Apollo (*Met.* 1.490–567), immediately preceding the episode. Like Apollo, Jupiter vainly boasts of his divine powers (*nec de plebe deo, sed qui caelestia magna/ sceptra manu teneo, sed qui uaga fulmina mitto*, 1.595–6).

[71] At this point one may remember Lucretius' discussion of the origin of language (5.1208–90). Io has taken an evolutionary step backwards.

the gods enter into the central arena of mutable shapes in which the mortals are simultaneously connected and alienated from the divine and animal world as the quintessential "other." Ovid's leveling of the playing field points out the complexity of the central question of the mortals' place in the world when confronted with the other in the form of gods and animals. Any shape harbors the possibility (one could even go so far as to say probability) of being something other than it seems.

In the episode of Jupiter seducing Europa, the simile shows up Jupiter's disguise as a bull, and thus reinforces the notion that the temporary change of costume does not entail a change in the god's identity. Let us turn now to a similar passage that explores the encounter of god and mortal, the story of Apollo and Coronis (*Met.* 2.542–632) with focus on a controversial simile that compares Apollo in his moment of grief to a cow. Similes, as already noted, undermine the gods' complete control as to how they appear and thus offer an additional perspective on the divine in the poem.

The story is told by a raven which, as punishment for telling Apollo about the unfaithfulness of his lover Coronis, is changed from white to black. Apollo's reaction at the betrayal is rage, the epic wrath (*ira*) which leads him to killing her. In dying, Coronis reveals that she is pregnant with their son Aesculapius (*Met.* 2.608–9). Apollo repents of what he has done and then proceeds to save the baby from his mother's womb, although he fails to save Coronis herself.[72] Apollo's grief as a manifestation of a human emotion in divine terms offers an intriguing complex of their mutual dependence.

According to both epic and tragic etiquette the gods must not mourn or come into immediate contact with human death. Ovid is not only aware of this convention, he points it out explicitly to the reader (*neque enim caelestia tingi/ ora licet lacrimis, Met.* 2.621–2).[73] Ovid's explicit avowal of acceptable divine behavior in the Europa episode suggests that it should not be seen as a parenthetical aside. In both the Jupiter episode and this one these declarations should alert the reader to the question whether the gods' indulgence in human(-izing) emotions does in fact detract from their divinity. Miller's study of the lamentations of Apollo suggests that

[72] For a structuralist reading of the myth that makes the mortal female an ultimately dispensable agent in creating the immortal male, see Burgess (2001).

[73] Bömer (1969–86) and Bömer (1958) for parallels. *Fast.* 4.521–2 shows Ceres shedding something like a tear: *dixit. et ut lacrimae (neque enim lacrimare deorum est)/ decidit in tepidos lucida gutta sinus.* Ovid's careful phrasing with *ut* draws attention to the representational gap of explaining divine things in human terms.

the god has a marked "humanity" that is brought out in three episodes that show the god confronting the death of a beloved mortal.[74] We must therefore conclude that Ovid intentionally explores the difficulty of portraying divine grief.

That the gods can and do feel grief for the death of a beloved is well known from the stories of the deaths of Sarpedon in the *Iliad*, or that of Hippolytus in Euripides' *Hippolytus*. These scenes both mark the ultimate divide between mortal and immortal, and the limits of divine power in the face of death. The divide is further emphasized by the prohibition from showing tears.[75] Thus, by convention, divine grief is implied but not shown. By contrast, Ovid lingers on this moment.

Apollo's futile attempts at saving Coronis from death mock his divine identity (*Met.* 2.618) as Apollo the healer about to deliver his son, Aesculapius, patron of medicine, into the world. Aesculapius' gifts are a direct consequence of Apollo's failure to cure mortal bodies. In an interesting twist, Ocyrhoe prophesies that the as-yet unnamed Aesculapius will bring Hippolytus[76] back to life (*Met.* 2.644–8), for which Aesculapius is struck by lightning by Jupiter before achieving deification by the intervention of Apollo. The passage is thus signaled as being an exploration of mortality.

Ovid's description of Apollo's emotion as he repents his action stands in contrast to the god's earlier distanced ease in acting out his rage. The divine instruments that he used to kill Coronis are now hateful to him (*Met.* 2.615–16). He virtually rejects his divinity and is described in humanizing terms as lover, not god (*paenitet heu sero poenae crudelis amantem, Met.* 2.612).[77] This process culminates in the simile that renders the sound of Apollo's voice (*Met.* 2.619–25):

> quae postquam frustra temptata rogumque parari
> uidit et arsuros supremis ignibus artus,
> tum uero gemitus (neque enim caelestia tingi
> ora licet lacrimis) alto de corde petitos
> edidit, haud aliter quam cum spectante iuuenca
> lactentis vituli dextra libratus ab aure
> tempora discussit claro caua malleus ictu.

[74] Miller (1999), 413. He discusses the deaths of Coronis, Cyparissus, and Hyacinthus.

[75] While scholars regularly cite Euripides *Hipp.* 1396 as a parallel for this prohibition, its intertextual importance has been ignored. Ovid's parenthesis *neque enim caelestia tingi/ ora licet lacrimis* is in fact an exact translation of Euripides' line, and signposts the connection between the two myths.

[76] Hippolytus acknowledges his debt to him at *Met.* 15.533–4.

[77] Miller (1999), 414 points out the double focalization (Apollo's and the narrator's) of the word "*crudelis.*"

After he sees these things tried in vain and the funeral pyre prepared and her limbs about to be burnt on top of the fire, then indeed he expels sighs (since heavenly faces must not be touched by tears), emerging from the bottom of his heart, not unlike when, while the mother cow is watching, the hammer, balanced off the right ear, shatters with a clear blow the hollow temples of the suckling calf.

The most obvious observation about this simile is also the most significant. There seems to be an odd lack of correspondence between tenor and vehicle. Bömer criticizes the simile for its lack of precision ("nicht exakt durchgeführt"),[78] while Barchiesi correctly observes the intended complexity ("una voluta complicazione nell'intreccio verbale")[79] that makes possible a multiplicity of perspectives, animal, human, and divine. It is worth the while to disentangle this knot of (failed) correspondences in detail.

To begin with, the tenor of the simile is Apollo's *gemitus ... alto de corde petitos*. In most interpretations and translations the vehicle is the lowing of the mother cow. Yet Ovid's syntax does not allow for such neat correspondence. The cow is not the subject of the *cum*-clause nor is she given a verb to express sound but, underlining her role as a bystander, relegated grammatically to the ablative. The correspondence between the god and the animal is thus in the seeing (*vidit–spectante*).[80] Feldherr has shown the precarious position of the spectator both for the characters and the reader.[81] The watching can be turned around on the one watching. In this simile, both god and cow are said to be watching, thus calling attention to the human reader's own place as spectator. In fact, there is no human element in this simile. The reader as spectator is doubled by the cow who watches the spectacle. In both Lucretius' and the *Fasti*'s version[82] the cow is ignorant of the fate of her calf; in the *Fasti* version the sacrifice context is even suppressed.[83] In those versions, the cow's roaming in nature is contrasted with the cultural artifice of sacrifice. In both these versions, the emphasis is on the separation and the mother's ignorance of what happened to her calf. In the *Metamorphoses*' version instead Ovid uses the presence of the cow at the sacrifice to show an uncanny and ominous, almost human, awareness of the animal's role in the spectacle. The reader,

78 Bömer (1969–86). 79 Barchiesi (2005b).

80 So Barchiesi (2005b); the Italian translation (by Ludovica Koch) reads "somiglia a una giovenca che guardi vibrare il martello." The translation still inverts the position of finite verb and participle in the Latin sentence.

81 Feldherr (1997) on how the spectator turns into the spectacle.

82 Lucr. 2.352–9; *Fast.* 4.459–62

83 Feeney (2004), 14 argues that the sacrifice is implied in the wider context of the Agonalia.

conditioned by the preceding tales of metamorphoses which emphasize the human consciousness of the victims turned animals, can empathize.

How does this scene define the encounter between mortal and immortal? The complicated sets of correspondence in this simile serve to underline the difficulty of coping with this encounter. In the most straightforward interpretation, Apollo is compared to the cow, in which case the killing of his lover Coronis is equivalent to the sacrifice of the calf. This drawing of parallels then turns the erotic relationship of Apollo to Coronis between male god and female mortal into the mothering bond between female adult animal and male calf. Moreover, one should note that Apollo's agency in the narrative as the guilty killer is displaced in the simile by the agentless *malleus*, the instrument of the killing. A second set of correspondences is set up by the mothering bond implied in "lactenti." Coronis as mother to Aesculapius corresponds to the mother cow and the calf, even though he is not yet born. And yet another layer is added if we compare the diction of Coronis' death and Apollo's belated reaction. In line 606, Coronis, hit by the arrow, gives out a groan (*icta dedit gemitum*). Apollo's groan thus echoes that of Coronis (*gemitus … edidit*) while his wound is transferred to the figurative language of the simile (*tempora discussit claro caua malleus ictu, Met.* 2.625)

This plethora of possible interpretations of the simile should not be interpreted as a refusal to come down on any side. Quite on the contrary, it reveals the complexity and interdependency of all the elements in the picture. The simile is so difficult and so jarring because it does not offer a clarifying illustration but insists on serving up the tangled relationship of the divine, mortal, and animal roles in sacrifice. Barchiesi remarks on the unprecedented threefold perspective of sacrifice.[84] The god suffering a human emotion is compared to a suffering animal (not the sacrificial victim, however).[85] The sacrifice that should give the god joy is turned on the god himself.

In this imagery of wrong turns and displacements the middle and center focus is curiously empty. The syntactically correct correspondence to Apollo's groan is not the lowing of the cow but the sound that the hammer makes when cracking the victim's skull. The god's groan, made even

[84] Barchiesi (2005b): "Il modello di Lucrezio, II, 352 sgg. (…) viene posto in forte contrasto con l'azione divina proponendo una visione inedita del sacrificio animale (cfr. Callimaco, fr. 75,10–1 Pfeiffer), umana e divina allo stesso tempo."

[85] The displacement of the awareness of the animal's role from victim to mother cow is another innovation by Ovid. In Callimachus, fr. 75 Pfeiffer, as in Pythagoras' speech (*Met.* 15.130–5) it is the victim itself that sees the sacrificial knife.

more physical (human- or animal-like) by the exertion expressed in *alto de corde petitos*, is placed at the very moment where the ritual *favete linguis* demands complete silence from the human audience and makes audible the hammer's impact. By locating the sound of the god's voice at this moment the simile conveys the transcendental nature of his grief.

The irony of using a sacrifice simile lies in the god's presence that is both real and implied in the ritual context. It has a parallel in the simile discussed earlier of Mercury being compared to a kite at sacrifice (*Met.* 2.716–21). The bird of omen as well as the sound of the sacrificial victim's skull signal moments of divine presence to the participants. Thus both similes accurately convey the feeling of the meeting of mortal and divine. Ovid's near-clinical precision in the details of this simile is not meant to distance the reader but to make him flinch, to feel the same emotions as both cow and god.

Sacrificial imagery in epic similes is unusual in Greek literature. In an article comparing Homer's and the Greek tragedians' use of sacrificial imagery, Seaford concludes that sacrifice in the main narrative is the norm for epic, thereby affirming the superiority and moral principles of the gods, while sacrifice in similes is a deviation employed by the tragic poets to mark the perverse nature of tragic death.[86] A notable exception to this rule is the tragic death of Laocoon as told in *Aeneid* 2.199–231 who is overtaken in the act of sacrificing a bull. As he struggles against the serpents, he lets out a noise that is rendered in a simile (*Aen.* 2.222–4):

> clamores simul horrendos ad sidera tollit:
> qualis mugitus, fugit cum saucius aram
> taurus et incertam excussit cervice securim.

At the same time he raises a dreadful noise to the stars: such are the bellows when a wounded bull has fled from the altar and shaken off from his neck an ill-aimed axe.

The simile reverses the roles of sacrifice and shows the priest himself at the mercy of divine wrath, the very thing that sacrifice seeks to regulate. The scene of the simile showing the polluted sacrifice itself (the bull escapes), comments on the impiousness of the god's action and implicitly rejects the charge of impiety that is leveled against Laocoon later (*Aen.* 2.229–31).

Not only does Ovid's simile on Apollo contain an element of tragic contamination in this supposedly epic poem, but this perverse connotation is applied to a god. This innovation comes out clearly when one compares

[86] Seaford (1989).

the two other sacrificial similes in the poem which also concentrate on the moment of killing. The first example comes from the story of Erisychthon (*Met.* 8.761–4):

> cuius ut in trunco fecit manus impia uulnus,
> haud aliter fluxit discusso cortice sanguis
> quam solet, ante aras ingens ubi uictima taurus
> concidit, abrupta cruor e ceruice profundi.

As his impious hand makes a wound in the trunk, blood flows from the gaping bark, not unlike what happens when an enormous sacrificed bull breaks down in front of the altar and blood flows from its severed neck.

Erysichthon's impiety is spelled out earlier in his refusal to give sacrifice and thus acknowledge the gods (*Met.* 8.739–40). The sacrificial simile thus underlines the sacrilege in the felling of the trees by its perverse application to an impious action. The passage is fascinating since the use of anthropomorphic metaphor represents the nymph as human as well as the tree she inhabits (*contremuit gemitumque dedit Deoia quercus,/ et pariter frondes, pariter pallescere glandes/ coepere* . . ., *Met.* 8.758–60; *sanguis*, 740).

Another parallel can be found at *Met.* 12.247–9 in the battle of the Lapiths where Amycus is compared to a priest at sacrifice (*rapuit funale . . . / elatumque alte, veluti qui candida tauri/ rumpere sacrifica molitur colla securi*) focusing on the human role in sacrifice. The comparison builds up an absurd contrast between the occasion and the ill-omened battle at the beginning of the marriage which in itself is a distorted narrative of an epic battle and again involves a hybrid creature, this time half-man, half-horse.[87] In all three applications of the sacrifice simile, bringing together the extremes of pious and impious behavior in tenor and vehicle creates tension that calls attention to the distortion of the respective roles in the order of sacrifice.

Apollo's and Mercury's similes, by contrast, since they concentrate on the gods' presence, grow even more complex by their imagined, but not ordinarily visible, role in sacrifice. However, in the poem, the gods' position as characters allows this presence to be both real and mediated: while they are plainly visible to the reader from outside the scene, their real presence inside the story is mediated through the simile's focalizers. The displacement of Apollo's grief to the simile offers a chance to meditate at one remove on the intermingling and substitution of human, divine, and animal species in the poem. Unlike the description of Jupiter as an

[87] See Chapter 3 for a more detailed discussion of this simile.

animal, likening Apollo's grief to a scene of sacrifice reinforces the notion not of the god's otherness that he shares with the animals but the god's connectedness to the human species in his tragic error. Ovid shows that we can empathize with the divine and the animal world to comprehend the essentially human feeling of grief.

We have focused so far on the conventional representation of the gods as well as the need for them to disguise themselves as they enter the world of the mortals. Yet even the depiction of their true shape is based on the conventional anthropomorphism. This means that the gods are essentially borrowing whatever form they assume. In the following discussions, the simile becomes a means to penetrate the disguise and aims at representing the true shape of the divine while at the same time it points to the circular logic inherent in the need for comparison in order to imagine the gods.

Both disguises and the traditional insignia of divine identity are random and interchangeable, functioning as a costume which does not penetrate to the layer of identity. Ovid makes the reader aware of this convention when he proposes an interchangeable image of Cupid and Adonis (*Met.* 10.515–18):

> laudaret faciem Liuor quoque: qualia namque
> corpora nudorum tabula pinguntur Amorum,
> talis erat; sed, ne faciat discrimina cultus,
> aut huic adde leues aut illis deme pharetras.

Even envy would praise his face: since he was like the paintings that depict the bodies of naked Cupids. So that the insignia may make no difference: either add the slight quiver there or take it from here.

Adonis is Cupid without a bow, or Cupid is Adonis with one. The comparison of Adonis to a picture emphasizes a beauty that is more than mortal because it is idealized and artificial. In the qualifying statement that follows, the comparison dissolves, as tenor and vehicle are shown to be interchangeable (*ne faciat discrimina*, 517). The parallel imperatives *adde* and *deme* give the impression that Ovid is painting the picture at the same time as he is making the comparison with it.[88] Adonis is no longer similar to Cupid, he is identical to him except for the extraneous detail of costume (*cultus*). Hardie[89] shows the further implications of this congruency in the context of the story of Venus' love for Adonis, provoked by the unintentional wounding of Cupid's arrow when he embraces his mother.

[88] See the discussion of *Met.* 1.400–6 in the first chapter. [89] Hardie (2004), 100–1.

In the same episode, Venus, the goddess of love and sex, dresses herself up to resemble the virgin goddess Diana[90] to make Adonis fall in love with her (*Met.* 10.533–6). By changing costume, she essentially denies her identity. Rather than using her own powers of seduction, she pretends to be Diana in following the idealized image of her as the model for involuntarily attracting desire. Her costuming is especially ironic since the passage alludes to Euripides' *Hippolytus* in which Aphrodite and Artemis are seen as polar opposites.[91]

The emphasis on disguise and costume as the gods manipulate their image to deceive mortals raises the question of what lies beneath it. The question of their true identity is no concern to themselves as they can always change back. However, it is of crucial importance to the experience of the characters within the *Metamorphoses*. To perceive the true shape of the gods means to experience epiphany.[92] Until that moment the human character cannot be sure of a god's identity.

The problem is brought up deviously by Juno as she assumes the disguise of Semele's old nurse Beroe and cautions her not to trust Jupiter's professed identity without a sure sign (*Met.* 3.273–86):

> Surgit ab his solio fuluaque recondita nube
> limen adit Semeles nec nubes ante remouit
> quam simulauit anum posuitque ad tempora canos
> sulcauitque cutem rugis et curua trementi
> membra tulit passu; vocem quoque fecit anilem
> ipsaque erat Beroe, Semeles Epidauria nutrix.
> ergo ubi captato sermone diuque loquendo
> ad nomen uenere Iovis, suspirat et 'opto
> Iuppiter ut sit' ait, 'metuo tamen omnia; multi
> nomine diuorum thalamos iniere pudicos.
> nec tamen esse Iouem satis est; det pignus amoris,
> si modo uerus is est, quantusque et qualis ab alta
> Iunone excipitur, tantus talisque rogato
> det tibi complexus suaque ante insignia sumat.'

With these words she rises from her throne and, hidden in a golden cloud, approaches Semele's doorstep. Nor does she remove the clouds before she has

[90] *Met.* 10.536: *fine genus vestem ritu succincta Dianae.* Cf. Venus as Diana in *Aen.* 1.325–30.

[91] Hardie (2004), 103.

[92] I should qualify this statement by pointing out that epiphany may be experienced in other ways as well, including dreams and sensory impressions other than visions. See Versnel (1987), Pfister (1924), and Lane Fox (1986), 102–67. However, I am here exclusively concerned with what lies beneath the more conventional representations, that is in stripping the disguise the god chooses for himself.

disguised herself as an old woman and put some grey hair on her temples and furrowed her skin with lines and carried her crooked limbs with trembling gait. Even her voice she made sound ancient. She was Beroe herself, Semele's Epidaurian nurse. And so after they had started talking and after a long while came to the name of Jupiter, she sighs and says: "I only wish it is Jupiter but still I fear it all; many men have entered chaste bedrooms under the name of the gods. Even for him to be Jupiter is not enough; let him give proof of his love if only he is true, and of such size and kind as he is received by lofty Juno, such an embrace ask that he should give you and take up his insignia."

Juno sounds sincere as she expresses the wish (*opto Iuppiter ut sit*, 281) which is the direct inversion of her actual desires. Moreover, her phrasing of this thought in a wish with the attendant subjunctive conceals her own secure knowledge of Jupiter's identity as Semele's lover. Juno's own disguise as Beroe[93] adds irony to her pretence of cautioning Semele. Juno not only disguises herself in the usual manner (*simulavit*, 275), she goes so far as to alter her voice (*vocem quoque fecit anilem*, 277)[94] – in short she completely usurps the nurse's identity – she *is* Beroe (*ipsaque erat Beroe*, *278*).

For Jupiter, on the other hand, identity is not enough, she claims (*nec tamen* ***esse*** *Iovis satis est*). He has to show proof (*pignus amoris*, 283). The phrase recalls Dido's wish for a child, a miniature Aeneas, especially since the phrase *Tyria paelice* (*Met.* 3.258) for Europa is surely meant to invoke Juno's continuous hatred for the city.[95] The real *pignus amoris* in this tale is of course the baby Dionysus, as Juno is well aware (*concipit (id deerat!) manifestaque crimina pleno/ fert utero*, 268–9).

Juno as the nurse warns Semele of mortal lovers who pretend to be immortal (281–2). This caution firmly establishes the epistemological divide between Juno and Semele. The rules of the fictional world of the *Metamorphoses* have, in fact, proven the opposite of Juno's warning. Rather than being attracted by the declaration of divine identity, the human fears it. The best example for this is Io's reaction to Jupiter's declaration of his godhead (*Met.* 1.595–7): '*Nec de plebe deo, sed qui caelestia magna/ sceptra manu teneo, sed qui vaga fulmina mitto./ ne fuge me!*' (*fugiebat enim*).

When Jupiter unwillingly gives in to Semele's demand that he appear in his true shape, Semele is incinerated along with her house (*Met.* 3.307–9). Jupiter's true identity when he makes love to Juno on equal, divine terms

93 See Wheeler (2000), 88–90 for the Virgilian roles of Juno and Beroe and how Ovid conflates them.

94 This begs the question what Juno really sounds like. Any disguise invites inquiry into what is being disguised.

95 Virgil *Aen.*5.570–72: *Iulus/ Sidonio est invectus equo, quem candida Dido/ esse sui dederat monumentum et pignus amoris.*

(*quantusque et qualis ab alta/ Iunone excipitur*, 284–5) is too powerful.[96] Divine lovemaking is too great for ordinary mortals to sustain. It has cosmic dimensions and implications. In the case of the gods as rapists "gender revelation equals penetration," as Richlin succinctly puts it.[97] The gods' true shape is so mysterious because seeing the divine is at worst lethal, or at least blinding.[98] Even with the god willing to reveal his or her identity, the sight is barred either out of piety (note the ritual proskynesis of Arachne's fellow-workers when Athena reveals herself, while Arachne stands out in braving the sight of the goddess, as she has claimed before, *Met.* 6.42–5), or for sheer physical difficulty. Thus in Phaethon's visit to Sol in the second book, Phaethon cannot come closer because his eyes hurt (*Met.* 2.20). Sol notices and takes off the helmet[99] so that Phaethon can see his face and thus confirm his father's identity.[100] Later, after he has sworn the oath, Sol implores Phaethon by asking him *aspice vultus* (*Met.* 2.92). To recognize the true identity of the divine is thus dangerous for mortals. To see a god is to come face-to-face with him and thus assert an equality in a relationship which does not allow it.

Epiphany thus challenges the poet twice over. The gods' own shape is unknowable and thus cannot be represented, but at the same time the existence of these stories titillates the reader with the idea that he will see vicariously and safely what the character must not see but does. The paradox comes out, for example, in the *Homeric Hymn to Aphrodite* when Aphrodite cautions Anchises not to talk about their encounter or else Jupiter will strike him with a thunderbolt. Yet the poem itself is testament to the telling of the story.[101] Thus the story has to give the illusion of allowing us to slip into the character and see what he sees while at the same time not giving anything away.

How then to represent what amounts to a vacuum of representation in the material sense? The simile opens up a negative space that is circumscribed by tenor and vehicle – an outer form that holds an inner emptiness. Instead of describing the divine in real terms, the simile offers the reader an impression that captures but does not equate the experience of

96 Juno's reference to conjugal lovemaking recalls Jupiter's ruse of appearing as Alcmena's husband.
97 Richlin (1992), 161
98 Callimachus (*Hymn* 5.101–2): ὃς κε τιν' ἀθανάθων ὅκα μὴ θεὸς αὐτὸς ἕληται/ ἀθρήσῃ μισθῶ τοῦτον ἰδεῖν μεγάλω.
99 Cf. Hector in *Il.* 6.466–75, another instance of a father recognizing his son.
100 Sol offers proof of his identity after it is no longer needed at *Met.* 2. 91–2: *do pignora certa timendo/ et patrio pater esse metu probo.*
101 *Hymn. Hom. Ven.* 286–8.

seeing the divine. What do the gods look *like* when they do not put on a likeness? "There is no there there," to quote Gertrude Stein.

The story of Pomona and Vertumnus is the last love story in the poem. The wooing of Vertumnus follows a series of fruitless and bizarre disguises until Vertumnus switches gender and impersonates an old woman. The story, as Lindheim has shown,[102] plays on the manipulation of image. Vertumnus' final disguise is the most effective, even if the least verisimilar. Even though he behaves in contrast to his appearance,[103] Pomona does not suspect anything. The story finds its climax when Vertumnus puts off the disguise and shows himself to Pomona in an epiphany (*Met.* 14.765–70):

> Haec ubi nequiquam formae deus apta senili
> edidit, in iuuenem rediit et anilia demit
> instrumenta sibi talisque apparuit illi,
> qualis ubi oppositas nitidissima solis imago
> euicit nubes nullaque obstante reluxit;

When the god, disguised in the shape of an old woman, had fruitlessly spoken these words, he returned to being a youth and took off the props of the old woman and revealed himself to her as when the shining image of the sun has defeated the clouds set against it and has grown bright again with nothing in its way.

The simile is particularly apt because it mimics the force of the epiphany[104] as Pomona is blinded by the sight of Vertumnus. The reader's gaze[105] too is blinded since despite the illustrative function of the simile he is unable to discern the image of Vertumnus. The sun coming out from behind the clouds is in effect the best smokescreen to avoid the need for detailed description. As we have seen, it is physically impossible to see the sun straight on. Vertumnus in fact does not resemble the sun but rather the *solis imago*, that is the simile itself is a deflected image and not a natural manifestation. He is "likened to a likeness," as Lindheim points out.[106] What is more, he might even impersonate the character Sol raping Leucothoe (*Met.* 4.230–3).

[102] Lindheim (1998).
[103] *Met.* 14.658–9: *dedit oscula, qualia numquam/ vera dedisset anus …*
[104] Bömer (1969–86) ad loc. interprets *apparuit* as the signal for epiphany.
[105] Lindheim (1998), 33 points out the invoked complicity of the reader in appreciating the perfection of Vertumnus' disguises: "Thus the response of the viewer to the sartorial displays acquires primary importance. 'He was able to seem' (*poterat … videri*, 646), 'you would have sworn' (*iurasses*, 648), 'you would think' (*putares*, 650) all highlight the tension between performance and 'reality'."
[106] Lindheim (1998), 33

The secondary literature on this passage[107] is mostly taken up by discussion of whether it is a rape scene (*vimque parat*) or a falling in love (*mutua vulnera sensit*). Rather than coming down on either side, the indeterminacy of the simile suggests a sudden emotion (*sensit*) but preserves an impenetrable intimacy to Pomona's feelings. Despite her resistance to Vertumnus' disguises earlier, she is now also captured by the image, *figura* (770). The simile takes account of the fact that the real appearance of the gods is mysterious and ineffable. There is therefore no way out of the representational crux as far as the gods are concerned, although the simile comes close in deflecting the inquirer's eye.

Representing divine power through comparison with the sun and sky in the simile reflects the magnitude of their emotions on a cosmic scale. While the natural phenomena in the sky can be observed from a distance, they remain intangibly abstract for humans though powerfully tangible in their consequences; in fact, such phenomena may be used as proof for the presence of the divine in the world.[108] The explosive potential of mortals encountering immortals is brought out in the simile's vehicle that brings the cosmos in the reach of the humans, if only through seeing the divine on earth. A classic cautionary tale, the Actaeon myth (*Met.* 3.131–251), constitutes one of the central passages in discussing the morality of the Ovidian gods. It is introduced, maybe by Ovid speaking *in propria persona*, as a mistake, not a crime, and the punishment that Diana exerts finds a divided echo.[109]

The build-up to the actual scene of seeing Diana naked is purposely suggestive. The spot is described as secluded (*in extremo … recessu*, 157) and the description of her habitual bath ritual, complete with undressing, builds up the anticipation by its sensual language: (*virgineos artus liquido perfundere rore*, 164; *depositae … pallae*, 167; *vincla … demunt*, 168; *sparsos per colla capillos/ colligit in nodum*, 170). Into this picture of relaxed intimacy stumbles Actaeon (*non certis passibus errans*, 175). He sees Diana despite the nymphs' attempts at covering her (*Met.* 3.181–5):

[107] In favor of the interpretation as rape: Richlin (1992), Gentilcore (1995), Parry (1965). Against: Johnson (1997).

[108] Cf. Horace *Carm.* 3.5.1 *Caelo tonantem credidimus Iovem regnare …* Contrast Lucretius' praise of Epicurus defying superstition, in a passage that deliberately uses metaphorical language to reduce the association to the absurd (Lucr. 1.66–9: *primum Graius homo mortalis tollere contra/ est oculos ausus primusque consistere contra,/ quem neque fama deum nec fulmina nec minitanti/ murmure compressit caelum …*)

[109] The passage is framed by two statements on divine justice: *Met.* 3.141–2: *at bene si quaeras, Fortunae crimen in illo,/ non scelus invenies; quod enim scelus error habebat? Met.* 3.253–5: *Rumor in ambiguo est; aliis violentior aequo/ visa deo est, alii laudant dignamque severa/ virginitate vocant.* Cf. *Tr.* 2.103–8 where Ovid compares himself to Actaeon.

tamen altior illis
ipsa dea est colloque tenus supereminet omnes.
qui color infectis aduersi solis ab ictu
nubibus esse solet aut purpureae Aurorae,
is fuit in uultu uisae sine ueste Dianae.

Still the goddess herself is taller than they and towers over them all as far as the neck. The color that clouds use to have when tinged by the stroke of the sun or the color of purple dawn: that was the color of the face of Diana, seen without her dress.

Instead of describing her body, Ovid instead focuses on her the color of her blushing face (*vultu*).[110] With this gesture of gentlemanly restraint, Ovid avoids repeating Actaeon's offense. Even more, he implicitly praises her divinity by describing her as standing above the rest. Unfortunately, her conspicuousness draws attention to the fact that she cannot hide her nakedness. But it is the focus on Diana's blush that pays homage to her prime attribute, perpetual virginity. Since he does not mention her body but only hints at her nakedness, the mystery of what Actaeon has seen remains. The blush marks Diana as even more desirable because it emphasizes the inaccessibility of her body.

Ovid's refusal to describe Diana's body recalls the ethical code of the elegist.[111] The event in fact is almost a mirror to the faux epiphany of Corinna: the mystery of her anonymity retains the ambivalence of her status. In the *Amores*, the *candida diva* transgresses the space of the sleeper and evokes epiphany in a parallel scene of undress. The fact that Ovid himself does not spread the word makes all the more cruel and impressive Diana's punishment that seeks expressly to prevent vulgar gossip: *nunc tibi me posito velamine narres,/ si poteris narrare, licet* (*Met* 3.192–3). In a strange twist of the fictional world intruding on Ovid's own poetic license, there is no story.

If we look more closely at the simile itself, the image that is conjured appears curiously abstract as it focuses on color alone. The comparison makes the reader complicit in Actaeon's involuntary lingering gaze. Sunrise and sundown typically invite long contemplation, as a purely aesthetic and serene experience.[112] The abstract quality of this image might suggest that Actaeon does not even know what he has seen and is still trying to figure it out. The simile might also contain a cue in invoking the boundaries

110 Anderson (1997) ad loc. suggest that this might be the only part he actually gets to see.
111 cf. Ovid *Am.* 1.5.25.
112 I do not agree with Bömer (1969–86) ad loc. who interprets Diana's heightened color as fury ("Zorn") that has cosmic implications. The image of sunrise or sundown to me suggests calm, not agitation.

of the day marking the transgression of the divide between mortal and immortal. Ovid's choice of simile thus also underlines the cosmic impact of a human recognizing a god. The contrast is heightened by the use of an everyday image (*solet*, 184) to describe the epiphany. Finally, in the association of sunrise and sundown as the images for human life as day and death as night there might be a hint already of his later punishment.

The simile thus stands in for seeing things straight on. Rather than showing the mystery, Ovid uses the simile to heighten the reader's frustration at not getting beyond the text. He uses the reader's own imagination to complete the picture following the poet's suggested lines with his own creative potential. The awareness of the fictional divide between reader and character is thus brought to the fore.

That the story appears in book 3 is no coincidence, as this book has as its unifying theme the identity of the divine and the need for mortals to find proof for it. As well as the stories of Actaeon, Semele, and Teiresias, the book also contains Bacchus' proof of his divinity, through the tragedy of Pentheus and in an embedded cautionary tale told by himself. While disguise and uncertainty about the gods is a constant theme throughout the *Metamorphoses* it might be of even greater importance in this context in which seeing is literally believing – but too late.

The simile of Diana's blush prepares the ground for another encounter between mortal and divine. This single exception in which such a cosmic simile is applied to a human actually confirms the connection between natural forces and the divine. When Minerva reveals herself to Arachne, the latter's temerity to challenge the goddess is reflected in the simile of her inscrutable blush, compared to the sky at dawn (*Met.* 6.45–9):

sola est non territa uirgo
sed tamen erubuit, subitusque inuita notauit
ora rubor rursusque euanuit, ut solet aer
purpureus fieri, cum primum Aurora movetur,
et breve post tempus candescere solis ab ortu.

The maiden alone is not frightened but blushes yet; at once a red hue marks her face against her will and vanishes again, as air is used to become purple when struck at first by the dawn, and after a short time grows white from the sunrise.

Against her will (*invita*, 6.46), Arachne's blush betrays her awareness of the consequence of challenging the divine, but it is gone within the space of the simile as if the color was no more than an optical illusion. The grandeur of the image thus marks simultaneously her *pudor* (blush as tenor of the simile) and her hybris (sky as vehicle of the simile). In a similar vein, the wool she uses is likened to clouds (*nebulas aequantia*, 6.21); later, the dyed wool that is used in the contest is compared in a simile to the color of the rainbow, a phenomenon that connects the extremes of mortal and immortal (6.63–7):

> qualis ab imbre solet percussis solibus arcus
> inficere ingenti longum curvamine caelum,
> in quo diversi niteant cum mille colores,
> transitus ipse tamen spectantia lumina fallit,
> usque adeo quod tangit idem est; tamen ultima distant.

Just as the rainbow tends to dye the wide sky in a giant curve as the sun's rays are shot through with rain, and in it shine a thousand different colors, yet still their overlap tricks the attentive eyes to the point that where it touches, it is the same; still the edges are unlike each other.

Arachne is messing with cosmic dimensions as she offers a revelatory view on the divine. In manipulating perception through artistic illusion, both in the prime material that deceives the eyes (*spectantia lumina fallit*, 6.66) and in the result that tricks the viewer (*verum taurum, vera freta putares*, 6.104), she challenges the divine control of the cosmos.

Representing the divine in a poem which has as its theme the manipulation of shapes through the divine by necessity reconfigures the respective positions of human, divine, and animal. While anthropomorphism may offer an easy way out of the dilemma, Ovid seems to call this convention into question. The simile's in-between status seems suited to the approximation of the sublime, as it suggests similarity while not insisting on congruence, on being. If the human condition in the poem is marked by the continuous conflict of "being" in spite of the change of shape, then the divine condition is a continuity of semblances that never reaches the essence of being. The figure of the simile offers a way to render the sublime in the interstice that exists in the approximation of tenor and vehicle. Any simile has points of similarity and contrast; the negotiation of these two poles may offer a way to comprehend the divine that defies categorization in terms of the natural world. The simile's openness as a figure shows the divine as exceeding identification with the natural world, be it the cosmos, the animal "other," or the augmented human form.

CHAPTER 3

The simile and genre

The previous two chapters have traced the fine line that divides human from animal and mortal from immortal. The continuous transformations, permutations, and disguises seem to reverberate as the faint echoes of the primal chaos in which nothing kept its form (*nulli sua forma manebat*, *Met.* 1.17). The same potential for entropy applies to the poem at large – the great variety and constant modulation of genres in the episodic structure challenges the poem's epic credentials. But if, as Hinds has suggested,[1] genre may be demarcated by a line that becomes visible only after it has been crossed, the epic simile offers a particularly poignant line of attack. On the one hand, it bears its generic affiliation in its very name; on the other, the flexible hinge of its form allows a step outside the narrative proper and offers a refractive view of it.

In defining the epic simile, most scholars agree on such criteria as length, complexity, or verbal correspondence between tenor and vehicle. The purpose of these definitions consists mainly in distinguishing the epic simile from other related figures of speech (such as short comparisons) within a single text or a single author's work, in order to gauge the overall number and thus the relative simile density within that context. However, an even more basic definition is possible: a simile is epic by virtue of its epic context. This seems to be borne out by Brunner's observation of the comparative rarity of long similes (from two to seven lines) in genres other than epic, in both Greek and Latin literature.[2] The epic simile is deeply intertwined with the tradition of the genre, playing a crucial part in constructing its discourse.

The term "Homeric simile," used interchangeably, points to the ultimate source for any epic simile. Thus allusion adds another dimension to this generic expectation as similes from Homer afford his successors themes on which to play their variations. The play with the allusion allows for a way

[1] Hinds (1987), 102. [2] Brunner (1966), 355.

of distancing and defining their epic vision against that of the father of the genre, while at the same time upholding the characteristic form itself. Any simile works on at least two levels, content (subject matter) and application (the function of the simile in the narrative context), affording at least two possible modes of allusion. Some similes from Homer have acquired the power of stock-in-trade for epic, a kind of short cut to allude to bigger themes. The lion simile, for example, exalting a hero's prowess in Homer, is used in Apollonius Rhodius' reworking of the model to portray a new kind of hero, and so marks not only a poetic innovation but also a new vision of epic masculinity.[3]

The assumption that the simile is epic by default is challenged by the new, generically multifaceted world of the *Metamorphoses*. The debate over the poem's status as an epic has lately given way to a provisional truce among scholars who declare it epic on account of meter, length, and scope.[4] Farrell's seminal article on the "dialogue of genres" within the poem has opened the discussion beyond the binary opposition of epic versus un-epic.[5] Central to the construction of this discourse is the epic simile which, once liberated from the context in which it was taken for granted, can now infuse the narrative with epic flavor. The simile itself, in both form and subject matter, becomes an active participant in articulating this dialogue.

Solodow groups the simile together with other epic features such as catalogues and battle scenes in Ovid's repertoire of epic features.[6] However, a look through Ovid's toolbox reveals that these elements are hardly conventional. Few would mistake for example the account of the fight of the Lapiths (*Met.* 12.219–35) for one of Homer's battles, or the catalogue of Actaeon's dogs (*Met.* 3.206–25) for that of the Greek army before Troy. Lacking an overall consistency of tone, Ovid's similes engage with the generic modulation and contrasts of the narrative. Of all the epic devices, the simile is the most flexible since it can be inserted without disturbing the narrative structure (as a catalogue would). Ovid uses similes to this effect in the *Amores*, in which they do not change the genre but represent a thorn in the side of elegy.[7] Since any comparison entails both similarity and difference, the simile is ideally suited to mediate the "dialogue of genres" that governs the poem and to stress the distance or closeness to the epic genre. Short of being ornamental epic deadwood, the simile fulfills an active role in shaping this process.

[3] Effe (2001), 152–3. [4] Harrison (2002), 87. [5] Farrell (1992).
[6] Solodow (1988), 18. [7] Boyd (1997), 90–131.

What makes a simile an epic simile? Brunner, in his work on similes in the *Metamorphoses*, found two obvious criteria to answer this question, length and subject matter. Similes of two to seven lines in length occur only 42 times in Ovid's corpus, 38 of which are in the *Metamorphoses*.[8] In terms of subject matter, similes in the *Metamorphoses* are drawn from imagery that emphasizes grandeur, as for example in depicting the forces of nature. Brunner's findings led him to affirm Heinze's characterization of the *Metamorphoses'* style as epic (*deinon*) versus the elegiac tone of the *Fasti* (*eleeinon*). He concluded that the epic simile "serves to provide epic flavor to material basically not of an epic nature."[9] Heinze's strict dichotomy of genre has been countered by Hinds who showed that the generic ambiguity of both poems problematizes the issue of genre.[10] The reappraisal of Heinze has obvious consequences for Brunner's thesis. Instead of seeing the epic simile as self-contained regardless of the context in which it is used, it appears profitable to examine exactly how its epic flavor interacts with the generically diverse mixture of the *Metamorphoses*, including its more "epic" portions.

Formal criteria, such as length or subject matter, do not take into account how these elements react with the narrative. Thus a lion simile might look like an epic simile without actually being epic in its application or tone. In fact, it seems self-evident that the subject matter should follow the conventions of the genre since if the simile is to work as an epic additive it needs to be recognizably epic. Allusion to the Homeric repertoire of imagery such as lions, bulls, and forces of nature thus corresponds to the bigger frame of epic itself. However, subject matter alone need not indicate epic grandeur and seriousness. The obvious counter-example is parody, which counters the gravity of the simile with the levity of context. Beyond parody, however, a simile at odds with its context disrupts the homogeneity of discourse and allows epic and other genres to be played out against each other. In this way the epic simile is made to "stage" epic. While potentially any simile in the *Metamorphoses* can perform this function, some similes seem to stand out in particular.

The "staged" quality of these similes derives in part from the specific allusion to a Homeric model that grounds the simile in the epic tradition even if its application or variation takes it far away from that tradition. Conte distinguishes between two modes of allusion, integrated and reflective, which he associates with Virgil and Ovid, respectively. They are summed up by Segal in his preface to Conte's book:

[8] Brunner (1966). [9] Brunner (1971), 363. [10] Hinds (1987), 115–34.

The Virgilian "integration" (as Jackson Knight called it) blends the allusion into a new synthesis that minimizes the juncture; the Ovidian mode is to call attention to the artifice involved in the allusion, to break the frame and make the enframing structure visible. For Conte both are rhetorical figures of a sort, the former (Virgilian) analogous to metaphor, the latter (Ovidian) analogous to simile.[11]

An important consequence results: if allusion is analogous to simile in Ovid, then allusion by means of simile may be thought of as compounded allusion, emphasizing not only the relationship between the two poets but also the method of their respective use of the simile to create an epic narrative. While Virgil integrates the allusion-through-simile by using the simile in the context of a traditionally epic narrative, Ovid distances the simile from its context, allowing it to reflect on its traditional role in creating the epic discourse. Thus not only the simile itself but the very fact of its use becomes a matter of challenging the norms of the genre and defining poetics in the face of tradition.

CEYX

The story of Ceyx and Alcyone occupies a special territory in the discussion of genre in the *Metamorphoses*. Its detail and length mark it as a self-sufficient epyllion. In the wider structure, it functions as a prelude to the 'epic' section in the subsequent books in which Ovid engages with the characters from Homer and Virgil. The poem's capability of demarcating the line at material that appears "more epic" than what precedes it is testament to its ambivalent status as an epic. In Otis' view, the contrast makes the story's celebration of conjugal love stand out as the structural centerpiece of the *Metamorphoses*.[12] He sees Ovid's manipulation of traditional epic instruments (the simile) and topoi (the storm, the sleep scene) as a way to distance his new vision of epic from that of his predecessors. Stressing the transition over the divide, Holzberg instead sees these elements as modulating the transition between elegiac and epic modes at this juncture.[13] On all accounts, Ovid's unorthodox treatment of these epic building blocks makes their importance in constructing genre stand out.

In particular, Ovid's daring reinvention of the epic simile in the storm scene deserves special attention. Otis' detailed analysis of the passage shows how the build-up of similes that liken the storm to soldiers besieging a

[11] Segal in Conte (1986), 12; Conte (1986), 52–69. [12] Otis (1970), 261.
[13] Holzberg (2002), 139–40.

city animates the storm as a quasi-human adversary.[14] The setting of the scene at night and the storm itself which erases distinctions between sea, underworld, and the heavens render the storm in demonic imagery. The series of similes progresses from the inanimate (*aries*, *Met.* 11.509), to the animal (*utque solent … leones*, 11.511), to the human (*ut miles*, 11.526). The density of the double simile in lines 508–11 lends a metamorphic quality to the images. The first simile reactivates the dormant metaphorical potential of the battering "ram" that is named after the animal. In the next image, the animals simile *par excellence*, lions, displace human warriors in fighting against shields and spears. Thus the traditional associations are condensed within the vehicle itself (battering ram/ram; lions/warriors). The rapid association that lets the disjointed elements flash briefly recreates the confusion of the tempest.

The similes increase in length and complexity with the result that the sea springs to life as a fully realized character in its own right, complete with emotions and intentions (*spe*; *accensus amore*, 527). Ovid treats the sea sometimes as one (*fluctus*, 529), then separate parts (*pars … pars*, 533–4), or even single waves (*unda velut victrix sinuataque despicit undas*, 553) which enhances the impression of a collective made up by individuals. The increasing length but even more so the emotional intensity of the similes grow along with the narrative action of the storm, building up a crescendo that unloads in a climactic simile (*Met.* 11.524–32):

> dat quoque iam saltus intra caua texta carinae
> fluctus; et ut miles, numero praestantior omni,
> cum saepe adsiluit defensae moenibus urbis,
> spe potitur tandem laudisque accensus amore
> inter mille uiros murum tamen occupat unus,
> sic, ubi pulsarunt nouiens latera ardua fluctus,
> uastius insurgens decimae ruit impetus undae,
> nec prius absistit fessam oppugnare carinam
> quam uelut in captae descendat moenia navis.

The flood now too jumps into the densely fitted hollow of the ship; and as a soldier, standing out from the whole number, after he has leaped often at the walls of the city being defended, takes hold of his aim at last and inflamed by his desire for praise, among a thousand men is yet the only one to seize the wall, just so, when nine waves were beating the high sides, the surging impact of the tenth wave came crashing down more devastatingly, and did not leave off battering the exhausted ship until it descended as it were the walls of the captured ship.

[14] See Otis (1970), 238–46 for an exemplary close reading.

The Homeric source of this simile describes Hector in the battle at the ships (*Il.* 15.621–8). Ovid, in inverting the original simile's tenor and vehicle, comments on Homer's own technique which had reactivated the dormant resonance of the storm for the beached ships of the Greeks that form the camp, itself a stand-in for Troy. The storm in the vehicle of the simile thus recalls the proper use of the ships. Ovid's allusion to this climactic scene in the *Iliad* imports the emotional charge of that battle into the Ceyx passage.

This pillaging of Homer for material may also be read as a programmatic statement on Ovid's position in the literary tradition. By switching tenor and vehicle of the Homeric simile, Ovid manages to compress this climactic battle scene in the space of a few lines, subjugating it to ancillary status. The reference is both specific and general: for the reader who recognizes the Homeric allusion, the anonymous *miles* must be Hector, especially since the lion simile (*Met.* 11.510–13) that Ovid applies to the wave marks the hero in the context of the *Iliad* (*Il.* 15.630–3); and yet, his anonymity makes it clear that Ovid alludes to epic battle scenes in general, and thus to the tradition of the epic genre as a whole. Ovid's engagement with Homer through the simile, the Homeric narrative device *par excellence*, thus also points to his position in the tradition of the genre. The inversion of the two elements leads to a change in the relative dimensions, foregrounding the storm in favor of the battle scene. Likewise, in the ensuing "epic narrative" Ovid will retain Homer's cast of characters but will change the relative proportions, with the Trojan War as backdrop to the formerly marginal, now pulled in front.[15] Solodow remarks on Ovid's habit, saying that in the Hecuba episode: "he places private suffering above national catastrophe."[16] The inversion of the simile's images likewise magnifies the singular death of Ceyx into a tragedy of epic proportions, invoking the topos of *urbs antiqua ruit*.

Since tenor and vehicle do not have equal weight, reversing their positions alters the hierarchy of the image. The vehicle exchanges its ancillary position for one of dominance, and vice versa. The respective roles circumscribe the world of the narrative. While the tenor is anchored in the narrative, the vehicle is by definition an escape from that reality, connecting the reader's reality with the emotions and experiences of the epic heroes. Homer's similes offer, as has often been pointed out, a temporary

[15] Ovid uses a similar technique in the *Heroides* in which the subjectivity of the heroines' letters result in a radical shift in perspective.

[16] Solodow (1988), 141.

break from the narrative, especially from the monotony of battle. Porter, in an article that emphasizes the contrast introduced by the simile into the Homeric narrative, writes:

> The rapid and intense epic narrative is magically suspended by the simile's sudden influx of *lyric description and feeling*, and the reader is given a brief glimpse of these many aspects of the world which are largely absent from the poem ...[17]

While Porter does not claim that the simile belongs to another genre, his phrasing is intriguing. The simile does introduce another mode into the narrative, demarcating the line between the reality of the battlefield and the rest of the world. By temporarily opening up the field of vision beyond the battlefield, the simile reveals the narrow focus on war of the narrative as a whole. In doing so, it demarcates the boundaries of epic as a narrative that pushes all other aspects of human life to the margin. Paradoxically, in using the reader's shared experience of these aspects, the simile's reality effect supports and makes plausible the epic fiction. Even when describing a storm, Homer will use contrast in the similes. Thus he compares Odysseus' raft to thistles blown in the wind (*Od.* 5.328–30), widening the picture beyond the imminent threat. By contrast, Ovid's battle similes compress the emotion in animating the forces of nature and show the storm as forcing epic confrontation onto the declared pacifist Ceyx (*cura mihi pax est*, *Met.* 11.297).

Ovid's move to reinforce the storm's epic credibility leads to a kind of epic overload, mingling the spectacular description of the storm itself with visions of the siege and sacking of a town. The similes grow in intensity and length and threaten to drown out the action of the storm itself. This is especially apparent in lines 525–36 in which simile and narrative blend to such an extent that it becomes hard to distinguish one from the other. Ovid starts off with an *ut–sic* construction, but returns to simile within (!) the *sic*-clause (*velut in captae descendat moenia navis*, 11.536). After only two lines, another simile, comparing the reaction of the sailors to the inhabitants of a fallen city, continues the earlier simile virtually without interruption by any narrative proper. The use of the simile thus helps create a parallel narrative, its irruption into the narrative mimicking the action of the waves. The density of epic codemarkers in this passage makes the storm look like an "epic ekphrasis".[18] The inversion of tenor and vehicle from the Homeric model reduces the martial action to a miniature

[17] Porter (1972), 11 (italics mine). [18] Otis (1970), 245.

vignette, while its subject matter continuously threatens to overwhelm its confines.

Inverting the simile's proportions creates an oddly lopsided view that draws attention to the very different weights of such scenes in the overall epic plot. Storms and battles are in fact not equivalent but opposing scenes in epic narrative. While battles offer an opportunity of winning glory in the face of death, storms function as a subversive element in the story, threatening to cancel out not only life, but renown. Drowning is the antithesis of an heroic death. In the middle of the storm, both Odysseus (*Od.* 5.306–12) and Aeneas (*Aen.* 1.94–101) express envy for those fallen at Troy who had a heroic death on the battlefield.[19] The vividly imagined heroic action of the storm accentuates the total absence of human heroics. The sailors' attitude is one of complete passivity (*Met.* 11.539–43); Ceyx himself is not mentioned until line 544. The energy of the battle simile only underscores the helpless suffering of the humans.

The inversion of the simile displaces Ceyx and makes the sea the real hero of the passage. Ceyx's helplessness fits with the elegiac persona he presents and marks him as being out of his element in the exaggerated epic context. Thus the simile's inversion of storm and battle also represents a reverse mirroring of genres. In the *Tristia* Ovid styles himself after Odysseus, proving that he is more epic than the epic hero (*Tr.* 1.5.57–84). In the storm scene at the beginning of his *Tristia*,[20] he fears not death itself but the wrong "genre" of death[21] (*Tr.* 1.2.51–6):

> nec letum timeo, **genus** est **miserabile** leti;
> demite naufragium, mors mihi munus erit.
> est aliquid, fatove ferrove cadentem
> in solida moriens ponere corpus humo,
> et mandare suis aliqua et sperare sepulcrum
> et non aequoreis piscibus esse cibum.

I do not fear death, it is the kind of death that is lamentable; take away the shipwreck and death will be a gift. It is worth something, having fallen by fate or steel, to put one's dying body in the solid earth, and to leave something to one's own and to hope for a burial and not be food for the fish of the sea.

[19] The first death at Troy, that of Protesilaus, is strictly speaking not on the battlefield but still at sea (*Met.* 12.66–8).

[20] Ovid had tried out the battle-storm image in *Tr.* 1.2.48–9: *Nec levius tabulae laterum feriuntur ab undis/ quam grave ballistae moenia pulsat onus.* Cf. *Met.* 11.508–9: *nec levius pulsata sonat quam ferreus olim/ cum laceras aries ballistave concutit arces.*

[21] My wording does not seek to imply that *genus* should be literally translated as *genre*.

While Ovid's persona aspires to epic status, the *genus miserabile* of drowning fits elegy's obsession with such a death. In fact, Alcyone's entreaties to her husband earlier to let her come with him (*Met.* 11.440–3) might come straight from the romantic vision of Propertius. Like Ceyx (*Met.* 11.545–6), Propertius wants his love buried in earth rather than at sea (2.26C.43–4):

> certe isdem nudi pariter iactabimur oris:
> me licet unda ferat, te modo terra tegat.

> At least we will be tossed equally naked onto the same shores:
> The sea may bear me, as long as earth covers you.

Ovid's persona in the *Tristia*, a misplaced epic hero in the context of elegy, inverts that of Ceyx, an elegiac hero misplaced in epic.

HECUBA

In contrast to the misplaced Ceyx, the character of Hecuba is equally at home in two genres, epic and tragedy. The story of Hecuba's revenge on Polymestor challenges the boundaries of both epic and tragedy. Hecuba, originally a character of Homeric epic, had been reinvented as a tragic heroine. Ovid's narrative is to a large extent based on Euripides' version of the myth, down to the almost verbatim translation of individual lines.[22] The reversal of her fortune from queen to slave of war constitutes a declension of genre as well, from epic to tragedy. She is thus, to use Hinds' term for Medea, an "intertextual heroine," at home in different genres.[23] At the same time, Ovid's treatment of the episode within the *Metamorphoses*, and more precisely within the expressly "epic" part of his poem, turns her into an epic character again, if only by virtue of being a character in epic. Her paradoxical status in genre terms is acted out in the narrative as she commences her defining tragic action reassuming her former epic identity as queen of Troy (*tamquam regina maneret, Met.* 13.545). The modulation between epic and tragic modes in the *Metamorphoses*' narrative thus makes Hecuba an "intratextual heroine," a character that belongs to both genres simultaneously.

Ovid's "re-epicising of the tragic plot" within the framework of the *Metamorphoses* employs traditional epic features.[24] A crucial role for the negotiation between these two genres falls to the epic simile that likens Hecuba to a lioness raging at the loss of her young (*Met.* 13.545–53):

[22] Hopkinson (2000), 24. [23] Hinds (1993). [24] Hopkinson (2000), 24.

qua simul exarsit, tamquam regina maneret,
ulcisci statuit poenaeque in imagine tota est,
utque furit catulo lactente orbata leaena
signaque nacta pedum sequitur quem non videt hostem,
sic Hecabe, postquam cum luctu miscuit iram,
non oblita animorum, annorum oblita suorum,
uadit ad artificem dirae Polymestora caedis
conloquiumque petit; nam se monstrare relictum
uelle latens illi, quod nato redderet, aurum.

And while she raged, as if she were still queen, she decided to take revenge and was wholly the image of punishment, as a lioness rages when bereft of her suckling cub; having found the tracks of feet, she follows the enemy that she does not see, so Hecabe, after mingling her grief with wrath, forgetful of her age but not her passions, strode to the contriver of the dreadful slaughter of Polymestor, and sought parley, saying that she wanted to show him some remaining gold that she was hiding, to give her back her son.

The simile's obvious epic heritage has been traced back to the Iliad (*Il.* 18.318–22). Even without the precise model for this simile, the association of Queen Hecuba with the lioness, the queen of the animal kingdom, would retain its epic flavor since lion similes are a hallmark of epic. Thus Hopkinson writes that the simile gives back to Hecuba her "epic dignity."[25]

The assumption of this epic role marks a crucial point in the narrative. At the sight of Polydorus' dead body, the Trojan women shriek while Hecuba falls silent (*obmutuit illa dolore, Met.* 13.538). Ovid thus recreates in his narrative the dramatic silence of staged tragedy. The outward action is halted while the reader is made to follow the gradual change in Hecuba's emotions, as if watching her onstage. Her lack of speech is accompanied by a lack of motion (*duroque simillima saxo, Met.* 13.540) in a formulation that is clearly meant to recall Niobe's petrification at the death of her children (*Met.* 6.301–9). Hecuba could turn into another Niobe, one feels. Instead, the reference accentuates Hecuba's daring: unlike Niobe whose loss of voice and movement reflect feminine passivity as a socially acceptable reaction to grief, Hecuba's turn to revenge marks her as transgressing expectations of gender.[26]

[25] Hopkinson (2000) ad loc.

[26] Cicero contrasts Niobe and Hecuba in their grief (*et Nioba fingitur lapidea propter aeternum, credo, in luctu silentium; Hecubam autem putant propter animi acerbitatem quandam et rabiem fingi in canem esse conversam. Tusc.* 2.26.3)

Hecuba's emotions change from grief to rage (*seque armat et instruit ira*, *Met.* 13.544). The simile presents the climactic point of this development after which the action picks up again (*vadit*, 551; *conloquiumque petit*, 552). It works as a bridge within the period (545–53) from Hecuba's decision to avenge her son (545–6) to the action she takes (551–2). The length of the resulting period gives the impression that Hecuba cannot be stopped in her action. Despite the simile's epic ancestry, it is used to convey the pivotal moment in the tragedy. Thus Ovid is able to recreate within the confines of the epic narrative the stage effects of the tragic version.

While the model for this simile has been recognized in Homer's simile of Achilles (*Il.* 18.318–22), the resonance of this allusion has not been fully explored.[27] Homer's simile also comes at a crucial moment of the epic narrative. It describes Achilles mourning for Patroclus, a scene that prepares the hero's re-entry into battle. While his companions mourn Patroclus, Achilles draws rage from the death of his friend in order to avenge his death. In the *Iliad*, the lion simile, the epic simile *par excellence*, is associated with Achilles in particular.[28] Like the hero's armor, the lion simile symbolizes Achilles' warrior persona, which he is about to reassume. Ovid's close modeling of his simile after Homer's thus shockingly equates the polar opposites of Achilles and Hecuba at the moment in which each prepares for action.

This allusion becomes even more potent as one notices the important differences in the details that Ovid seeks to emphasize. Homer's simile compares the close relationship of Achilles to Patroclus in terms of the parental bond between lion and cub.[29] Ovid contrasts with this Hecuba's real maternal bond with Polydorus. Not only does he make a point of the female gender of the lion (*leaena*, 547) but he imagines the cub as still dependent on its mother's milk (*catulo lactente*, 547) which increases the pathos of Polydorus' death and recalls the pathos of Hecuba's appeal to Hector (*Il.* 22.79–81). Moreover, whereas Homer's simile talks of cubs in the plural even though Patroclus is one person, Ovid's simile has the cub in the singular despite Hecuba's loss of all her fifty sons.

The greatest difference in the two versions, however, concerns not so much the vehicle but the tenor of the simile. The gender of the lioness, her

[27] Hopkinson (2000) ad loc.

[28] Arist. *Rh.* III.3.1406b. Intriguingly, in the same passage he quotes Plato *Resp.* 469D, who compares those who strip the dead to dogs who bite at stones (i.e. cowards).

[29] Lonsdale (1990), 11: "Many of the great animal similes that mark the strong bond among the Achaian warriors, such as the mother cow shielding her new-born (17.4 ff.), or the lioness tracking down the hunter who has stolen her cubs (18. 318 ff.), counterbalance the domestic encounters possible in the house of Priam."

proverbial protective instinct toward her young, and her regal stature all fit Hecuba perfectly, one might say even better than Achilles. Ovid treats the simile in an extremely conservative manner, adjusting only the details. The very traditional nature of the simile contrasts with the way in which it is applied. Women in epic are not compared to lions (or lionesses). The lion is a warrior symbol, belonging to the male domain. Thus Hecuba and her daughter, at *Aen.* 2.513–5, for instance, are compared to doves. The gender segregation in the similes, associating women with the weak and flighty, is a logical consequence of the situations in which women find themselves. The *Aeneid* simile describes the women cowering by the altar – women in traditional epic certainly do not go on the warpath, as Hecuba does. Hecuba's behavior is thus thoroughly epic, as illustrated by the epic simile, and thoroughly un-epic in that the simile has a woman for its tenor.

Hecuba's rage makes her assume an epic warrior's persona, and thus destroys the compartmentalization of male and female in war, and the poetry of war, epic. Earlier in the *Metamorphoses*, Hecuba had equated Polyxena's death by sacrifice with her other sons' death in battle (*Met.* 13.495–500).[30] To reinforce the point, Ovid uses deliberately martial language to describe her. She is not overpowered by her rage but controls it as a weapon: *seque armat et instruit ira.*[31] Hecuba's figurative taking up of arms thus corresponds to Achilles' literal one. The women who help her are similarly arraigned in martial order as *agmina matrum* (560). Hecuba's rage has epic proportions: *ira* gets mentioned an exceptional four times in the narrative (543, 548, 559, 562). Hecuba shares this emotion with only one other character in book 13, the epic hero Ajax. The women's figurative usurpation of the epic warrior role can only be ended by real violence when the Thracians charge at the women with stones and other weapons.

Switching the genre back to tragedy, however, reveals a familiar pattern of portraying women who usurp male roles as bestial, even monstrous. Euripides himself draws on the same image of the lioness with her cubs when the nurse describes Medea poised for action (*Med.* 187–9), contrasting the lioness' maternal instinct with the perversely twisted mind of Medea. Her act of killing her children in rage at Jason unites the simile's victim and perpetrator in one. Instead of meshing with the narrative, the image stands out as being "curiously inappropriate here, since the lioness uses all her strength and wiles to protect her offspring whereas Medea will

30 See Keith (2000), 124.

31 Note also the use of the transitive verb in line 550: *postquam cum luctu miscuit iram* suggests her control over the emotion.

use all hers to destroy her children."[32] Euripides deliberately creates a lack of correspondence to show Medea's lack of humanity – she is even more bestial than the anthropomorphized lioness.

Ovid also confuses gender roles in misapplying the traditional male simile to describe a female character, which seems to reinforce the stereotyping of tragedy. At the same time, however, the great care that he takes in preserving the original allusion in its epic context seems to imply that Hecuba is on some level the equal of Achilles. If Achilles' rage at Patroclus' death is justified in the *Iliad*, then so is Hecuba's, in a circle of vengeance and counter-vengeance that perpetuates the hatred. Priam's gesture of reconciliation (resisted by Hecuba) was meant to end this circle. Its reactivation through Hecuba's revenge counteracts the closure of the *Iliad*, as Hecuba herself reasserts her former identity.

The simile blends sympathy for the animal, imagined in anthropomorphic fashion, with fear of its savage nature. This duality foregrounds the problem of how to judge Hecuba, an issue that is still being discussed in respect to Euripides' play. Ovid concludes the episode by offering the unanimous reaction to Hecuba's transformation into a dog: pity.[33] The sympathy extends to Ovid's discretion as he implies rather than exploits her metamorphosis. He renders only her changed voice, not her body (*Met.* 13.567–9):

> at haec missum rauco cum murmure saxum
> morsibus insequitur rictuque in verba parato
> latravit conata loqui.

But she goes after the hurled rock with bites, and with a hoarse growl, the mouth opened wide for words, she barks, trying to speak.

In Euripides' version, by contrast, the dog imagery prevails. Not only does Polymestor curse the Trojan women as bitches (*Hec.* 1060–5), his own dog-like appearance once he is blinded (*Hec.* 1058–9) is mirrored by Hecuba's own metamorphosis as punishment of stooping down to the level of her enemy in acting out her revenge.[34] Kerrigan writes on Euripides' treatment:

[32] Bongie (1977), 28 n.35

[33] The internal audience stands in for the audience of tragedy and directs the reader's response. Ovid singles out Juno as being unusually sympathetic (*illius fortuna deos quoque moverat omnes,/ sic omnes, ut et ipsa Iovis coniunx sororque/ eventus Hecaben meruisse negaverit illos, Met.* 13.573–5). Perhaps because she is the only queen in epic who knows the power of *ira*?

[34] On the canine imagery in Euripides' *Hecuba*, see Mossman (1995), 194–202.

> ... but there is also a comic grotesquerie in this abasement of the tragic queen to the four-legged dogginess of her foe – something which Ovid, characteristically, adumbrates in his account of Hecuba's transformation.[35]

While commentators on Ovid tend to read the lion simile as a precursor of Hecuba's bestial state, the simile does not so much anticipate as contradict her later humiliation. Ovid's lion simile completely overshadows the image of her later metamorphosis.

Lions and dogs are at opposite ends of the animal spectrum as symbols for bravery and cowardice, respectively. The complete reversal of the image anticipated in the simile thus reflects Hecuba's fall from epic figure to tragic victim. The epic simile paradoxically enhances the tragic nature of the episode by contrasting figurative grandeur with pitiful reality.

It is thus possible to read the "epic simile" in both the tragic and the epic mode. The simile itself functions as a "pivot" between the two genres, a polyvalent sign that can be read either way, depending on the expectation of genre that the reader brings to the text. As Conte observes:

> The task of changing the whole structure in this way is assigned to a difference in the constellation of the signifying elements ... Behind the unchanging objects and words emerges the power of the relations and systems of signs that are literary genres.[36]

The figure of the epic simile itself, despite its obvious generic heritage, may be used to modulate genre and to exploit the divergent literary history of Hecuba's character. The epic simile is not a simple tool to inject epic flavor into the narrative and smooth over the generic provenance of the material. Rather, it plays its own constitutive part in marking and playing with the conventions of both epic and tragedy, retaining the distinct flavors of each.

APOLLO AND DAPHNE

Reading a character's generic identity in such a polyvalent system then also contains the danger of misinterpretation, especially when one of the characters happens to be divine. The story of Apollo and Daphne stands out in scholarly literature as one of the most discussed episodes of the poem. Nicoll was the first to point out its programmatic function for the epic as a whole. As the first love story of the poem (*primus amor*, *Met.* 1.452), it squares off the generic registers of elegy and epic against each

[35] Kerrigan (1996), 194. [36] Conte (1994), 109.

other in the encounter of Apollo and Cupid. Apollo's dual status as both the patron god of poetry and a character in the poem who is subject to the poet leads to a struggle for authorial control over an epic simile that is seen as determining the genre of the encounter.

Nicoll argues that Cupid's derailing of the epic project by shooting his darts should be seen as a corrective to the overly pompous epic poetics of the beginning.[37] Indeed, the previous, more conventionally epic beginnings of the poem continue to result in calamitous destruction, thereby stalling rather than advancing the plot. The slaying of the monster Python by Apollo is the last in this line, the monster being another error of nature that needs to be removed as if the repeated creation of the cosmos demands continuous emendation (*illa* [sc. *tellus*] *quidem nollet, sed te quoque, maxime Python,/ tum genuit*, *Met.* 1. 439–40).[38] Cupid's sabotaging act breaks this cycle of repetitive beginnings. In deliberate imitation of Apollo's plague-bringing arrows that open the dramatic action of the *Iliad*, he wounds Apollo. Ironically, the latter's healing powers are no defense (*remedia* [*amoris*]) against this sudden love "sickness" (*Met.* 1.521–4).

As much as Cupid's interference seems to derail the epic project, it really sets it on the tracks. *Amor* will work as a major motivational engine for this epic; the forward motion of the plot is reflected in the dynamic of the subsequent chase. Ovid thus inverts the usual narratological associations of epic and romance, as Quint describes them: "To the victors belongs epic, with its linear teleology; to the losers belongs romance, with its random and circular wandering."[39]

Ovid marks this fresh beginning with the words *primus amor*, a tag that oscillates between epic or elegy.[40] *Amor* is the topos that conventionally marks the threat of digression and generic contamination. This conventional strategy of "essentialising epic" defines the boundary of the genre by threatening transgression, as Hinds has demonstrated.[41] What appears at first to be an interruption reveals itself as a nod to Ovid's loyal followers that they will at last be satisfied in their expectations of the erotic poet. The new turn of events also reinforces and exemplifies Ovid's dictum that

[37] Nicoll (1980), 181: "We may, therefore, feel that Apollo's feat is tainted by being described in terms which are much too reminiscent of the jargon used by the followers of Callimachus when referring to grand epic." He cites especially the description of the Python as unusually large (*tot iugera … prementem*, *Met.* 1.459) and, worse, bloated (*tumidum*, *Met.* 1.460).

[38] Note also that this latest creation is only partly original, as if to emphasize the lack of progress: *edidit innumeras partimque figuras/ rettulit antiquas, partim nova monstra creavit* (*Met.* 1.436–7).

[39] Quint (1993), 9. [40] Due (1974), 112 for epic; Nicoll (1980), 176–7 for elegy.

[41] Hinds (2000).

epic is all about *amor*.[42] Love is what makes the world go round and the plot go forward.

The motif of the chase is central to this self-positioning in the epic genre. Ovid uses the scene to allude to the legendary pursuit of Achilles and Hector in Homer (*Il.* 22.131–246), and Aeneas and Turnus in Virgil (*Aen.* 12.741–90) in which the final chase exemplifies the climax of a linear epic. There can be only winners or losers.[43] This world-view finds its figurative expression in the predator–prey simile in the second stage of the chase. While the first simile in Homer compares the two heroes to horses competing in an athletic setting (*Il.* 22.162–6), the predator–prey configuration in the subsequent similes (falcon/dove, *Il.* 22.139–42; hound/fawn, *Il.* 22.189–93) prescribes the roles of natural antagonists. Already in Homer, the scene is marked by a high degree of meta-literary awareness, on the parts of both the narrator and the characters, of the fixed roles that are being played out on both the literal and figurative level. Thus the narrator comments on the charged terms of this race by emphasizing the "inadequacy of the games simile even before he [sc. the narrator] employs it."[44] At the conclusion of the race, Achilles reinforces the terms of the previous predator–prey similes as he refuses Hector's attempts at negotiations with a reference to the animal world (*Il.* 22.261–7).[45]

While commentators and scholars routinely point out Ovid's allusion to these models, an interpretation has been elusive. Yet the re-contextualization of the epic cliché, not merely the recognition of it as a source, is crucial for understanding Ovid's own position in the epic line-up. Ovid locates the scene at the beginning of his epic and thus literally turns its symbolic nature on its head. Since it is no longer the decisive outcome of the wider conflict, the chase is robbed of its significance beyond the single episode. What is more, in the course of the *Metamorphoses* it will be replayed in countless variations, diluting its force by repetition. At the same time, the ambiguity of metamorphosis replaces the strict opposition of life and death, as the reader's expectation of a clear outcome, set up by

42 Cf. Ovid's judgment of the *Iliad* in *Tr.* 2.371–4. See Hinds (2000) for *amor* as the catalyst of the epic genre.

43 Quint (1993), 4–5.

44 Quint (1993), 4 on *Il.* 22.161. In terms of the plot, the race looks ahead to Patroclus' funeral games, celebrated in book 23, but it also, in mentioning the prize of the game (a tripod or a woman), loops back both on the origin of the conflict (Helen) and the beginning of the poem itself (the quarrel of Agamemnon and Achilles over Briseis).

45 Achilles compares the hostile relationship of lions and men, as well as lambs and wolves. Homer might allude to Achilles' association with the animal and consequently his perceived exemption from the laws that govern human behavior.

the simile, is ultimately frustrated. Nonetheless, evoking the typical situation aims at convincing Ovid's readers of his epic credentials. He uses the very familiarity of his models gradually to lull the reader into accepting his radical rewriting of epic conventions.

The force of this epic acclimatisation is played out explicitly in the predator–prey simile that is used to characterize Apollo. As Daphne turns to flee, Apollo disavows the comparison which she seems to provoke by her behavior (*Met.* 1.504–7):

> nympha, precor, Penei, mane! non insequor hostis;
> nympha, mane! sic agna lupum, sic cerua leonem,
> sic aquilam penna fugiunt trepidante columbae,
> hostes quaeque suos; amor est mihi causa sequendi.

Nymph, I beg you, Peneus' daughter, stay! I am not following as an enemy, nymph, stay! So does a lamb flee from a wolf, a deer from a lion, so do doves flee on trembling wing from the eagle, all enemies to each other; the reason for my pursuit is love.

When the race starts in earnest, the narrator takes over, picking up the predator–prey roles of the previous simile with a vengeance (*Met.* 1.533–9):

> ut canis in uacuo leporem cum Gallicus aruo
> uidit, et hic praedam pedibus petit, ille salutem,
> alter inhaesuro similis iam iamque tenere
> sperat et extento stringit uestigia rostro,
> alter in ambiguo est an sit comprensus et ipsis
> morsibus eripitur tangentiaque ora relinquit;
> sic deus et uirgo est, hic spe celer, illa timore.

As when a Gallic dog sees a hare in an empty field and makes with his feet for the prey, the other for his life. One, as if about to latch on, expects every moment now to catch it and with its snout sticking out grazes the other's tracks; the other is unsure whether it has been snatched and tears itself out of the snap itself and leaves behind the snout that touches it, just so the god and the maiden, he swift with expectation, and she with fear.

While Apollo's disavowal of the predator role is primarily intended to stop Daphne's flight, his choice of the figure resonates on the level of poetics as well. According to Apollo, it is Daphne who provokes the association with the predator–prey simile. *Because* she is fleeing, he is forced to pursue.[46] Thus, inverting the usual order of the simile, the *sic*-clause begins

[46] Hornsby (1970), 134 describes Aeneas' ethical dilemma in identical terms: "Because of Turnus' frightened flight, Aeneas is forced into pursuit ... By forcing Aeneas to pursue him, he again forces

a comparison which finds no corresponding *ut;* quite on the contrary, Apollo repeats that it is not a fitting comparison (*Met.* 1.507). He offers an explicit reading of the simile (*hostes quaeque suos*, 1.505) that he claims is at odds with his intentions (*non insequor hostis*, 504) and points out that his real reason, accurately enough, is *amor*, the very opposite of *bella.* Apollo's protestations at the clichéd feel of the situation, when read at the level of aesthetics, as befits his role as patron god of Ovid's poetry, seeks to uphold the generic purity of the episode, separating erotic from martial conquest. Daphne's reaction of instant flight is contrary to the pose of seduction. Apollo, in his new role as *amator*, employs the epic cliché to distance himself from the genre, a move that is well known from elegiac poetry. ***Non*** *insequor hostis* may be read not only as a rejection of epic, it is the (negatively defined) genre code for elegy. For this stance, the simple evocation of the cliché is enough: the enumeration of animal of prey and their predators is deliberately artless; no scene is sketched even in traces – these are all examples that can be filled in by any reader of epic, stock themes of the epic repertoire. Whereas Apollo claims to have undergone a genre change already, from epic conqueror to elegiac lover, Daphne's reaction strikes him as being stuck in an epic world-view which knows only the binary opposition of male and female, predator and prey, hunter and victim.[47] Apollo's manipulation of the poetically correct reading of the episode through his application of simile, as his emendation of Daphne's fleeing figure and hair ('*quid si comantur?*', 498) reduces the scene to pure aesthetics.

In rejecting the clichéd image of the hunt, Apollo at once suggests and rejects the epic perspective, simultaneously proposing what the situation looks like while denying the validity of this impression. His protest foregrounds the importance of genre in shaping our expectations, of genre as an imposed filter through which the reader interprets a given situation, in this case the pursuit of one character by another. Daphne flees from Apollo *as if* she were a Hector or a Turnus. The allusion to these legendary battles seems grossly exaggerated, a rhetorical strategy that seeks to align temporarily the reader's view with that of Apollo.

Aeneas to fight on his terms, terms which gain him only a little time. In the simile, Aeneas is reduced to an animal, just as Turnus is; he becomes like a hunting dog."

47 Ironically, Daphne's vehement rejection of sex sets her up as a rape victim. See Heath (1991). For the displacement of the martial through the erotic pursuit in Ovid's epic see also the allusion to the Apollo–Daphne scene in the similes at *Met* 11.771–6, that describe Aesacus, a "*Troius heros*" (773) who dies before he reaches the battlefield.

Ovid's Apollo recalls Horace's persona, in his attempts of amatory persuasion in *Odes* 1.23 who likewise exaggerates his amorous rejection by Chloe by couching it in mock-epic terms (*Vitas inuleo me similis, Chloe/ … / atque non ego te tigris ut aspera/ Gaetulusve leo frangere persequor*). While lion and fawn are "creatures of speech,"[48] evocative of epic violence, Horace's play on these images does not foreground problems of genre for Horace's own poetics, especially since the image is split up between the first and fourth stanzas and is not presented in the *ut–sic* formula of epic. Horace uses the topos without compromising the generic orientation of his work.[49]

By contrast, Ovid's Apollo not only uses the strictly epic form of the simile, enhancing it by the repetition of examples, but also does so in ambiguous generic territory, the gray zone between the polar opposites of *amor* and *bella*. Apollo's status contradicts the inferior position which the elegiac lover is supposed to assume. Not only is he a male divine figure encountering a female mortal in a setting that carries with it instantaneous associations with rape, he is an epic figure who has just shown his martial prowess in slaying the Python. Thus what looks like epic must be epic, and Apollo's attempt at amatory persuasion is contradicted by the image it invokes.

As the race turns serious, the narrator takes over from the temporarily silenced Apollo (*Plura locuturum timido Peneia cursu/ fugit cumque ipso verba imperfecta reliquit, Met.* 1.525–6)[50] and picks up on the roles of the predator–prey simile in elaborate detail, stretching out the agonizing pursuit for maximum suspense. The imposition of narratorial perspective purports to give an objective view of the situation, and reasserts the narrator's right to control the story, contradicting his character outright. But is this move completely without self-interest? The shift in perspective implies the focalization through the hypothetical presence of a third party; here, this view coincides with Cupid's actual presence (*utque monebat/ ipse Amor*, 1.531–2). Cupid's role as the hunter marks him as the voyeuristic presence behind the chase, similar to the divine audience of the final combat of Homeric and Virgilian epic. One should note that the hunt of dog and

48 The phrase is Lonsdale's (1990).

49 Davis (1983), 37 n.40: "Such disclaimers in un-heroic contexts gain some irony from the fact that predatory similes are ultimately derived from epic (read non-erotic) sources …" In this case, Ovid combines the tradition of his sources, both epic and non-epic. Apollo's attempt at amatory persuasion resembles that of Polyphemus in Theocritus *Id.* 11.24, who likewise battles the expectations of his epic vs. erotic persona.

50 Cf. the narrator's similar takeover mid-verse from Mercury: *talia verba refert, restabat verba referre* (*Met* 1.700).

hare, while inspired by animal instinct, reflects an artificial environment controlled by humans for their pleasure (much as the athletic scene in the Iliadic simile), not the natural violence between wild animals. By externalizing the figure of the hunter, Ovid alludes to a notorious problem in the Virgilian model for this simile, namely the identification of Aeneas with the hunter and/or his dog (*venator, Aen.* 12.751; *Umber*, 12.753). Hornsby has demonstrated that this is a critical issue in Virgil's debasing characterization of Turnus as animal-like, whereas Aeneas is specifically excluded from such comparisons.[51] In Ovid, Apollo and Daphne are both reduced to instinctive behavior, under the tight control of the scene by instinct incarnate itself (Amor/Cupid) whose double nature is shown in the two arrows (*Met.* 1.470–1).

The progression from Apollo's rejection of the simile's roles to the narrator's explicit reaffirmation of them gives the reader an odd feeling of satisfaction. The familiar form of the simile guarantees acquiescence in its validity and appropriateness. Perfect symmetry governs everything in this set-up: from the two arrows (*Met.* 1.469–71),[52] to the opposing pairs of male/female, immortal/mortal, predator/prey. It is easy to overlook the complete reinvention of the simile itself. Anderson comments that Ovid "eroticizes the epic,"[53] a common reading that nonetheless calls for its reversal: does Ovid equally "epicize the erotic"?

Apollo's earlier contrast between *hostis* and *amor* has collapsed by the second simile. The predator–prey formula of the epic simile has been reappropriated for the erotic chase. What makes this so easy is the fact that the imagery of the hunt coincides with both the associations of love and war.[54] Thus the epic simile, used conventionally to denote war, can be reimagined as denoting eros. Ovid had already followed through on the equation of opposites, love and war, in *Amores* 1.9 (*Militat omnis amans*), chiefly by treating the figurative language of love poetry as literal. Here, he uses the figurative language of war, and more particular an allusion to the decisive final scenes of Virgil's and Homer's epic, to show that the two really do coincide.

Whether Ovid eroticizes the epic or epicizes the erotic then depends largely on the perspective one takes. The former seems to imply a tendency to soften the epic; the moral seriousness of epic is relieved, or undermined, by the lighter, frivolous tone of erotic role-playing. The latter view, hardening the erotic, brings out the underlying violence in this and

51 Hornsby (1970), 135 n.5.
52 Barchiesi (2005b) ad loc. comments that the two arrows are Ovid's unique invention.
53 Anderson (1997) ad loc. 54 Davis (1983), 25–42 focuses only on the hunting aspect.

subsequent stories of "*amor*."[55] Ovid effectively yokes together the themes of *bella* and *amor* through his reworking of the epic simile that applies to both.[56] For the remainder of the poem, the predator–prey simile will come to be associated almost exclusively with rape, so for example in the stories of Philomela (*Met.* 6.516–8; 527–30) or Arethusa (*Met.* 5.626–9).

Looking back to Homer from Ovid, the limits of persuasion and violence stand out even more clearly. As Hector ponders the imminent encounter with Achilles, he indulges in a daydreaming monologue.[57] At last he calls himself to order with a reminder of reality, explicitly contrasting the martial with the erotic. Achilles and Hector are *not* a boy and girl in love, he says (*Il.* 22.126–8):[58]

> **οὐ** μέν πως νῦν ἔστιν ἀπὸ δρυὸς **οὐδ'** ἀπὸ πέτρης
> τῷ ὀαριζέμεναι, ἅ τε παρθένος ἠΐθεός τε,
> παρθένος ἠΐθεός τ'ὀαρίζετον ἀλλήλοιν.

Now there is no way to talk to him about the oak and the rock, the things that maiden and youth, maiden and youth talk about with each other.

Despite the change from epic to erotic encounter in Ovid, the scene of the chase plays out in a disturbingly similar fashion. When Apollo fails in his attempts to seduce Daphne by amatory persuasion (talking like a boy to a girl) he resorts to violence. The roles of the simile appear in hindsight to be inevitable. Its familiar form casts in stone the violent conflict of conqueror and defeated that lies at the heart of epic, and extends its reach to the conflict of desire.

ACHILLES AND NESTOR

While the epic simile may serve to accentuate the diverse generic provenance of an episode, the ultimate litmus test for its epic credentials must be its reaction with an overtly epic context. Instead of blending seamlessly with its contextual background, as might be expected, it plays a

[55] On the gendered opposition of epic and elegy as *mollis* and *durus* respectively, see Sharrock (2002b), 106 and n.42.

[56] While "A is like C, and B is like C, so A must be like C" is a logical fallacy, the sharing of associations nonetheless brings together the two genres.

[57] The phrase ἀπὸ δρυὸς οὐδ' ἀπὸ πέτρης connotes the different genre of Hector's escapist fantasy. It recalls the fairy tale of human beings arising from trees or stones, as pointed out by the A and T scholiasts. Cf. *Od.* 19.163, where Penelope asks the 'stranger' Odysseus about his provenance (see Russo [1985] ad loc.) and Hesiod *Theog.* 35. Daphne's escape from the certain ending thus marks the fairy-tale origin of the epic *Metamorphoses*.

[58] Gender roles cast Hector as the victim throughout, including the simile of *male* falcon and *female* dove (*Il.* 22.139–44).

central role in directing the reading of the "epic" sections of the poem. Ovid's oblique position vis-à-vis the tradition of Homeric and Virgilian epic comes out most clearly in the battle scenes, especially in the latter part of the poem. Since by universal definition, including Ovid's own, epic is about war (*arma ... violentaque bella*, *Am.* 1.1.1), the challenge in depicting battle scenes is also an exercise in poetic self-assertion against the dominance of this essentializing tradition of the genre. The challenge is twofold: how to incorporate this material in the context of this radically different poem that finds its universal themes in stories of love and metamorphosis; and how to treat the material itself in order to accentuate its generic provenance.

In book 12, Ovid thematizes the two aspects of epic performance, namely battle itself and singing about battle, when he shows Achilles' duel with Cygnus (*Met.* 12.70–145) followed by Nestor's tale about Caeneus and the battle of the Lapiths and Centaurs (*Met.* 12.169–535). Nestor's account of a past battle overshadows Achilles' performance by far in both length and drama. The insertion of Nestor's reminiscences during this lull from the battlefield ironically picks up his efforts in the *Iliad* at getting Achilles back to fighting by recounting his own martial achievements (e.g. *Il.* 11.655–803).[59]

Central to the interpretation of the episode is the timing and location of Ovid's confrontation with the *Iliad*.[60] Instead of concentrating on the peripheral but successful battles in the regions around Troy which Achilles recalls as winning him glory (*Met.* 12.108–14), Ovid chooses the time of the siege, noted paradoxically for the absence of action. Nestor's story functions as a substitute for the battle scenes of the *Iliad*,[61] while Ovid's manipulation of the perception of time by such devices as flashback narrative reinforces the illusion of narrated, as well as narrative, time passing.[62] This contrast between little action and long narration stages the conceit of rewriting the *Iliad* as an almost historiographic exercise. While the "facts" of what happened cannot be altered, the speeches of the characters are open to the poet's imagination. The careful manipulation of the

[59] In the same account Nestor also talks about his brothers being killed by Hercules (*Il.* 11.690–3), a detail left out in this passage but that Tlepolemus makes him remember (*Met.* 12.536–40).

[60] Musgrove (1998), 223 remarks on the directness of this confrontation: "Since the Centauromachy actually has a Homeric origin (*Il.* 1.247–84) and recounts that most epic type of scene, the battle, we cannot use the explanation that Ovid is playing one genre off another, nor can we argue that the epic fom is undercut by the intrusion of another genre, or Homer by the intrusion of the Cyclic poems."

[61] Ellsworth (1980), 25–6. [62] Musgrove (1998).

existing characters thus preserves Homer not merely as a text but as a quasi-historical world unto itself.

Opening the scene at Troy, Ovid passes swiftly towards martial action. The preliminaries to Achilles' encounter with Cygnus are narrated with great urgency (*iam ... iam ... iam*, *Met.* 12.71–3), passing over summarily the many victims of both Cygnus (*nec ... exiguo ... / sanguine*; 70–1; *mille viros*, 72) and Achilles (*totaque ... sternebat ... / agmina*, 74–5) to heighten the suspense for the duel. In explicit deference to literary history, Homer's canonic version must be preserved: the paradox of depicting battle without killing off major characters has Hector spared (*decimum dilatus in annum/ Hector erat*, 76–7) while Cygnus stands in as a double. Yet despite seeking Cygnus out personally, Achilles does not recognize his opponent (or pretends not to), promising him only the consolation reserved to insignificant characters (*Met.* 12.80–1): '*quisquis es, o iuvenis' dixit, 'solamen habeto/ mortis, ab Haemonio quod sis iugulatus Achille.*'[63] The drive of the narrative makes us expect a decisive if inferior duel, a prelude double to Hector's encounter with Achilles.

Meeting Homer on his own turf comes close to squaring the circle for a poet of Callimachean allegiances, given that the attempts of the Cyclic poets at this were despised by Callimachus, a rejection of epigonality that forms a central tenet of his poetical program. Ovid's solution consists in disabling epic warfare by magic, matching invulnerability with violence, which stands for both the temptation and the impossibility of imitating Homer's battle scenes. Even the least significant death at Troy has been catalogued by now, leaving no room for telling an as yet untold story. Through the application of magic a kind of double reality results which is rendered by a series of short comparisons. For example, Achilles' spear, while sharp and intact, strikes bluntly (*utque hebeti pectus tantummodo contudit ictu*, 85); he questions his martial prowess (*ante actis veluti male crederet*, 115) even though he can see the "mountains" (*aceruos*, 113) of bodies killed earlier (*et feci et video*, 114) but Cygnus' body seems made out of rock (*velut muro solidaque a caute*, 124), an allusion perhaps to Astyages' amazement at hitting stone instead of his enemy (*Met.* 5.203–4).

After the third unsuccessful shot at Cygnus, Achilles loses control (*Met.* 12.102–4):

[63] This seemingly irrelevant skirmish will be the cause of his demise (*Met.* 12.580–96). Ovid evidently enjoys playing with the grave pathos of predetermined outcome.

> haud secus exarsit quam circo taurus aperto,
> cum sua terribili petit inritamina cornu,
> poeniceas uestes, elusaque uulnera sentit.

He rages in heat not unlike a bull in an open circus, when it lunges at its provocation, a purple cloth, with its frightful horns and feels the wounds that it misses.

While the association of bull and hero's strength is conventional material, the closest parallel is the simile comparing Turnus, as he prepares for the last fight in the *Aeneid*, to a bull raging against a tree. The simile illustrates his futile emotion and inferior animal instinct, thus turning the display of martial valor into a foreboding symbol of his defeat.[64]

Ovid takes Virgil's degradation of the traditional association of animal and hero one step further as he introduces the anachronistic setting of the circus and parades Achilles, a victim of his own warrior instinct reacting to Cygnus' taunting, in a game of illusion. Instead of the calibrated symmetry of e.g. the predator–prey simile type, the one-sided manipulation of the bull shows Achilles' isolation as he virtually fights himself. Cygnus' mirroring of Achilles' own (quasi-) invulnerability reduces the duel to the absurd. The bull feels the blows he is meant to inflict (*elusaque vulnera sentit*, 104) as if reflecting the wounds back onto the attacker. Ovid uses a similar bull simile when deconstructing Hercules' heroic persona (*Met.* 9.204–6):[65]

> dixit, perque altam saucius Oeten
> haud aliter graditur, quam si uenabula taurus
> corpore fixa gerat factique refugerit auctor.

Thus he spoke and roamed wounded all over lofty Mount Oeta not unlike a bull which bears a hunting spear stuck in its body while the doer of the deed has fled.

In both cases, the bull's powerful anger contrasts with the manipulated setting in which there no longer is a visible opponent (*factique refugerit auctor*, 206; *poeniceas vestes*, 104). Instead of legitimizing the hero's savage instinct by reference to natural violence, the simile pits animal instinct against the institutions that mark human superiority: the hunt and the amphitheater, the latter a stylized version of the former.

The association of the two heroes via the bull simile may allude to the variant of the Cygnus myth in the *Shield of Heracles*, wrongly attributed to

[64] *Aen.* 12.101–6: *his agitur furiis, totoque ardentis ab ore/ scintillae absistunt, oculis micat acribus ignis,/ mugitus veluti cum prima in proelia taurus/ terrificos ciet atque irasci in cornua temptat/ arboris obnixus trunco, ventosque lacessit/ ictibus aut sparsa ad pugnam proludit harena.*

[65] Bömer (1969–86) ad loc. thinks this is a real, not a staged hunt of either wild bulls or domesticated ones that were left to roam in the summer.

Hesiod, in which Hercules successfully subdues his foe (*Sc.* 416–20).[66] In fact, Achilles' dubious victory is called *labor* as well as *pugna* (*Met.* 12.146), recalling Hercules.[67] Moreover, the shield itself depicts the battle of the Lapiths and Centaurs (*Sc.* 178–90), Nestor's subject matter. The poem thus presents a promising intertext to the passage here, in that it advertises its epigonal relationship to the *Iliad* not only in its subject matter, Hercules' shield, but also in the disproportionate amount given to ornamental ekphrasis instead of actual fighting. In the *Metamorphoses*, the proportion of Achilles' abbreviated martial action to Nestor's overlong speech shows a similar asymmetry and relegates Achilles himself to the position of emulating admirer. Ovid thus engages not only with the *Iliad* but also, self-deprecatingly, with the tradition of the Cyclic poems.

The anachronistic break introduced by the amphitheater alerts the reader to his own role as spectator, offering a meta-poetic stance on Ovid's manipulation of the reader's expectations of an epic duel. The simile adds a visual layer, yet has the paradoxical effect of removing the epic pretense of the duel, making the reader see through appearances and thereby inverting momentarily the real and the illusory. In fact, Cygnus appears to be a red flag more than he is a soldier: he even comments himself on the artificiality of his armor, which is not functional but decorative (*Met.* 12.88–92).[68] The scene is set up to look like a battle but is rigged to fail in order to preserve the unique encounter of Hector and Achilles.[69] By introducing the anachronistic setting of the amphitheater, Ovid appeals to the reader's urbanity which can find pleasure in such a spectacle. Presenting the battle as entertainment also preserves the conceit that nothing of significance happened in the years prior to the action of the *Iliad*.

Reality intrudes only briefly when Achilles tests his spear on Menoetes, whose death is passed over without further comment. Ovid's Lycian Menoetes is a double of Virgil's Arcadian Menoetes (*Aen.* 12.517–21),[70] the last victim of Turnus in the *Aeneid* and symbol for the human price of war. Virgil composes a moving apostrophe to this insignificant soldier, portraying him in a vignette. By contrast, Ovid cursorily identifies him not as individual but as one of the multitude (*Lycia de plebe*, *Met.* 12.116)

[66] See Janko (1986).

[67] Cf. also Perseus' Herculean *labor* of slaying the sea monster (*Met.* 4.739). See Keith (2002a), 240.

[68] Ironically, his armor is used not to defend but to attack him.

[69] Much as the duel between Paris and Menelaus (*Il.* 3.325–82) which offers (or threatens, in terms of plot) to end the Trojan War and thus the epic action in the *Iliad* before it has begun.

[70] *Aen.* 12.517–520: *et iuuenem exosum nequiquam bella Menoeten,/ Arcada, piscosae cui circum flumina Lernae/ ars fuerat pauperque domus nec nota potentum/ munera, conductaque pater tellure serebat.*

and refuses to linger on the dying body, breaking with the epic convention that affords even the lowliest character such consolation for his death. Even more poignant, Cygnus' body vanishes at the precise moment of death, which is elided by focusing on the helm straps instead (*vincla trahit galeae; quae … / elidunt fauces, et respiramen iterque/ eripiunt animae, Met.* 12.141–3). Ovid's battle scene then frustrates the reader by withholding closure through the traditional elements of epic, death and the pathos of dying. In this the reader may identify with Achilles, searching for the violence (*elusaque … vulnera*, 104) demanded by the generic code.[71]

Even though Achilles is declared victor, the outcome remains ambiguous, as the duel is called *labor* as well as *pugna* (*Met.* 12.146), and the Greek warriors' attempts at instant codification of the deed as epic fail at its miraculous component (*visum mirabile … invictum*, 165–66).[72] Zumwalt notes that the obsessive retelling of the warriors' own deeds, rather than celebrating those of heroes past, defeats the very purpose of heroic song.[73] The exclusive focus on the subject of war (*pugnas, hostis, pericula*, 12.160–1) reflects the coarse tastes of this internal audience. The narrator's parenthesis (*quid enim loqueretur Achilles,/ aut quid apud magnum potius loquerentur Achillem?*, *Met.* 12.162–3) may be read as a comment on Achilles' presence suppressing other genres and voices, reducing epic to martial action. When Achilles asks Nestor about Caeneus he naturally expects a military setting (*qua tibi militia, cuius certamine pugnae,/ cognitus, Met.* 12.180–1).

While Achilles' deed qualifies as epic in terms of setting and characters, it ultimately fails to satisfy due to the miraculous escape of Cygnus, an atmosphere of low pressure (hypo-epic) that is now corrected by Nestor's tale, generally characterized as hyper-epic because of its gory detail. Although any epic action in Ovid is highly self-reflexive, the introduction of Nestor as internal narrator, attempting to boost morale, reinforces this meta-epic dimension. The figure of Nestor connects not only generations of heroes but also generations of texts, namely Homer and Ovid. As a live presence of this past, Nestor becomes the voice of epic inside Ovid's poem, his credentials assured by the similar role he played in Homer, where he upholds the heroic code by comparing the Iliadic heroes to

[71] See Feeney (1999a), 182–3 on the reader's desire for violence as a key ingredient for the enjoyment of epic. From Cygnus' perspective, metamorphosis may seem preferable to death, but his fame is limited by the fact that he is one of three swans mentioned in the poem (alluded to in the periphrasis of the swan as *volucrem Phaetontida, Met.* 12.581). Caeneus' fame rests on being called *unica avis* by Mopsus (*Met.* 12.531).

[72] See Griffin (1977) on Homer excluding magic from epic in contrast to the Cyclic poets.

[73] Zumwalt (1978), 214.

former generations. He thus stands for a kind of Ur-epic[74] which informs the epic code by comparison. Choosing Nestor as an internal narrator then should guarantee the purity of epic vision, especially since the fight between Lapiths and Centaurs is developed from a kernel in the *Iliad* (*Il.* 1.247–84).

Nestor's awareness of his role as epic narrator and of the demands of his audience comes out in the shorthand with which he introduces the scene: *captaeque erat urbis imago* (*Met.* 12.225). The transference immediately establishes the epic credentials of the story and promises outrageous killings and spectacular sights.[75] At the same time, the term *imago* draws attention to the staged quality of this account, a self-awareness of performing epic. Thus the very invocation of the epic cliché reveals a certain distance from the genre, without necessary implying parody. Rather, the interplay between frame and content, style and subject may be seen to question a static concept of epic as an unchanging tableau which employs generic markers as if painting by numbers.

The dilemma of the generic nature of this account grows even more complex when one recalls the main narrator's use of the storm simile at the beginning of book 5, the double of the ensuing scene of a wedding disturbed by violence, in which magic finally wins over might (*Met.* 5.5–7):

> inque repentinos conuiuia versa tumultus
> adsimilare freto possis, quod saeua quietum
> uentorum rabies motis exasperat undis.

You could compare this banquet turned suddenly to a brawl to a sea, whose calm the savage rage of the winds whips up with beating waves.

If we accepted the epic status of that story, can we deny it to Nestor?[76] This acknowledgment of audience manipulation challenges the reader to decide actively either to go along with or refuse the classification of the episode as epic.[77] It also draws attention to the effectiveness of generic

[74] Musgrove (1998), 229 n.26

[75] Rossi (2003), 28. Keeping in mind that the *urbs–capta* motif itself is a reaction to epic in other genres, namely tragedy and historiography, and is only assimilated into epic by Virgil: Rossi (2003), 17–25.

[76] Keith (2002b) discusses the passage as a "sustained meditation on the action of heroic, particularly Virgilian, epic," 109. See also Baldo (1997).

[77] In this I follow Farrell's (1994) lead expressed in a book review: "But it seems to me equally useful to question the premise that epic, either the [sic] epic or any epic, 'is' either one thing or another. Rather than make this assumption, I hope that the results reached by both Quint and Wofford will encourage future students of epic to adopt a phenomenological approach to genre and to admit that genre itself and the relationship of any single poem to its genre(s) is to a large degree whatever its readers make of it."

markers such as similes and conventional themes in establishing such a genre identity.

The Centaurs' enthusiastic shouts for *arma, arma* seem to echo Nestor's audience's single-minded desire for a narrative of violence. Their intrusion on the wedding scene immediately changes the atmosphere of the story, symbolized in their misappropriation of domestic (*res epulis quondam, nunc bello et caedibus aptae*, *Met.* 12.244) and sacred objects as their weapons.[78] The start of the battle is marked by an intensifying simile (*Met.*12.245–50):

> Primus Ophionides Amycus penetralia donis
> haud timuit spoliare suis et primus ab aede
> lampadibus densum rapuit funale coruscis,
> elatumque alte, ueluti qui candida tauri
> rumpere sacrifica molitur colla securi,
> illisit fronti Lapithae Celadontis ...

First Amycus, son of Omphion, did not shrink back from despoiling the inner sanctum of gifts and first snatched up from its position a candelabrum thick with flashing torches, held up high, as if one about to sever the sacrificial white neck of a bull with an axe, he dashed it in the head of the Lapith Celadon.

The simile's invocation of religious ritual underlines Amycus' blasphemous action, not only in misusing the sacred object but in using the wrong one, and thereby inflicting a particularly gruesome kind of wound. The pose of the Centaur emphasizes the relative height (*elatumque alte, Met.* 12.248) of his semi-equine body, and makes him even more conspicuous. The centaur's sacrilege legitimizes the ensuing violence from the human perspective, but the comparison goes even further in that it invokes the very institution that ritually enacts the divide between (killing) human and (dying) animal and thus stands in flagrant contrast to the centaur's own hybrid nature. As the simile focuses on the pause just before the fatal blow (*molitur*, 249) in which all eyes are drawn to the victim, it creates a moment of suspense in the narrative, finally released by the emphatic *illisit* of the next line.

The graphic nature of the developing account needs little further illustration by similes which seem instead intended to characterize the centaurs as savage monsters.[79] The wounding of Charaxes by the centaur

78 For the misappropriation of sacred objects as weapons cf. *Met.* 5.56–8, *Aen.* 12.298–301.

79 The lines of a third simile (*Met.* 12.435–8) are suspect and so are not part of my discussion. Nonetheless, they seem to allude to Polyphemus who is first seen making cheese (*Od.* 9.246–9), then crushing the brains of Odysseus' companions (*Od.*9.287).

Rhoetus recalls the blinding of the Cyclops from the Odyssey (*Met.* 12.274–9):

> correpti rapida, ueluti seges arida, flamma
> arserunt crines, et uulnere sanguis inustus
> terribilem stridore sonum dedit, ut dare ferrum
> igne rubens plerumque solet, quod forcipe curua
> cum faber eduxit lacubus demittit; at illud
> stridet et in tepida submersum sibilat unda.

The hair burned, seized by a rapid flame, like a dry cornfield; and in the wound the burnt-in blood makes a terrible sound with a hiss such as reddening iron often tends to make, which the smith with curved tongs takes out and lowers in the water but it hisses and sizzles even submerged in the lukewarm water.

Labate has argued that this Odyssean echo[80] in Ovid serves as a reminder of the Homeric prototype of such a fight with monsters, widening the scope of epic beyond Iliadic battle scenes.[81] Indeed, Nestor resembles Odysseus in his function as internal narrator and claim to be an eyewitness to the bizarre. However, an important difference emerges. The simile in Homer characterizes Odysseus' use of superior human skills in order to overcome a man-eating monster and emphasizes the divide between wilderness and civilization.[82] Ovid instead uses the similes to show the centaurs' perverse nature, making them the odd men out in a conventional battle narrative. Both sacrifice and the construction of weapons are distinct human behaviors that mark the divide from the animal world. The problem is therefore not the simile's vehicle but its tenor. The enormous range of the epic simile is only possible because of the undisputed human status of the tenor that grounds it. Thus a hero may be compared to any number of things (animal, rock, force of nature, woman) without compromising his identity. By contrast, the centaurs' ambiguous nature, half-man, half-animal, makes such comparisons inherently problematic. Comparing the centaurs' fighting to distinctly human acts thus emphasizes their approximation to the status of being human but their ultimate failure to attain it.[83]

Later on in the same episode, Ovid likewise deconstructs the foundation of the epic simile when he plays with its metamorphic possibilities.

[80] *Od.* 9.387–94. [81] Labate (1997), 162.

[82] Pucci (1997), 118–20 discusses Odysseus' rhetorical construction of the Cyclops as his un-civilized "other."

[83] Cf. also the challenge that Caeneus poses to the centaurs' *vir-tus* in terms of gender (*Met.* 12.499–506), Keith (1999).

He uses an epic simile traditionally used in battle scenes, the comparison of spears to hail, both equally menacing.[84] Ovid picks up this image to illustrate Latreus striking Caeneus in the face (*Met.* 12.478–81):

> furit ille dolore
> nudaque Phyllei iuuenis ferit ora sarisa;[85]
> non secus haec resilit, quam tecti a culmine grando,
> aut si quis paruo feriat caua tympana saxo.

He rages with grief and strikes the bare face of the young son of Phylleus with a spear; it bounces back not unlike hail from the top of a roof or when somebody strikes a hollow drum with a small pebble.

While the simile starts out as an echo of traditional topos, Ovid has changed the *tertium comparationis* from the hail's danger to its bounce, thus retaining the traditional image but completely changing its focus. Moreover, he adds a frivolous twist in the subsequent image of the pebbles. It seems that the menacing weapons change mid-air into a child's game, disabling the epic seriousness of the fight. What starts out as a grand epic gesture is thwarted by Caeneus' magical inviolability. The change is also reflected in the oscillating meaning of *ferire*, as if the attacker's intention had suddenly changed (*ferit*, 479; *feriat*, 481; cf. also *furit*, 478).[86]

Nestor's account ends with a simile that involves his audience and returns it back to the reality of the Greek camp. He describes Caeneus who has been buried under a mass of trees (*Met.* 12.518–22):

> modo se super aera frustra
> tollere conatur iactasque euoluere silvas,
> interdumque mouet, ueluti, quam cernimus, ecce,
> ardua si terrae quatiatur motibus Ide.
> exitus in dubio est ...

Now he tries in vain to lift himself towards the air and rid himself from the woods tossed on him, and from time to time he moves like lofty Mount Ida, look, the one we see, when it is shaken by the motions of the earth. The outcome was uncertain.

[84] See Baldo (1995) for parallels in earlier epic, especially in Virgil, for example *Aen.* 9.669–71; an even more intriguing parallel is the use of the epic simile in the games in the boxing match between Entellus and Dares (*Aen.* 5.458–60), standing out in the Odyssean half of the *Aeneid.* Ovid's entertainment through narrative violence thus mimics the violence sublimated into games at this point of the *Aeneid.*

[85] Bömer (1969–86) ad loc. and Solodow (1988), 77 notice the anachronistic detail of the Hellenistic weapon. Ovid plays with the notion of anachronistic discrepancy between Iron Age and bronze weapons in the *Iliad.* On anachronism, see Chapter 4.

[86] As with *vulnera* (*Met.* 12.104) above.

Again what appears as a conventional epic simile undergoes change through the context in which it is used. Comparisons with natural forces in Homer evoke the impression of an overwhelming foe, often in the collective, especially when seen from afar.[87] Despite being close to asphyxiation, Caeneus' body still appears larger than life against the multitude of his attackers, and gives the impression of gigantic proportions. Ironically, the uprooted trees are not a result of Caeneus' own movements but had been hurled by his opponents. The simile thus captures the centaurs' lingering unease over the final destruction of Caeneus. It effectively hides the moment of transition so that Nestor can truthfully claim that the outcome was uncertain, suggesting either death by asphyxiation or metamorphosis into a bird, as declared by the seer Mopsus. Nestor's sardonic comment on Mopsus' spontaneous acclamation of the bird as unique, *unica avis* (*credita res auctore est, Met.* 12.532)[88] shows a disarming awareness of how narrators manipulate their audiences. What was a source of frustration and a blemish on Achilles' war record, the lack of closure, becomes, with roles reversed, Nestor's boast of not admitting defeat. There is a certain irony in replicating the cover of the trees on Caeneus' body in the covering of the narrative with a simile since Caeneus can no longer actually be seen but only intuited through movement. In fact, he not only looks like but is no more than a pile of trees, a mirror image of the mountains that are left anthropomorphically "naked" (*Met.* 12.512).[89]

Nestor actively engages his internal audience in envisioning the scene by drawing their attention to their present surroundings (*quam cernimus, ecce, Met.* 12.520). The immediacy of that comparison cannot be reached by the reader who has to develop the image in his mind's eye instead. Unlike Horace who invites the addressee/reader to share the imaginary view of Mount Soracte (*vides*),[90] Ovid's pointed distinction of internal and external audience excludes the reader and draws attention to the different horizon of Nestor's audience for whom Troy is not an imagined place but reality. The protreptic function of this simile connects the present landscape with the fabled past. Every time the soldiers look at Mount Ida they will in their mind's eye see the giant Caeneus and be inspired, like Nestor, to fight. Like Nestor's famous proclamations on the superior strength of former heroes, the simile functions as an almost tangible reminder of that past. The division between external and internal audience is even more

[87] *Il.* 2.780–5 compares the Greek army advancing against the Trojans to an earthquake.
[88] The scene itself recalls the manipulations of bird omens to political ends.
[89] In a Homeric simile (*Il.* 12.131–4) the Lapiths are compared to trees that cannot be uprooted.
[90] Horace *Carm.*1.9.

striking when one recalls the deliberate anachronism of the simile that compares Achilles to a bull in the arena discussed earlier. Both similes emphasize the different historical position of characters and readers, and drive home the strange power of literature to overcome this barrier. By "going in," Ovid can position himself anterior to Homer, showing not only an Achilles who is not yet "Achilles" but also a kind of epic narrative that is not the *Iliad*.

Nestor (or Ovid, by proxy) has delivered what his audience demanded, a bloody narrative of battle, but he has also managed to sneak in two metamorphoses, a divine rape, a love story, and hybrid monsters – in a word, the *Metamorphoses* in miniature. In putting this tale in the mouth of Nestor, Ovid inverts the history of the genre, claiming that his own poem is going back to the roots and that the exclusive focus on war as the defining feature of epic is the aberration. If Nestor himself is made to sound like Ovid, then this reductive idea of epic is not intrinsic to the genre but rather shaped by the unimaginative, repetitive *sermones* (not *carmina*) of the warriors.[91]

It is then not so much a question of epic and un-epic elements played out against each other as a change of the parameters of the genre. The manipulation of the epic simile to illustrate "incredible" situations such as fighting an invincible opponent or the dubious heroic status of the half-animal centaurs stretches these conventional elements to the breaking point. While Nestor's centauromachy is in many respects a redundant double of the fight between Perseus and Phineus in book 5, Ovid's indulgence in having him speak at length purports to be a response to the reader's hunger for "more of the same." Ovid goes to great lengths to emphasize the total lack of story material at Troy itself (discounting the events covered in the *Iliad*),[92] but hints at the limitless supply of myth that lies just outside this precisely circumscribed field, in the incidental memories of a much larger poetic tradition, through its intermediary Nestor.

[91] Zumwalt's distinction (1978). Barchiesi (1997), 140: "Ovidio sembra accennare un' origine del genere epiço in questi garruli intrattenimenti presso i fuochi di bivacco."

[92] Thus taking literally the Homeric technique of recounting the story of the war through the action of a few days. Ovid pretends to accept that there was no more fighting to tell.

CHAPTER 4

Simile and fictionality

The view of Mount Ida at the conclusion of the last chapter has already pointed to the paper-thin divide between fiction and reality, with the physical landscape around Troy partaking as much of the fictional world as it does of the real world. While fiction usually borrows from the real world for greater plausibility, the *Metamorphoses* claim a mutual dependence of the two, aiming to relate a hidden truth that can only be unlocked through storytelling. The world of the *Metamorphoses* is a fictional world that purports to explain the origins of the real world, transforming it from the template into the remains of the story. The malleable character of the poem thus extends to its own identity as fiction, full of incredible but "true" stories. The physical reality of the transformed body delivers the ultimate proof, pointing out of the fictional world towards the reader's reality and anchoring the story's truth outside of the text. At the same time, a pronounced awareness of the trespass of the reader inside the text is marked by frequent apostrophes, invitations for judgment, and not least in the mirroring of narrator and audience in the many proxies that tell the story.

This strategy of positing an inside and outside of the story creates a sense of the permeability of the text, in both directions. It adds an extra dimension to the contained fictional world, marking points of entrance and exit. The simile likewise opens up the narrative to a temporary glimpse outside, disrupting its flow yet deepening the fictional illusion. The simile's focalization lets the reader look through the eyes of an internal character. Yet it also uses objects and experiences from the real world, providing a sense of tangibility and assimilating the fictional world to the reader's extra-textual experience. In this act of assimilation, the simile embodies the connection of real and fictional world.

Yet the simile's distance to the narrative may also be exploited for staging the conditions of fictional belief. Just as the text may stage its own textuality in showing self-aware characters and narrators, the simile may be made to reflect on the nature of illusion. Key to this is the illusory quality of the simile itself; it is a textual chimera, a mental image provoked by words alone. As such it holds up a mirror to the illusions of the text, reminding us that the persuasive force of fiction is founded on similarity. Characters that are like human beings act in a world like our own; our mental images supply the rest. Through the manipulation of these mental images the reader crosses the boundary between reality and fiction; the similes in this chapter all reflect on this elusive moment.

While truth and illusion may seem absolute terms, deciding between the fictional and the real in the *Metamorphoses* is largely a matter of subjective perspective, and this conflict plays out most prominently in stories in which a character is trapped by an illusion, for the most part visual. The fact that Ovid's characters are deceived by their eyes (rather than by their other senses) makes it possible for the fictional divide to be framed in terms of the contest between verbal and visual art. The impact of visual immediacy on the character who accepts the illusion is as important as the verbal description that can reveal both the trick and the reality. Dramatic irony results from the reader's superior knowledge of the situation over the naive pronouncements of the character.

This principle is at work in the episode of Narcissus (*Met.* 3.407–510), in which the reader is aware that Narcissus is looking at his own mirror image whereas Narcissus is slow and not altogether successful at this realization. Conversely, the reader cannot grasp precisely what Narcissus sees since he lacks the visual immediacy that is both mediated and obfuscated by the ekphrastic description of the image. Hardie draws an analogy between Narcissus and the reader both trying to reach beyond what he terms the "looking-glass of the text."[1] The simile, as verbal counterpart to the visual *simulacrum*, presents the interface for this exchange.[2] Similes punctuate and define the narrative at dramatic moments, progressively building up, and capture in the medium of imagery the complications and contradiction of the visual and verbal impressions.

NARCISSUS

Narcissus' story is unique among those told in the *Metamorphoses* because it involves a character who does not lose the visual aspect of his self by

[1] Hardie (2002), 146–7, 163. [2] Hardie (1999).

transformation into something else but is, quite the contrary, reduced to this crucial surface aspect of human identity.[3] Io's existential horror when she confirms her altered aspect in the reflection of the lake contrasts forcefully with Narcissus' desire for his human counterpart in the mirror.[4] Yet both reflect the anxiety that their appearance does in some sense constitute their identity. For most victims of metamorphosis, the change in appearance equals social exclusion, as they are no longer recognizable as human, let alone as an individual, but are equally excluded from their new community.[5] For Narcissus, the opposite is true: shunning all social contact, he finds an idealized audience of one in his mirror image. When he realizes that he is alone, the loss of validation of his identity by another human being literally ends his existence.

In the Narcissus story, the conflict between looking like and being oneself is illustrated using techniques of visual and narrative realism, making the reader and onlooker an active participant in judging the validity of Narcissus' existence. The almost imperceptible cracks of the surface multiply by degrees as Narcissus' image is conveyed to the reader. Similes punctuate not only the three most important moments in the narrative (i.e. first recognition, breakdown, and death) but are employed in rendering the visual crises of this progression as well.

The crucial moment of Narcissus' first awareness of his reflection is marked by a short simile (*Met.* 3.418–19):

> adstupet ipse sibi uultuque immotus eodem
> haeret, ut e Pario formatum marmore signum.

He stares at himself in amazement and remains motionless with the same expression, like a statue hewn from Parian marble.

This simile is the first look the reader gets at the image that entrances Narcissus after the building of suspense in the preceding verses that describe his reaction (*imagine correptus formae*, 3.415–17), and sets off an avalanche of descriptive detail. The perfectly calibrated symmetry of line

[3] Even the flower that eventually replaces his body (*nusquam corpus erat; croceum pro corpore florem/ inveniunt, Met.* 3.509–10) recalls his beauty, i.e. his physical self, in its colors and drooping head.

[4] The verse break mimics the shock of her new appearance: *novaque ut conspexit in unda/ cornua, pertimuit seque exsternata refugit* (*Met.* 1.640–1). The synthesis of these two characters appears to be Cipus who sees his horns in the mirror and touches them for reassurance: *Aut sua flumina cum vidit Cipus in unda/ cornua (vidit enim) falsamque in imagine credens/ esse fidem, digitis ad frontem saepe relatis,/ quae vidit tetigit, nec iam sua lumina damnans/ restitit* (*Met.* 15.565–9).

Cf. Bettini (1991), 17–18 on Sosia looking at himself in the mirror (Plautus *Amph.* 441–7).

[5] Cf. Callisto: *saepe feris latuit visis oblita, quid esset,/ ursaque conspectos in montibus horruit ursos ...* (*Met.* 2.493–4).

418 renders the static pose (*ipse* and *immotus* form the center of their separate, respective halves; yet taken together they also link them as the epicenter of the fixed self around which everything revolves)[6] and replicates in the word order the mirror effect, while the enjambment of *haeret* creates a pause that stages the simile. The simile thus opens the self-contained circle of Narcissus' viewing to allow the reader to participate in the spectacle. Significantly, the description of Narcissus' beauty has been delayed until this moment even though its effect on others is noted at several points in the text.[7] The meeting with the mirror image is thus literally the first glimpse of Narcissus, reifying both what is in front and what is inside the mirror.[8]

Hardie remarks on these lines:

> The boundary between art and reality is overstepped by the application of the simile not to the inanimate object of Narcissus' stupefied gaze, the reflection, but to his own living person; *but since the reflection is of himself, the simile applies equally to the object of his gaze. He is his own simile.*[9]

With this double take on what is real and what is representation Ovid manages to reproduce for the reader the mirror experience, to create before his mind's eye both the original Narcissus and his marble double. Ironically, the use of the statue simile in describing Narcissus' looks for the first time points to the inherent tension of this representation: there is no prior hierarchy of copy and original or, for that matter, mirror image and originating source. The trick in the application of the statue simile lies in the fact that the reader is not able to compare Narcissus' looks with anything; he has never seen him before. This move prepares the reader for the subsequent takeover of image over substance as Narcissus' reflection becomes ever more lifelike while his own body declines.

In focusing on Narcissus himself instead of the reflection, Ovid preserves the mysterious pull of this image, shading it from the reader who is forced to extrapolate by using his superior knowledge of mirrors' reflective properties. This mental translation seems innocuous enough until one

[6] For the role of *ipse* in objectifying the self, see Hardie (2002), 278 and n.40.

[7] Cf. reaction to Narcissus (except of course for blind Teiresias): as a baby, *iam tunc qui posset amari*, *Met.* 3.344–5; as a youth, … *poteratque puer iuvenisque videri:/ multi illum iuvenes, multae cupiere puellae/ sed fuit in tenera tam dura superbia forma*, *Met.* 3.351; and, most importantly, as seen by Echo (*adspicit*, 356; *vidit et incaluit*, 371); her focalization returns in line 494.

[8] The simultaneous creation of original and copy has a counterpart in the sculpting simile in book 1 (Deucalion and Pyrrha) which is discussed in Chapter 1. Cf. also Lucretius' etymology of *simulacrum* as deriving from simultaneity (*simul ac*), Hardie (2002) 151 n.15.

[9] Hardie (2002), 146 (emphasis mine).

realizes that with each turn the image is altered to some degree. Hardie's phrasing elides the significant, though infinitesimally small *ut* of the simile.[10] Narcissus is *not* his own simile and the simile does not apply *equally* to both the reflection and the body. It is worth noting the exiguous asymmetry that exists between these images.[11] While allowing for their superficial similarity as representations of Narcissus (be they verbal or visual),[12] it is also necessary to keep them apart in their distinctness and see the translation of one into the other as a problem of ekphrasis, beginning with the double-edged simile itself, both verbal and visual simulacrum,[13] which subverts the implicit hierarchy of tenor and vehicle, original and copy. Paradoxically, the very sameness of the visual surface highlights rather than obscures differences on a more profound level.

The reduction of Narcissus to his visual aspect suggests that there is no substance behind the superficial resemblance. As Frontisi-Ducroux notes, commenting on the phrase *imaginis umbrae* in the authorial intrusion (*Met.* 3.434), Narcissus appears to be nothing but image.[14] Yet the exaggerated emphasis on sameness should make us suspicious of exchanging one for the other ontologically. Narcissus may look like a statue in his motionlessness, giving the impression that viewer and viewed have exchanged places; his pose, however, betrays his engaged consciousness.[15] Nor are marble statues and mirror images identical: one is a representation that is meant to exist without a referent; the other exists only as long as the referent is present.[16] Much of the dramatic irony in the subsequent description stems from the conflict with this static initial image of the marble statue and the quite different properties of the mirror image.

The reader may thus identify with Narcissus himself who expresses the frustration at his inability to cross the boundary of the water's surface to complete union with his alter ego: *exigua prohibemur aqua* (3.450).

10 See also Barchiesi (2007) ad loc.: "Narciso è anche l'immagine di Narciso vista nell' acqua, e la statua è insieme la persona e il suo rispecchiamento."

11 Cf. Mencacci (1996), 117–18 for Augustine's observation that the mirror image resembles us while we cannot resemble the mirror image (*Soliloquies* 11.6.11).

12 I count four: the creation of Narcissus as character through the text, the mirror image, the statue itself, and the simile that compares him to the statue.

13 Hardie (2002), 163.

14 Frontisi-Ducroux (1997), 216 : "Comme si le caractère immatériel du reflet gagnait par contagion – parallèlement à ce qui se passe en amour – le modèle."

15 Henderson (1979) ad loc. criticizes Ovid's simile as ***in-congruous***: "the *signum* can hardly be lying flat."

16 Statues replace the body they are modeled on, thereafter being independent of it. In fact, statues of the divine must have this separation: while they are modeled on a mortal, they represent the divine.

Paradoxically, the only boundary is the medium that constitutes the image. As signaled by the statue simile, looking at Narcissus is an aesthetic experience – Narcissus is not so much human as a work of art produced by nature. Despite the pronounced solipsism of its subject, in this passage different perspectives converge. It is not focalized through Narcissus' eyes[17] but rather the narrator's, and the mediation of the image through this outside focalization at times puts verbal and visual image at odds, offering different visions. The description, moreover, is not of the mirror image, focalized through Narcissus' eyes, but of Narcissus himself focalized through the eyes of the narrator, who translates his own visual impression of this textual character for the reader. The first simile then functions as a warning and an indicator to read the form in front of the mirror ekphrastically, that is in an awareness of the transformative process the image undergoes as it is conveyed to the reader.

Fowler pointed out the effectiveness of focalization in making the reader identify with a character, thereby allowing him to cross into the reality of the story. By forcing the reader to look through the eyes of the character he is made to assimilate the consciousness of the character, noticing the exact same fragments of a given piece of art. The conceit that character and reader "look" at the exact same picture, however, does not preclude their divergent interpretation. As Fowler observes, what the reader loses in visual immediacy he makes up for in the wider textual perspective of the experience, integrating the ekphrasis into the plot of which the character is unaware in his subjective stance.[18]

Fowler chooses as his example Aeneas looking at the murals in the temple of Juno at Carthage. The similarity of Aeneas and Narcissus as "special cases of viewer in that they gaze on images of themselves" is noted only in passing by Hardie, yet it is highly relevant to Narcissus' conflict.[19] Aeneas, in his role as epic hero, is used to seeing himself objectified and talking of himself as a character,[20] and can therefore recognize the story in the murals as an event in which he has taken part, aligning himself with the reader's view of himself as a character (*se quoque principibus permixtum agnovit Achivis, Aen.* 1.488). Narcissus, even though ostensibly looking at himself, sees another living person instead of an image. It is surely significant that this is Narcissus' first experience of solitude (*Met.* 3.379). Unaware of

17 *Pace* Salzman-Mitchell (2005b), 94.
18 Fowler (1991), 31–3.
19 Hardie (2002), 146.
20 See the progression in the narrative as he prepares to meet Dido. He recognizes himself in the murals (*Aen.* 1.488); Ilioneus talks about him before Dido (544); Dido wishes for his presence (575–6); he reveals himself (595–6).

anything but his subjective experience, he has no abstract notion of the self and thus cannot imagine that the reflection is not a real person. The mirror thus reflects Narcissus' own fictionality: as a product of the text, a fictional character, he is no more real than his mirror image. Yet inside the fictional situation the reader identifies with the verisimilar character and rejects the "illusion" of the reflection. While Aeneas and the reader both share the view of his externalized self fixed in the artwork that records the past, Narcissus' image is unstable, as visual and textual image are developed at the same time.

In describing the figure of Narcissus, the gap between character and reader becomes apparent. The most obvious difference lies in Narcissus' naivety in observing his mirror image as opposed to the narrator's (and reader's) extreme sophistication with which the experience of viewing is described. In order to translate Narcissus' admiration for what he sees for his urbane audience, that is to represent credibly Narcissus' state of irrecoverable innocence, Ovid has recourse to the visual clichés of ekphrastic description. Thus the pretense of reading Narcissus' thoughts as he marvels at the image, though outwardly presented as explicit, embedded focalization (*spectat*, 420; *cuncta miratur*, 424), goes against the logic of this bucolic character who is not even aware of the image-making properties of water.[21]

The objective focalization allows for a double vision which is the very opposite of Narcissus' subjective perspective. This division shows in the use of active/passive reflections without change of tense (*qui probat, ipse probatur/ dumque petit, petitur*, 426), as opposed to Narcissus' later active/active constructions in his speech, crucially accompanied by a change of tense to evoke a sense of communication (*cumque ego porrexi tibi bracchia, porrigis ultro*, 458).[22] The superior knowledge of narrator/reader is expressed most clearly in the ironic double construction in line 430: *quid videat, nescit: sed quod videt, uritur illo*. Narcissus is the exact opposite of the reader in his immediate physical reaction that is an almost simultaneous reflex to what he sees. The reader is absolutely clear about what kind of image Narcissus sees, his mirror image, and how it behaves (summed up by the narrator's exclamation in lines 432–6) but is barred from truly seeing the image itself unless translated through the textual medium that both allows and withholds access to it.[23] While Narcissus' own focalization

[21] See de Jong (2004), 102–14 for the terminology. Narcissus' ignorance is astonishing, given that both his parents are water deities (*Met.* 3.342–4).

[22] For the latter, see Brenkman (1976), 313. [23] Hardie (2002), 147–8.

is explicitly marked by noting the watery medium of the image (*lacu*, 476; *unda*, 486; *in solitam undam*, 499), the image itself is never described. To see this image is only possible through Narcissus' eyes, that is his consciousness. The mirror image thus remains elusive for the reader who has only indirect access to it by "looking" at the original Narcissus, thereby increasing the sense of the mirror image's irreality. This phantom image really is nowhere, as the editorial intrusion reminds Narcissus (*quod petis, est nusquam*, 433, echoed ironically in the final disappearance of his body: *nusquam corpus erat*, 509) .

It is worth noting here some properties of mirror images as distinct from visual art. Narcissus' reception of his mirror image is couched in terms of art criticism which in turn come into conflict with the properties of the mirror image. The most poignant contrast lies in the opposition of art and nature. While the pool resembles a mirror as the descriptive adjective *argenteus* alludes, it is actually a part of the natural landscape. The natural mirror of the lake suggests a lack of agent. Nobody is holding the mirror, nor is Narcissus fooled by a naturalist ruse. His delusion originates in himself while the pool merely reflects anything that is put opposite its surface. There is no temporal delay for the image to come into being which would alert us to a manufactured origin. The lack of discrimination in subject matter is another sign of the artlessness of this image, seeing that the selection of subject is one of utmost importance to the artist. The staged "coincidence" of Narcissus' encounter is especially poignant as the Narcissus theme was one of the most popular subjects in ancient art.[24] Finally, one should consider the medium: water. While water must be stagnant to be able to reflect an image, the ephemerality of the mirror image recalls its fluid potential. The reflection differs from conventional visual art in two important aspects: it is dynamic, and it is inherently transitory. The dynamic of the image is what fools Narcissus; unlike the viewer of a realist piece of art who wishes static art to be imbued with life, Narcissus is not deluded in his mind when he notices that the image moves or changes color – it really does. At the same time, the image is not fixed in the medium, that is pigment or marble: it has no material tangibility of its own.

Intriguingly, these differences mark precisely the limitations of visual and verbal art that are played against each other in the tradition of ekphrasis, static versus dynamic, simultaneous versus sequential action,

[24] Elsner (2000), 91–100 discusses the prominence of Narcissus in both Hellenistic and Roman visual art and ekphrastic descriptions (with pictures).

diachronic versus synchronic. The mirror image may thus present a kind of compromise between the two modes of art, as is the verbal trick of mirroring words which performs simultaneously a visual trick on the page. Ovid's textual medium then surpasses the visual in that it is able to render in its linearity what visual art cannot, the dynamic of this transient image. At the same time, he captures not so much the image itself as the experience of viewing, which he reimagines for the reader-as-viewer couched in the language of art criticism.

The visual multiplications of Narcissus' aspect as statue and mirror image, pretending to render exactly the same image countless times, obscure the fact that the real differences lie in the act of viewing. One should discern (at least) two viewers, Narcissus himself and the narrator, the one completely self-absorbed in his circle of mutual admiration, the other (almost) self-effacingly communicating what he sees to the reader.

The divergent focalization comes to a head in the moment of Narcissus' breakdown. At the end of his speech, Narcissus disturbs the waters with his tears and is no longer able to see the image (*Met.* 3.477–85):

> 'quo refugis? remane nec me, crudelis, amantem
> desere,' clamauit; 'liceat, quod tangere non est
> adspicere et misero praebere alimenta furori.'
> dumque dolet, summa uestem deduxit ab ora
> nudaque marmoreis percussit pectora palmis.
> pectora traxerunt roseum percussa ruborem
> non aliter quam poma solent, quae candida parte,
> parte rubent, aut ut uariis solet uua racemis
> ducere purpureum nondum matura colorem.

'Where do you flee? Stay, cruel one, and do not desert me who loves you,' he cried, 'allow a look at what cannot be touched and give some nourishment to this wretched one in his insanity.' While he grieves, he rends his garment from the top of his face and strikes his naked chest with marble hands, and the chest draws a rosy redness as it is struck, not unlike when apples, white on one side, grow red on the other, or like grapes that, not yet ripe, take on a purple color in variegated clusters.

This is the only time in the whole story that the circle of eye contact is broken and Narcissus cannot see a reciprocal action.[25] The perspective changes back from the subjective viewpoint of the monologue to the objective narrator who describes the effects of the blows on Narcissus' body. Narcissus' breakdown is directly linked to his wish to look at the

[25] The break is signposted by verbal repetition: *liceat … adspicere*, 479; *adspexit*, 486.

image without touching it (*liceat, quod tangere non est,/ adspicere*, 478–9), as if he has finally caught up with the reader's aesthetic detachment. A topos in ancient art criticism is the temptation to touch sculpture and leave behind evidence of this erotic/aesthetic transgression in a red mark.[26] However, this thought is always expressed potentially – since the tactile sense would eventually override the visual deception. In Narcissus' case this potentiality becomes reality. At the exact moment he renounces the idea of touching the image, he (unwittingly) does so, reaching literally through the looking glass. The reddening in the mirror image thus constitutes for him the ultimate proof of the image's reality.[27]

The interruption in Narcissus' viewing reveals the narrator's own subjectivity and erotic bias. Alluding to the initial simile of the marble statue, he describes Narcissus' hands as *marmoreis palmis*. The transition from simile to metaphor shows how the distance between Narcissus and his reflection is closing in a partial fusion of image and body: "like marble" becomes *marmoreis palmis*, a partial substitution akin to Pelops' ivory shoulder. His hands appear no longer part of his living body, symbolizing the violence directed against himself as if it came from outside. The metaphorical use of *marmoreis* also emphasizes the hardness of the blows that Narcissus is inflicting which allows the reader to imagine his physical pain in greater clarity.

Unlike the marble hands, the living flesh appears more sensuously real, as opposed to the initial simile in which the statue image and the body were static and lifeless. Ovid inverts the conventional topos of the white marble coming to life in changing from white to red, in making the 'marble hands' effect the change on the living body, showing again the triangulation of art, mirror, and life.[28] The color simile, taken from the repertoire of love poetry, reveals the erotic entanglement of the narrator himself, falling under the spell of Narcissus' beauty which, from the day of his birth, has consumed anyone who saw him. A counter-movement develops between Narcissus' own and the narrator's gaze. Narcissus progresses from

[26] A brilliant example for this mixed motivation can be seen in Herodas 4.59–62 where Phile expresses her temptation to pinch the buttocks of a nude boy statue.

[27] The description of Narcissus has uncanny parallels with the evocation of the poet's beloved in *Amores* 1.7. Both seem to be made of marble (*Am.* 1.7.51–2) but their visual perfection is marred by erotic violence, making them more real; their silence is staged as unresponsiveness to the lover's entreaties (*Am.* 1.7.19–22); in both, the final breakdown comes through seeing tears (*Am.* 1.7.57–60).Hardie (2002), 163.

[28] Narcissus' lack of motion motivates the first simile whereas statues themselves seem always on the brink of movement. See Hardie (2002), 148–50. The simile thus reverses the lifelikeness of its content.

immediacy to distance, from erotic lover to art lover. While at first he tries to possess the image, taking in both the image and the water (3.415), he resigns himself in the end to looking, which serves as purely metaphorical *alimenta* to his erotic hunger. By contrast, the narrator's viewpoint changes from the distanced view of the marble statue to the natural, more immediate simile of apples and grapes, from looking at Narcissus as a statue to looking at Narcissus as erotic conquest. The cruel irony lies in the narrator's offering in the simile what Narcissus desires, a juxtaposition which Hardie observes:

> Narcissus' final dissolution is triggered by the sight of his blushing flesh compared in the simile at 483–5 to apples and grapes. The ultimate fruitlessness of Narcissus' desire is signalled *by his attempt to feed on a literary simulacrum*, or simile. Narcissus' abnormal erotic pathology becomes the common experience of every reader.[29]

While the juxtaposition of metaphor and simile is powerful in itself, the trick lies in the ambiguous reintroduction of Narcissus' viewpoint. As shown above, the narrator's focalization replaces Narcissus' at this point, to return only at line 485 with *quae simul adspexit liquefacta in unda*. But what exactly does the relative pronoun *quae* signify? While grammatically speaking it refers back to *pectora*, it could also be construed as summing up all of the preceding lines.[30]

Once again, subjective focalization conflicts with the idea of a stable image, identical for both narrator/reader and character. Narcissus sees the image in the water, signposted by *unda*, that is he sees the reflection of himself and not the original as the narrator/reader has just done, once again leaving the mystery of the mirror image intact through this summary wording. Even more to the point, Narcissus cannot see the very image to which the relative pronoun seems to refer, the apples and grapes of the simile. It is a truism that characters inside fiction cannot see similes but experience actions in the immediate moment.[31] Narcissus therefore sees only his blushing skin, whereas the mental eye of the reader is filled with a kaleidoscope of images, of marble hands, reddening skin,

[29] Hardie (2002), 163 (emphasis mine).

[30] Cf. the respective translations of Mandelbaum (1993): "when he sees this"; Humphries (1955): "He sees it all once more"; Koch (2007): " vede quel rosso."

[31] For a parallel in visual arts, one may compare Philostratus' address to Narcissus (*Imag.* 1.23.3), quoted by Elsner (2000), 103: "As for you, however, Narcissus, it is not painting that has deceived you, nor are you engrossed in a thing of pigments or wax; but you do not realize that the water represents you exactly as you are when you gaze upon it ..." The internal perspective of Narcissus is so natural (it is water, not pigment) that he is fooled by the natural artifice. Philostratus plays with the conceit that in naturalist art the subject seems to transcend the material from which it is made.

apples and grapes, etc. from which he must extrapolate Narcissus' aspect. The flattened-out perspective of the text on the page makes it look as if Narcissus were able to "feed on the simile" when in actuality he is not able to see it. As with the display of Narcissus' initial ignorance of the mirror effect, the narrator here again shows his knowledge, this time of the rules of fiction, is superior to the character's.

This textual stratagem recalls a visual counterpart of Narcissus, a fresco from Pompeii described by Elsner. A basin of water was put in front of a picture of Narcissus, as if his gaze could cross the divide between the two-dimensional picture and the three-dimensional room, between the world of imagination and reality.[32] In the same vein, Ovid's Narcissus is made to see more than he is actually capable of seeing because he ostensibly reunites his gaze with the narrator's.

Narcissus' reaction to what he sees in the water provokes the next visual crisis. Particularly striking is the density of similes here, progressing almost without interruption from one set of images to the next (*Met.* 3.483–95):

> non aliter quam poma solent, quae candida parte,
> parte rubent, aut ut uariis solet uua racemis
> ducere purpureum nondum matura colorem.
> quae simul adspexit liquefacta rursus in unda
> non tulit ulterius sed, ut intabescere flauae
> igne levi cerae matutinaeque pruinae
> sole tepente solent, sic attentuatus amore
> liquitur et tecto paulatim carpitur igni,
> et neque iam color est mixto candore rubori
> nec uigor et uires et quae modo uisa placebant
> nec corpus remanet, quondam quod amauerat Echo.
> quae tamen ut uidit, quamuis irata memorque
> indoluit.

not unlike when apples, white on one side, grow red on the other, or like grapes that, not yet ripe, take on a purple color in variegated clusters. As soon as he saw this again in the liquefied wave, he could not bear it any more: but as yellow wax begins to melt by a slight fire or morning frost under a warming sun, so he dissolves, consumed by love, and little by little is seized by the fire, and gone already is that color of white mixed with red, the vigor and strength and the things that just now were a pleasure to see, nor did the body remain, the one Echo had once loved. As she saw this, though angry at the memory, she grieved.

[32] Elsner (2000), 98–9: "On the ground below the image, it appears that there was a basin on a high stand containing water, in which not only would the painted Narcissus have been reflected, but also anyone who paused to look at the fresco with any care."

As in the hiatus of Narcissus' gaze in the previous lines, the description is focalized through the narrator, drawing an arc that ends in the view of a different focalizer, Echo. Narcissus' breakdown can be interpreted both as a physical breakdown (*non tulit ulterius*, 487) and as an inability to keep up the visual contact with his mirror image. Narcissus cannot bear looking any longer, and in the absence of Narcissus' gaze the object of his vision disintegrates just as it had come alive at the moment he notices it.

The disappearance of Narcissus' body begins surreptitiously with a couple of similes before proceeding to outright negation of the very qualities that rendered him attractive. Ovid's use of the simile enforces the sense of Narcissus' growing loss of substance. As noted in the chapter on metamorphosis, the simile can obscure the transformation by covering the action with the smokescreen of the image it presents. Here, by contrast, the simile enacts the attenuation of Narcissus' body by deconstructing the surface. The wax-and-dew simile undoes the apples-and-grapes simile, yet the almost immediate progression from one to the other emphasizes the detached quality of this visual impression. Narcissus is presented as a series of images that remove the sense of material tangibility that was built up in the preceding lines. After the lines of the simile, there are no more references to his body, either the parts or the whole.[33]

His progressive decline is not only rendered by the images of the simile but extends to the level of tense and mode.[34] In the vehicle, the inchoative verb *intabescere* and the present tense of the phrase *sole tepente* initiate the process that comes to an end in the tenor in which the passive (*liquitur*, *carpitur*) and perfect (*attenuatus*) dominate, thus blending object and illustration seamlessly.[35] The frontal position of the vehicle lulls the reader into a greater acceptance of the magical disappearance of Narcissus' body. In addition, the simile's imagery with its familiar air of domestic and recurrent scenes (*solent*) aims to naturalize the extraordinary event.

Narcissus' liquefaction begins in the image he sees (*liquefacta … in unda*, 486) and continues through the imagery of melting wax in the simile. As the deconstruction of Narcissus' body continues, the more concrete

[33] *Nec corpus remanet* (*Met.* 10.493) is a negative after-image suggesting an answer to the riddle of what Echo sees in line 498 (*quae tamen ut vidit*). It corresponds to her own identity that is reduced to reflecting sound. For more on Echo's mediating role see below.

[34] Cf. their earlier role in creating the mirror effect.

[35] Cf. also the simile of the melting snow at *Od.* 19.204–8 where the vehicle at first appears to be Penelope's tears, then her cheeks: τῆς δ'ἄρ' ἀκουούσης ῥέε δάκρυα, τήκετο δὲ χρώς./ ὡς δὲ χιὼν κατατήκε' ἐν ἀκροπόλοισιν ὄρεσσιν,/ ἥν τ'Εὖρος κατέτηξεν, ἐπὴν Ζέφυρος καταχεύῃ/ τηκομένης δ'ἄρα τῆς ποταμοὶ πλήθουσι ῥεοντεσ' / ὥς τὴς τήκετο καλὰ παρήια δάκρυ χεούσησ'

images of the simile in turn get replaced by the negation of abstract qualities, further enhancing the sense of receding/fading vision. The swift destruction of such ineffable qualities as color, vigor, and strength contrasts with the effort made earlier to invoke them; the prosaic *et neque iam color est mixto candore rubori* (491), cancels out the evocative fruit simile of lines 482–5. Just as Narcissus' beauty had been conjured up by the poet through the careful combination of body parts,[36] so now it is deconstructed through negation and abstraction.[37] The earlier fascination with that verbally rendered image now seems quaint: *quae modo visa placebant* (492) – "the things that were nice to look at just now" are already fading from memory in their particularity, as if not only the mirror image but equally Narcissus' body itself had been no more than a mirage. With this reverse ekphrasis Ovid demonstrates the superiority of verbal over visual art. While language can simply assert that a human body can burn and melt away, tearing down as well as building up a mental image, visual art is bound by its material nature.

The reference to the morning dew in the simile (*matutinaeque pruinae*, 488) is the first temporal marker since the beginning of the story where a break from the hunt around noon is implied (413). The intrusion of the temporal marker heralds the ending of the narrative illusion, the dream-like suspension of outside reality that lies at the heart of Narcissus' infatuation. The location of this myth, completely isolated and with no outside light, metaphorically creates its own cosmos in the circular gaze of Narcissus' and his mirror image (*geminum, sua lumina, sidus*, 420).[38] Despite the allusion to the topos of noontime seduction, the place is cool and dark, giving no indication of the time of day. Moreover, the bucolic interlude of Echo and Narcissus is situated between the mention of cities (*Aonias urbes* [339] and *Achaidas urbes* [511]), and the fact that the story is reported by *fama* (512), all suggest a vague provenance that seems to mock the reader's own desire for verisimilitude. The introduction of Echo as a witness to the disappearing act reframes this "anti-ekphrasis" in yet another mode. As Brenkman notes, Echo is incapable of communicating spontaneously, which calls into question the credibility of the story itself

36 Sharrock (1991), 36 n.2 excludes Narcissus for fear of having him overshadow his female counterparts, but says that her argument applies to him as well.

37 The same technique is used by Catullus in poem 43 (*Salve, nec minimo puella naso*) to give a kind of reverse negative of Lesbia's beauty.

38 *Geminum sidus*, a grammatical singular containing a double, encloses *sua lumina* to accentuate the uninterrupted circle of gazing.

and suggests a disintegration that does not halt at Narcissus' body.[39] Thus, even at the level of narrative the circular isolation finds representation.

The metamorphoses of Narcissus and Echo capture the illusory quality of this episode. As Narcissus' body vanishes, the place returns to its previous innocuous description of landscape with the single addition of the flower, recalling in the fashion of a simile two essential but abstract features of Narcissus: the gesture of his downward gaze and the color of his skin.[40] This token of his presence toys with the reader's desire for realism, for a material continuity which eludes the intrinsically changeable nature of the mirror image. Just as the similes of wax and dew give visual concreteness to Narcissus dissolving, so the flower promises tangibility, the promise that the story did not just trick the reader as the visual image tricked Narcissus. However, while the flower serves as a visual reminder of Narcissus, there is no continuity with his body or blood.[41] The significance of this break has been pointed out by Brenkman:

> The flower is the only access, at the level of the narrated event to the drama of Narcissus but it can have no meaning at that level since its significance emerges only out of the fabric of signs at play in the text.[42]

As if to call into question the whole aetiological enterprise of leaving marks of metamorphoses past in the landscape, Echo's metamorphosis is even more extreme. In her shame, she first hides her face with leaves (*pudibundaque frondibus ora/ protegit*, 393–4), thus assimilating herself to the landscape in disguise, before she turns into a rock (*ossa ferunt lapidis traxisse figuram*, 399). However, uniquely among stone metamorphoses, it is not the rock that takes her form but she who takes on the form of a rock (an oxymoron since rocks are precisely amorphous) which makes her undistinguishable from her surroundings. Without the intervention of the narrator, the record of both their existences would disappear, yet his own curious presence in the text resembles the ephemerality of his characters, at once real and imagined.

The stage of the natural landscape swallows up its human players (almost) without a trace and simply returns to its previous, seemingly innocuous, state. The images in the final couple of similes suggest the end of the fictional illusion. The melting wax that stands for artistic creation

[39] Brenkman (1976), 325.

[40] Note that the color adjective *croceum* derives from yet another flower.

[41] Barchiesi (2007) ad loc. notes the contrast to the flower metamorphoses of e.g. Hyacinthus (*Met.* 10.210–19), Adonis (*Met.* 10.731–9), and Ajax (*Met.* 13.394–8).

[42] Brenkman (1976), 326.

(both visual and verbal)[43] is ready to be fashioned into new shapes and stories, while the image of the warming sun connects the mythical landscape of the pool where the sun does not reach to the world of the reader from which the simile is taken. The verbal repetition at the beginning and the end of the story (*nullo sole tepescere*, 412; *sole tepente*, 489) closes the circle of illusion. The various images in the similes are all taken from outside this self-contained environment, referring to the world of art, agriculture, and domesticity. Made to illustrate the beauty of Narcissus, they not only capture perfectly his intrusion into this hyper-natural landscape but also claim the witnesses of narrator and reader as real presences in this story.

HOUSE OF SLEEP

The immersion of the reader in the text becomes even more pronounced in the textual fantasy of the House of Sleep. This allegorical set-piece reifies the abstract concept of sleep and dreams and allows the reader a glimpse behind the scenes. As the immaterial substance of dreams turns material, the simile straddles the divide between the two worlds and marks the transition.

The world of fiction and the world of the reader's experience touch in the simile which illustrates through triangulating comparison something in the text which cannot adequately be expressed in literal language. The simile's association of the familiarly quotidian with the unique moment in fiction provokes a sudden crossing of permissible frames of reference that assimilates the alien element and allows the reader to share the experience of the characters.

Whereas the simile keeps the two levels distinct, the structure of fiction appropriates the real world in using and rearranging its shapes and experiences to construct its own. Dreams, particularly literary dreams, also use characters and images that have been introduced before but rearrange them according to plausibility, not truth. The familiarity of shapes lures the reader or dreamer across the threshold of consciousness and allows him to accept an internal logic that defies the rational part of his brain. Once one is immersed in dream or fiction, stepping outside of it may seem impossible; even when the spell is broken, the experience may carry

[43] Cf. in particular the wax simile as Pygmalion's marble statue becomes flesh: *temptatum mollescit ebur positoque rigore/ subsidit digitis ceditque, ut Hymettia sole/ cera remollescit tractaque pollice multas/ flectitur in facies iposque fit utilis usu* (*Met.* 10.283–6); and Pythagoras on the migration of the soul: *utque novis facilis signatur cera figuris,/ nec manet ut fuerat nec formas servat easdem,/ sed tamen ipsa eadem est: animam sic semper eandem /esse sed in varias doceo migrare figuras* (*Met.* 15.169–72).

over in a sense of disorientation before reality asserts its dominance once again.[44] For the duration, however, the parasitic relationship of dream and fiction to reality is inverted.

The affinity of the two experiences finds expression in the device of the fictional dream as parallel narrative. Homer uses the device of the fictional dream repeatedly in the *Iliad*, but reserves its most effective use for a simile in the climactic scene of Achilles' pursuit of Hector (*Il.* 22.199–201):

ὡς δ'ἐν ὀνείρῳ οὐ δύναται φεύγοντα διώκειν
οὔτ' ἄρ' ὁ τὸν δύναται ὑποφεύγειν οὔθ' ὁ διώκειν
ὥς ὁ τὸν οὐ δύνατο μάρψαι ποσίν, οὐδ' ὅς ἀλύξαι

As in a dream a man cannot pursue the one who flees, nor can the other flee from the one who pursues, so can one not snatch the other with his feet, nor the other escape.

According to Scodel, the simile "contributes to the credibility of the action by offering the reader a comparison that makes its strangeness meaningful: the pursuit is assimilated to an uncanny (but universally human) experience."[45] While Scodel's emphasis is on the assimilating force of the simile, it is important not to downplay the unresolved tension of its image. The dream simile renders this climactic moment as a kind of para-reality. Unlike the immediately preceding simile of a natural chase (*Il.* 22.189–93), with its classic transference of human to animal (dog/fawn), the dream simile achieves almost complete visual congruence with the fictional reality of the text. Since the simile situation itself is imaginary and not real it makes palpable the divine influence in stalling the outcome.

The uncertain focalization of the simile adds to the uncanny atmosphere: Moulton remarks on the difficulty of knowing whether it is Hector or Achilles who is imagined dreaming.[46] This ambiguity is especially pronounced given that dreams are by nature the most subjective of experiences. In spite of its surcharge of anxiety, the simile therefore introduces a note of emotional detachment at this crucial moment. It renders the optical illusion of static immobility for the spectator of the race that is both maintained and can only be broken by divine intervention. It is left up to the reader to apportion his empathy for either character or indeed vacillate between the two. In using the dream situation as vehicle for the simile, Homer comments on the experience of fiction as one of simultaneously identifying strongly with the character while being aware of one's

[44] See Feeney (1993), 235 on the spell of fiction. [45] Scodel (1999), 9.
[46] Moulton (1977), 84. Both are only identified by their roles (the one fleeing, the one pursuing) in vehicle and tenor.

position as a spectator. The dream situation applies as much to the reader's rapt attention which he shares with the internal spectators as to the perceived psychology of the two heroes. It thus captures the surreal sense of vicarious participation in straddling the divide of being inside (vehicle) and outside (tenor) the scene.

Homer's dream simile is not as psychologically accurate as but also less partial than that of Virgil, who takes his audience into Turnus' mind, linking character, reader and poet together in a conspiratorial first person plural (*Aen.* 12.908–11): *ac velut in somnis, oculos ubi languida pressit/ nocte quies, nequiquam avidos extendere cursus/ velle videmur et in mediis conatibus aegri succidimus.* He prepares the simile by letting the reader share Turnus' dream in *Aen.* 7.421–59.

This association of dreams and the fictional experience is further expanded by Ovid in his full-blown allegorization of the House of Sleep (*Met.* 11.592–649), where the reader is invited behind the scenes and introduced to the production of dreams. In Ovid, the dreams form the tenor not the vehicle of a simile, thus inverting the Homeric and Virgilian model. Both Hardie and Tissol have remarked on the meta-poetical importance of this scene, pointing out the histrionic detail in the costuming as well as the speaking name of Morpheus, in which Ahl detects echoes of morphe, mors, and Orpheus.[47] Sleep, the producer of dreams that can take on any shape (*somnia quae veras aequant imitamine formas, Met.* 11.626), is the artist figure that most closely resembles Ovid (*mutatas dicere formas, Met* 1.1).[48]

The gradual approach to the House of Sleep allows the reader to take in the abundant details of the garden and the house that appeal to all the senses. True to the immaterial nature of his subject, Ovid's description is less description than invitation to imagine, drawing attention to the diffuse light and dissolution of borders. Tissol remarks that the technique of negation in particular opens up the possibilities for imagination.[49] The narrative flows uninterrupted until Iris comes to the center, Somnus' bed, which receives a meticulous two-line description (*Met.* 11.610–11).

Significantly, the dreams she encounters form the first and only barrier to her approach as can be seen from the first use of the verb *intravit.* They are described in a triple simile (*Met.* 11.613–17):

> hunc circa passim uarias imitantia formas
> somnia uana iacent totidem quot messis aristas,

[47] Hardie (2002), 278; Tissol (1997), 80–2; Ahl (1985), 59–60.
[48] Morpheus' role will be examined below. [49] Tissol (1997), 77 and n.121.

silua gerit frondes, eiectas litus harenas.
Quo simul intrauit manibusque obstantia uirgo
somnia dimouit, ...

Around him everywhere lay bodiless dreams imitating various shapes, as many as the crop has ears, the wood leaves, the shore sand spewed from the sea. As soon as the virgin goddess entered and removed the dreams in her way with her hands ...

The first impression is thus one of limitless abundance, conveyed not only by the quasi-proverbial images themselves but also by the triple structure of the simile, which piles one image on top of the other. The rapid sequence of proposed images illustrates the changeable nature of the dreams and the inability to fix them in a single static image. The simile is highly self-reflexive: since dreams exist for the sole purpose of imitation, illustrating them by way of a multiple simile creates the uncanny effect that they latch onto any image as soon as it is proposed. The verbal *simulacrum* illustrates, or rather performs, a visual *simulacrum*.

While the ostensible purpose of the simile is to illustrate their number (*quot*), its images give the illusion of visual concreteness to the bodiless dreams (*somnia vana*).[50] In letting the reader look at the *somnia vana*, Ovid meets the challenge of illustrating nothingness head on. One may compare the far more elusive formulation in Virgil's description (*Aen.* 6.282–4):

in medio ramos annosaque bracchia pandit
ulmus opaca, ingens quam sedem somnia vulgo
vana ferunt, foliisque sub omnibus haerent.

In the midst a dark elm stretches its branches and aged arms, a giant elm which they say among the people is the realm of the bodiless dreams; they stick underneath all the leaves.

Virgil's image of the dark tree hiding the dreams alludes to Homer's depiction of Hypnos sitting in the form of a bird in a tall fir.[51] However, Virgil's image does not make use of simile to illustrate the immaterial but rather hides the *somnia* in plain sight. He emphasizes the ambiguity of their existence by reference to folktale (*vulgo/ ... ferunt*) and limited visibility (because the elm is dark and huge). Then, by switching back to direct statement at the end (using the indicative instead of the expected

[50] Following Bömer (1969–86) ad loc. I understand *vana* as *bodiless, without substance (körperlos)*.
[51] For the controversy see Chapter 2.

infinitive) Virgil seems to suggest that they actually do exist. Their position on the underside of the leaves connects them to a physical reality that illustrates not only their number but also their parasitic nature. The collusion of what is actually visible (the leaves, the elm itself) and what is imagined (the dreams, the anthropomorphic metaphor of *bracchia pandit*) charges the physical environment with a ghost-like atmosphere that reproduces the emotional disturbance of Aeneas in the mind of the reader.

The dependence on comparisons for describing dreams can be detected even in the secondary literature. In discussing the two passages, Miller writes:

> Like Ovid, Virgil characterized dreams as insubstantial, but he has changed the *metaphorical shape* of these vain beings: instead of the *cobwebby, languorous creatures* of Ovid's imagination, now dreams roo[s]t *like bats* beneath the leaves of a tree, an *organic metaphor* in keeping, perhaps, with Virgil's chthonic, earthy placement of the realm.[52]

The metaphors Miller detects are her own; there is no mention of cobwebs in Ovid or of bats in Virgil. Rather, her metaphors reveal an apparently unconscious reaction to the image-making properties of the text that teases the reader with the paradox of an empty shape. The same effect can be observed in Näf's paraphrase of the Ovidian passage, talking about a variety of figures that can be discerned in the substanceless dreams.[53] And yet, nothing can actually be seen. Ovid is playing a trick on the reader's mind in suggesting a variety of shapes in the simile while limiting their function to illustrating their number. The visualization of their content is a reflex of the mind when confronted with the idea of nothing.

The images of leaves, sand, and ears of wheat render the impression of a pile of individual pieces that cannot be told apart because one looks exactly like the other. While these similes have many parallels in Roman and Greek literature, one Homeric precedent stands out: Iris herself uses the simile of the leaves and grains of sand (*Il.* 2.800–1) when talking in disguise to the Trojans about the size of the Greek army. If Ovid is indeed alluding to this Homeric simile, his quotation of Iris' own words further reinforces the idea that to her the dreams have as much tangible reality as humans. The simile thus combines two paradoxical notions: it lets the reader imagine what the dreams look like in an abstract pile while simultaneously blocking a glimpse of any particular dream.

[52] Miller (1994), 25 (emphases mine).

[53] Näf (2004), 95: "Rings um ihn [sc. Somnus] liegen wesenslose Träume, in welchen allerlei Gestalten zu erkennen sind."

The simile of the *somnia vana* stands out as the only simile in this passage. This is particularly noticeable against the backdrop of the storm scene in which similes threaten to drown out the narrative action, as if replacing literal with figurative scenes. In the context of the House of Sleep, with its principal preoccupations of shape-shifting and illusion this contrast is even more pronounced. The purpose of this passage is to give body to the immaterial; thus sleep is pictured as a sleepy man, the cave and gardens are full of physical manifestations of sleep associations, from the sleep-inducing scent of poppies and the sound of the burbling stream to the monochrome bedspread that implies the absence of light.[54] In this context, dreams form the only physical barrier to Sleep, but since they represent mental states their materiality remains ambiguous. The simile thus reflects appropriately their incomplete reification.[55]

Iris' removal of the physical barrier of dreams also removes the mental barrier and causes Sleep to awaken.[56] Iris' handling of the dreams demonstrates the effectiveness of the illusion – she has to remove the resistant (*obstantia, Met.* 11.616) dreams with her hands (*manibusque .../ somnia dimovit*, 616–17). Like a pantomime pretending to touch a wall, Iris' gestures give the illusion of body to the bodiless forms. As any reader of epic knows, it is the very nature of dreams that they cannot be touched or grasped: so, for example, the Sybil's warning that Aeneas' panicked wielding of the sword will cut through air (*Aen.* 6.290–4). Contrasting Iris and Aeneas, one sees that Iris is outside of the illusion and therefore can handle the dreams as things, whereas Aeneas' mind is complicit with the illusion and therefore meets with the paradox of the bodiless form.[57]

The simile of the *somnia vana* with its paradox of simultaneous immateriality and tangibility introduces the self-aware discourse of fictionality in this excursus. Ovid's House of Sleep tricks the mind with the imitation

[54] The contrast is intensified by Iris' multicolored robe that lightens up the room.

[55] Contrast Lucian *Ver. hist.* 2.34–5 who has fully personified dreams. Statius' description of dreams is probably inspired by Ovid; however, his have imaginary faces (*adsunt innumero circum vaga Somnia vultu/ vera simul falsis permixtaque tristia blandis, Theb.* 10.112–13). The lines are not extant in most manuscripts.

[56] Hardie (2002), 235 comments on the "absurdity of personifying a condition that is one of the depersonalisation of the waking individual." Iris has to break one illusion (the perfect personification of Sleep) in order to create another (the ruse of being able to talk to Sleep). Sleep has to step out of his role momentarily, but note that he immediately returns to sleep at Iris' departure (*Met.* 11.649) and thus gives plausibility to Alcyone's dream as conveyed telepathically through his own mental process.

[57] Feeney (1991), 202 points out the different names for Phobetor/Ikelos (*Met.* 11.640–1): one describes a human emotion, the other a simple fact. Apparently gods do not dream – they are missing from Ovid's enumeration (*Met.* 11.644–5). Iris' sleepiness arises from contamination that must be avoided (*labique ut somnum sensit in artus,/ effugit, Met.* 11.631–2).

of shapes known from the real world in order to illustrate states and experiences that are impossible to grasp literally. The pile of dreams represents an abundant potential of storylines with which we are teased but which we are also incapable of seeing, because that would mean telling the story, actualizing the dream in fictional narrative.

The dreams' meta-poetical significance becomes even clearer when one considers the inextricable relationship between things and writing about things that Ovid establishes both at the beginning of the Metamorphoses (*nam vos mutastis et illa*)[58] and in talking about the poem in retrospect in the *Tristia*: *sunt quoque mutatae ter quinque volumina formae* (*Tr.* 1.1.117) Although the *mutatae formae* are conventionally translated into the title *Metamorphoses*, the metonymy of the poem's title (just like Ovid's earlier *Amores*) vacillates between the subject and object of Ovid's writing, with the characteristic tease of transforming reality into fiction and vice versa. Like Ovid who calls the *Metamorphoses* his children (*orba parente suo, Tr.* 1.7.35), Sleep is surrounded by his children, the dreams (*Met.* 11.633).

The disruption of the narrative flow by the meta-narrative excursus of the House of Sleep, an Ovidian invention, is remarkable for its redundancy in plot terms. Whereas in Homer or Virgil Mercury or Iris delivers the message, here the message is relayed from Juno to Iris to Somnus who in turn gives the task to Morpheus. This explicit choreography makes possible the view of dreams as both things (or scripts) and performances. The different manifestations capture the two levels of fictional experience. A text is both a physical object that can be handled physically (or tossed aside) and a process of the imagination in which the characters come to life as though they were real persons.[59]

Morpheus exemplifies the latter in acting out the dream,[60] combining personification with impersonation. While he follows standard epic tradition for dream apparitions in taking Ceyx's appearance, there are numerous allusions to the dramatic stage, not least the description of his detailed preparation for the role. The distinction between Ceyx's face and body suggests that he is putting on a mask (*in faciem abit, Met.* 11.653). The body, by contrast, is a separate, verisimilar costume: not only the changed skin color but also the lack of clothes indicate the conventions of showing a shipwrecked character.[61] The phrase *exanimi similis* opens a chink in

58 Wheeler (1999), 12–13.

59 Propertius 3.3.18–19 has an imaginary female reader toss the book aside by her bed when her lover comes, thereby conflating her virtual and actual experience.

60 Cf. Juno's *somnia … narrantia* (*Met.* 11.588).

61 Cf. the importance of clothes for the survivors of the shipwreck in Plautus' *Rud.* 573–80.

this perfect costume. It may be read as "like *the* dead man (i.e. Ceyx)" or "like *a* dead man," altering Ceyx's shape for greater plausibility. Morpheus acknowledges that he does indeed look a bit too real, resembling no longer Ceyx but Ceyx's shade (11.659–60). Morpheus' nakedness is a disarming move: no clothes hide the "true" Ceyx, yet their very absence functions as Morpheus' costume. The privileged view of the naked Ceyx is meant to convince Alcyone beyond a doubt; the Homeric counterpart to this story is Penelope's intuitive recognition of Odysseus in the costume of a beggar.

Introducing the conventions of the tragic stage in this epic story results in a speech that is part tragic messenger speech (relating a death that has taken place offstage) part epic first-person narrative (authenticating the speech). Morpheus' impersonation of Ceyx makes possible the certain announcement of his own death with the absurdity of dream logic. "Ceyx" can simultaneously narrate how he was stopped from speaking by drowning (*oraque nostra, tuum frustra clamantia nomen,/ implerunt fluctus*, *Met.* 11.665–6) and assert the power of his voice (*ipse ego fata ... edo*, 668). Both statements are "true" in the sense that the reader has "witnessed" (i.e. read verbatim) the former (*Met.* 11.566–7), and is accepting the convention of the speaking dream at present.

Alcyone continues this blurring of boundaries when, awake and living, she claims she has died (*nulla est Alcyone*, 11.684; *nunc absens perii*, 11.700) and relives Ceyx's shipwreck metaphorically. Alcyone's absolute trust in the truthfulness of the dream resonates with the reader because her "emotional knowledge" of Ceyx's death fits perfectly with the reader's fictional knowledge. Yet neither Ceyx nor Ceyx's shade delivers the message.[62] The dramatic verisimilitude of the dream that is achieved by the use of Morpheus' superior acting skills, including his voice and hand gestures, also compromises the truth of the dream and foreshadows that Ceyx's death might not yet be final, even though it convinces Alcyone.[63]

Alcyone's unconditional belief in verisimilar products of the imagination reflects her ambiguous experience of reality. On waking, she repeats the dream in her own words, as if asserting its reality, then, as if by reflex, she transforms the "true" narrative of Ceyx's shipwreck into a literary lament, assimilating the external tempest to a feminine form as internal, emotional catastrophe (*Met.* 11.700–3). This reversal incidentally

[62] Since Morpheus is the imitation of an *imago*, the real Ceyx is, so to speak, doubly dead. Cf. Hardie (2002), 157 on Narcissus' mirror image presaging his death.

[63] Fantham (1979), 339–40, 344.

reveals her awareness of her role inside tragic conventions as a woman fixed to one location and living only vicariously through her imagination. Given her fertile imagination, the elaborate mythologization of the dream appears even more redundant. Alcyone is an ideal candidate for Lucretius' explanation that dreams are merely a replica of our waking preoccupations (Lucretius 4.962–7).[64]

Alcyone has anticipated disaster from the start, extrapolating narratives of shipwreck from pieces of timber and cenotaphs (*Met.* 11.428–9). What is more, as daughter of Aeolus she claims to have seen the (personified) winds at work from the perspective of a spectator (*Met.* 11.433–8), an outrageously fictional situation for which she claims reality status as eyewitness (*nam novi et saepe paterna/ parva domo vidi*, 437–8).[65] Finally, the change of perspective from land to sea in the tempest narrative itself is framed by reference to Alcyone's sleep as if the events formed a dream of which she is not aware. She retires to bed when she no longer sees the ship (*seque toro ponit*, 472) and the scene changes to the high seas. The shipwreck is over by morning (Lucifer, 570); and the attention reverts to Alcyone (*interea Aeolis*, 573). Thus fiction, imagination, dream, and reality create multiple layers in this narrative.

Using the dream as meta-poetic reminder of the power of the imagination in constructing the semblance of reality, Ovid at once lays bare his tricks and ensnares the reader with them. At the beginning of the passage, he shows dreams imagined from without as tangible illusions. But once the dream is actualized in the narrative, the reader becomes complicit in accepting its truth on the level of fiction. Ryan, in examining virtual narration in postmodern fiction, comes to a remarkably similar conclusion, using dream as metaphor for the fictional experience:

> We can no more observe the stages of our own immersion than we can watch ourselves fall asleep. It is only retrospectively, like a person who awakens from a dream, that the reader realizes that the picture world has come to be experienced as primary reality. Immersion cannot be reflected from within immersion, but it can be forcefully enacted by the text from a state of distancing. In this enactment, virtual narration functions as a launching pad, not as a destination. Its fate is to fade into real narration, so that immersion can be lived as well as signified.[66]

[64] Perhaps even more so because hers are already fictional constructs, not real actions as in the examples taken from the male world of labor that Lucretius gives.

[65] Otis (1970), 251 notes the absence of divine apparatus in the tempest scene which contradicts this view and which creates a contrast "between the real and the unreal, the demythologized storm and the mythologized sleep ... the most personal and subjective of events – the lover's dream – is deliberately objectified and clothed in the garments of epic fantasy and myth."

[66] Ryan (1995), 284.

In Ovid, the literary device of the fictional dream plays the relative values of truth and verisimilitude off against each other as illusion is employed to assert reality. But Alcyone is not the only victim of this illusionism. Tissol has remarked on the ironic obsession with truthfulness in the passage.[67] How true is Alcyone's dream for the reader? Her dream is both a manifest presence of Morpheus, and thus not a figment of Alcyone's imagination, and it is true because the dream speech affirms the earlier narrative by verbatim repetition.[68] The irony of a lifelike Ceyx declaring his own death becomes even more pronounced if one considers the narrative dead-end that shipwrecks usually represent: nobody is left to tell the story. Yet if the story can be told by Ceyx, then maybe he is not altogether dead.[69] The exaggerated verisimilitude of the dream raises doubts about its literal truth, thereby preparing the reader for the even more miraculous final scene in which Alcyone, transformed into a bird, manages to revive Ceyx.

While the dream, despite some amount of poetic license, still reflects a plausible situation of shipwreck and empathic communication, the ensuing scene is clearly marked as waking reality, and the stranger for it. Feldherr points out the disturbing effect of metamorphosis on the perception of reality in the mind of the reader as well as in that of the victim. Commenting on the beginning sentence of Kafka's *Metamorphosis*, he writes:[70]

> The first words, with their resemblance to the classic fairy tale beginning 'once upon a time', seem to offer one possibility: we can normalize this supernatural event by assuming the story belongs to a genre that doesn't ask us to take it seriously, and even rejoice in the distance that separates us from a fictional world where such things are possible. So for Samsa there is the fleeting possibility that he is still dreaming.

Alcyone's transformation happens simultaneously with the expression of doubt by the narrator, as if working verbal magic by abracadabra: *insilit huc,* ***mirumque fuit potuisse****: volabat* (11.731). Ceyx's return to life is

[67] Tissol (1997), 79–81. He seems immune to doubting his own fictional belief in the story, leaving Ceyx and Alcyone as the only victims of Ovid's manipulation of language.

[68] Contrast the far more skeptical treatment of Isis' dream apparition in *Met.* 9.687–8: *ante torum … / aut stetit aut visa est.* Isis is of course an exotic goddess so maybe the skepticism is directed at her divine existence as much as at the truthfulness of the dream.

[69] Tissol (1997), 81: "In the domain of the word, however, formal conventions rule both dreams and stages; the power of the word is so great that it must be kept at the cost of verisimilitude." Cf. also Rosati (1983), 133–4 on Dryope who continues to speak even as metamorphosis is silencing her.

[70] Feldherr (2002), 163. The sentence in question is: "As Gregor Samsa awoke one morning from uneasy dreams, he found himself transformed in his bed into a monstrous insect."/ "Als Gregor Samsa eines Morgens aus unruhigen Träumen erwachte, fand er sich in seinem Bett zu einem ungeheueren Ungeziefer verwandelt."

likewise presented at first as possible optical illusion, while the metamorphosis is achieved by a simple exchange of vowels that turns on the change from objective to subjective perception (*senserit … senserat*): *senserit hoc Ceyx, an vultum motibus undae/ tollere sit visus, populus dubitabat: at ille/ senserat* (*Met.* 11.739–41). Ovid's trick of expressing disbelief or a psychologizing explanation before asserting the incredible as plain fact disarms the reader's potential protests at this manipulation.[71]

Appropriately enough, metamorphosis provides closure for an episode that had destabilized the absolute boundaries between waking and dreaming, fiction and reality, experiencing and imagining the tempest. The fictional characters, now transformed into birds, become part of the reader's extratextual reality. For most of the narrative, both Ceyx and Alcyone in human form are invoked as no more than visions, mirroring the fictionality of their existence.[72] Conversely, in their final incarnation as birds they present an allegorized image of conjugal love reflected in physical reality.

The imaginary view from the shore, central for depicting Alcyone's perception earlier, cements the distance between internal and external audience and characters in the final scene. While the reader shares the ground under his feet with the common-sense *populus*, the birds on the horizon are immortalized in their instability as creatures between sea and air. The familiar anthropomorphization of the birds' behavior as memory of their human heritage adds plausibility to the metamorphosis.

The relief at having successfully assimilated fiction into the frame of everyday reality is, however, short-lived, as an anonymous old man points out a similar bird and takes it as starting point for the story of Aesacus (*Met.* 11.749–50). The physical world itself, as referent for the verisimilitude of the fictional world, is not an unchanging tableau: it is a point of departure as well as arrival in the myriad storylines it contains through the inextricable link between metamorphosis and storytelling. Story results in metamorphosis, as in the case of Ceyx and Alcyone, or the result of metamorphosis can trigger story, as in the case of Aesacus. The fictional characters themselves destabilize the boundaries of fiction even further: Ceyx himself is a storyteller before becoming the subject of story himself.[73] The staged coincidence of telling Aesacus' story reconnects the narrative arc to the scene of Troy and thus to the primary level of narrative. Ovid marks the disruption caused by the story for the wider temporal frame

[71] Hardie (2002),173–4.

[72] See Tissol (1997), 74–5 and Hardie (2002), 280–2 for the importance of names as stand-in for bodies.

[73] See Barchiesi (1989); Feeney (1991), 230–2; Wheeler (1999).

of the poem by presenting it as a white spot on the map of the internal audience,[74] as if canceling out the entire episode in which Priam's ignorance of the fate of his son mirrors Alcyone's:[75] *Nescius assumptis Priamus pater Aesacon alis/ vivere lugebat ...* (*Met.* 12.1–2).

In contrast to the incompleteness that, according to Ronen, characterizes fiction in general, the worlds of the fictional and the real in Ovid's poem are inextricably connected through the concept of metamorphosis.[76] Just as in Ovid's simile of the dreams, these stories are at once tangible in their physical reifications and inherently as transient and multiform as the act of narration that brings them back to (fictional) life. The glimpses in and out of reality render the fictional barrier permeable, and make us uncertain on which side we are actually standing, eliding the absolute boundaries between story and reality, inside and outside of the book.

ATALANTA AND HIPPOMENES

For the *Metamorphoses*, an aetiological poem, the relationship of fiction and reality may also be expressed though time: the fictional past accounts for the real present. Ovid's poem begins as the world comes into being and finds closure as it draws down the narrative to his own time when story-world and the reality of contemporary Roman reality coalesce. Despite this underlying teleology, the poem's frequent shifts in narrators and the associative style of its transitions constantly defy such linear chronology. Wheeler has shown how the poem's internal narrative time emerges as a competing guide from these temporal contradictions, ordering narrative from the inside as the narrator or characters refer to events by association.[77] Such detachment from conventional chronology is possible because reader and primary narrator share the same extratextual timeframe – that of the Roman present.

Ovid's aetiological poem abounds in expressions that show the traces of fiction in reality, in the form of tangible relics of a fictional past. Thus the

[74] I use the geographical metaphor deliberately. The locals, in the form of the *senior aliquis*, know the story, while Priam at Troy, the center of epic storytelling, is unaware of it. Ovid thus integrates the local and the global in his universalizing narrative. See also Hardie (2002), 85 on the commemoration of Aesacus' name despite his lack of epic heroism.

[75] Both lead to inappropriate ritual action. Alcyone pollutes the altar by praying for one who is dead; Priam builds a cenotaph for a living (albeit as a bird) person. See Hardie (2002), 84–6, 247–8.

[76] Ronen (1988), 497. For the application of the possible worlds theory on Roman poetry see Edmunds (2001), 97–101.

[77] Wheeler (1999), 117: "The ostensible linearity of a world history of metamorphosis thus furnishes a pretext for a second narrative, or metanarrative, which is that of the poem's own performance."

play with time is also a play of being inside and outside of the poem, with the physical reality authenticating the story. It is no coincidence that such pointers to the present often come at the end of an episode. The device emphasizes closure as the reader is released from the spell of fiction and into the banal experience of reality, the world of things. And yet these tangible objects are the traces and triggers of the ephemeral story, banal only for the uninitiated. Anachronism reverses that direction by escorting the reader across the threshold into the mythical past; Ovid's poem abounds in these, too.[78] The intrusion of contemporary detail in the mythical past reminds the reader of his role in reimagining it, as if leaving traces in fiction through his presence. The disruption is notable because the detail breaks the illusion of verisimilitude; it is real outside of fiction but not plausible inside it.

With the significant exception of the much-discussed Augustan references at the beginning and close of the poem, such anachronisms are not historical but rather accentuate the prototechnological, natural innocence of the mythical past as opposed to the sophistication of an undefined Roman present, that is between the experience of the fictional character and that of the reader.[79] While characters are bound by their location in the story, by limitations such as geography, gender, experience (sometimes overcome by their role as internal audience), the reader, whose limited insight resembles theirs in real life, shares the poet's universal view. Anachronism functions as a reminder of this conspiracy.

Anachronism, like dirt, is matter out of place, although it should not be brushed off as inattention. As a deliberately placed reminder of the extratextual reality, it lets down the fictional mask of the narrator in the same way as Ovid's frequent addresses to the reader, another break with epic conventions. What is more, Solodow notes that a distinction was made already in antiquity between anachronism in the narrative and anachronism in the simile. Scholiasts criticized the former while allowing the latter, arguing that the simile is an expression out of the mouth of the narrator.[80]

78 I am here narrowly concerned with the divide between the inside and outside of the poem. For the poem's internal anachronisms see Wheeler (1999), 117–39, Feeney (1999b), Gildenhard and Zissos (1999).

79 A deliberate break from Virgil who uses anachronism to predict the Augustan age. For the differences between Virgil and Ovid and more examples of anachronism, see Solodow (1988), 75–89. For anachronism in Virgil see Sandbach (1990).

80 Solodow (1988), 76 concludes: "Similes, then, we may dismiss from our consideration." He quotes (239, n.1) Hyg. ap. Gell. 10.16, Servius on Virgil *Aen.* 3.703, Norden on Virgil *Aen.* 6.2 with further examples, including the A and T scholia on *Il.* 21.362, Euripides' *Phoen.* 6, and Apollonius Rhodius *Arg.* 4.553.

Thus Latreus wielding a Macedonian *sarisa* in his fight with Caeneus (*Met.* 12.479) is an anachronism,[81] even more so because the detail is part of Nestor's internal narrative, but a simile comparing the boar in Meleager's hunt to a siege-engine is admissible because the simile provides distance from the narrative proper (*Met.* 8.355–61). On closer inspection however, one can see that both provide an effective commentary on the battle narrative. Latreus strikes Caeneus with an impossible weapon, unsurpassed in Ovid's own time but non-existent in the archaic age. The anachronism perfectly emblematizes the warrior's superior strength that becomes powerless in the face of Caeneus; it suggests that the weapon might as well not be there. The simile of the siege-engine in book 8 likewise comments on the epic action in this episode, particularly as it is used in a typically epic fashion to render the overwhelming size of the enemy, thus drawing attention to its own status as hallmark of the genre. Again, the anachronism 'modernizes' the quaint fight for Ovid's contemporary reader, while its hyperbole functions as a reminder that this hunt takes place outside the edge of epic proper, that is the sacking of cities and especially Troy, emphasized at other places by the appearance of pre-Homeric characters, such as Castor and Pollux before their catasterism (*At gemini, nondum caelestia sidera, fratres, Met.* 8.372).

Despite these similarities in effect, the formal distinction between anachronistic detail and anachronistic simile is valid since one places an object inside the fictional landscape while the other aims to convey an impression in the terms of Ovid's contemporary audience, leaving the scene itself undisturbed. However, the multiplicity of narrators in the poem complicates the matter considerably: in the *Metamorphoses*, the practice of metadiegesis frequently removes the primary narrator from view. A prominent example for such an anachronism is the infamous pipe simile in the Pyramus and Thisbe episode (*Met.* 3.120–24). This simile is highly disruptive both because the simile itself is at odds with the rural and ancient setting and because the character who utters it (one of the Minyeides) cannot be aware of Roman plumbing and thus is technically incapable of making the comparison. Ovid thus calls into question the independence of his characters by openly displaying his hand. Newlands has convincingly argued that in doing so he casts the Minyeides' exaggerated trust in art over nature as ignorance: "Ironically, the daughters of Minyas seem unaware of the warnings implicit in their stories."[82] The

[81] Solodow (1988), 240 n.5 discusses the instances of *sarisa* in Latin literature.
[82] Newlands (1986), 150.

anachronistic simile thus can be a tool of the contemporary primary narrator to show his control of the narrative and defeat his artist doubles, all of whom, as Leach has shown, lose the ability to practice their art and are destroyed (Arachne, Minyeides, Orpheus, Pygmalion).[83]

Among the anachronistic similes, the subcategory that alludes to the Roman stage promises a particularly intriguing insight into the negotiation of fictional illusion. Such similes alert the reader to the 'staged' quality of the text, not only in pointing to the provenance of Ovid's material from tragedy,[84] but also in foregrounding the transition of representation into reality. Feldherr describes the surreal effect of the near congruence of simile and narrative at *Met.* 3.111–14 as the sown men are compared to figures on a theater curtain: "Correspondingly Ovid omits the transition from simile back to narrative, as though the figures themselves have stepped off the curtain to become <<real>> warriors whom Cadmus encounters."[85] The anachronistic reference to the Roman theater makes the reader identify with Cadmus' uneasy role of spectator as the simile self-referentially plays with the crossing of the fictional boundary and 'stages' the reader's gradual immersion in the text.

The layering of multiple narrators is a prominent technique to achieve the total absorption of the reader in the story in which the act of storytelling becomes a way to suspend action on the primary level. The song of Orpheus occupies most of book 10 and features in miniature the practice of metadiegesis in the poem as a whole. The anachronistic simile that compares the color of Atalanta's body to marble tinged red by the awning in the theater (*Met.* 10.794–6)[86] shows the ripple effect it creates both in the tiers of narrators at this point and in the wider context of the scene and the poem.

That Ovid is aware of the anachronism can easily be shown by reference to it in Ovid's own *Ars amatoria*. As he gives a mock aetiology for sexual conquest in the theater using the rape of the Sabines as exemplum, he draws attention to the setting (*Ars am.* 1.103–106):

> Tunc neque marmoreo pendebant vela theatro
> nec fuerant liquido pulpita rubra croco;
> illic, quas tulerant nemorosa Palatia, frondes
> simpliciter positae scaena sine arte fuit

[83] Leach (1974). For a useful summary of the polarized discussion around Orpheus see Lateiner (1984), 27 n.65.
[84] Hardie (1990), 226 n.14. [85] Feldherr (1997), 37.
[86] *Pace* Bömer (1969–86) ad loc. and Salzman-Mitchell (2005a), 171 who stipulate a domestic context.

Back then there were no coverings hanging over the marble theater nor were the seats red with liquid saffron; there, the leaves that the woody Palatine wore, arranged simply, made a stage without art.

Ovid simultaneously suggest and removes the anachronistic detail of the awning, alluding to Propertius' technique in the opening poem of book 4 which evokes an archaic past by direct negative comparison with the elegance of contemporary Rome.[87] The simile thus evokes the fashionable urbanity of the present found in Roman (and particularly Ovidian) love elegy. What is more, Ovid's simile has its model in Lucretian color theory (Lucretius 4.75–83) where part of its magic is the evocation of the theater with complete disregard for the spectacle proper. In Lucretius, the audience of respectable Republican Rome, the mothers and fathers, as opposed to the lowlifes on stage, becomes the spectacle.[88] This inversion of spectacle and audience is useful to keep in mind in the following discussion.

The simile is anachronistic in a triple sense, not only because it is uttered by a fictional character (Venus) and applied to an archaic setting, but also because it is put in her mouth by Ovid's poet double, Orpheus, himself an archaic character. The intricate nature of Orpheus' song thus accentuates the anachronism of the simile. However, rather than seeing only the primary narrator behind the simile, we shall see how it influences the poetics of each in turn. The motivation of Venus, Orpheus, and the narrator are all connected.

To begin with the innermost level, Venus. Venus begins her storytelling with an Alexandrian footnote (*forsitan audieris aliquam certamine cursus/ veloces superasse viros, Met.* 10.560–1) that delays mentioning Atalanta's name until the oracle pronounces it in line 565. The most intriguing source text for this allusion turns out to be the song of Silenus in Virgil's *Eclogue* 6.60 where the story of Atalanta is paraphrased in one line.[89] The paraphrase thus evokes an irrecoverable vocal performance (explaining Venus' *audieris*) which survives only as subject of song but not as the song itself. Thomas has drawn attention to the intricate layering of narrators in this eclogue;[90] the allusion to it in Ovid thus simultaneously draws attention to his own layering of narrators as inspired by the Virgilian model. What is more, Silenus is a mock version of the Orpheus figure (Virgil *Ecl.* 6.25–30). Ovid's allusion to *Eclogue* 6 thus nods to the bucolic setting of

[87] Propertius 4.1.15–16: *nec sinuosa cavo pendebant vela theatro/ pulpita sollemnis non oluere crocos*. See Hinds (1987), 34–5 and n.30.

[88] Perfectly illustrating Lucretius' maxim of poetry being subservient to philosophy.

[89] *Pace* Knox (1986) who sees an allusion to the alternate version (Milanion) in Propertius 1.1.15.

[90] Thomas (1998).

the *Eclogues* which dominate both the external setting of Orpheus and the internal setting of Venus' song but makes Orpheus replace the famously ugly Silenus with the goddess Venus, proverbial for her beauty. Of course, Virgil himself alludes to Theocritus' third *Idyll* (40–3; 45–8) in which Silenus tells the story of Hippomenes/Atalanta and of Adonis/Venus as mythical exempla in order to win over Amaryllis.[91] The allusion creates a ripple effect – who has 'heard' Silenus' song, Ovid, Orpheus or Venus? Although it is obviously the poet who creates the allusion, its force is amplified by the implied consciousness of literary history which his fictional characters possess as artists in their own right, especially so since Virgil's *Eclogues* version plays with the ephemerality of song as opposed to writing. The background history of the song itself adds to the effect of the anachronistic simile as it openly acknowledges the presence of the reader in deciphering the allusion.

Venus, in Orpheus' characterization a careful poet in her own right, uses poetry in order to seduce Adonis as she relinquishes her pretended role as the huntress Diana. Seeking shade and rest from the unusual exhaustion (*insolitus labor, Met.* 10.554), she reassumes her identity (*adsuetaque semper in umbra/ indulgere sibi formamque augere colendo, Met.* 10.533–4). Venus draws attention to her proverbial beauty in a triangulating comparison with subject and addressee of her song that simultaneously deconstructs the prevalent standard simile of Diana as measure for a virgin's beauty (*Met.* 10.578–80):

> ut faciem et posito corpus uelamine uidit
> (quale meum, uel quale tuum, si femina fias),
> obstipuit tollensque manus 'ignoscite' dixit …

When he saw her face and, her dress cast aside, her body, like mine (or like yours if you were a woman) he was struck and raising his hands, he said: "Forgive me"…

In using herself as the object of comparison, Venus incarnates her own simile,[92] eliding the barrier between story subject and narrator, and alludes to her own status as object of artistic representation, most famously in the Aphrodite of Cnidos that corresponds exactly to the pose implied here (*posito … velamine*). Without the Diana costume (*Met.* 10.536), the naked

[91] Ovid's combination of both mythical exempla restores the Theocritean version from Virgil's who only mentions Atalanta.

[92] Note also the quasi-epiphanic reaction of Hippomenes (*obstipuit tollensque manus, Met.* 10.580). See the discussion in Chapter 2 (on Icarus and Daedalus) and the phrase *vidit et obstipuit* in conjunction with the divine.

Venus reveals herself as the ideal of beauty.[93] What is more, the bizarre reference to Adonis' hypothetical gender switch recalls that Adonis himself is very much an artistic creation. At his birth (*Met.* 10.515–18), Adonis is compared to a painting of Cupid in what Hardie has termed an approximative simile, a simile that is virtually congruent with what it aims to illustrate.[94] The parenthesis *si femina fias* corresponds to the earlier emendation of the picture *aut huic adde levis, aut illi deme pharetras* (10.518). From the outset, Venus sets up the Atalanta story as a thinly veiled double for her own attraction to Adonis when she alludes to their own artistic representations as forerunners of their fictionalized counterparts.

As Venus takes her audience inside the story, she explicitly focalizes the simile through its male protagonist, Hippomenes. While he muses on Atalanta's beauty, he is overtaken in his thoughts by the action (*Met.* 10.586–90):[95]

dum talia secum
exigit Hippomenes, passu uolat alite uirgo.
quae quamquam Scythica non setius ire sagitta
Aonio uisa est iuueni, tamen ille decorem
miratur magis; et cursus facit ipse decorem.

While Hippomenes pondered these things within himself, the maiden flew past on winged course, and although she seemed to the Aonian youth to go no less slowly than a Scythian arrow, still he marveled even more at her beauty; the run itself lent her beauty.

Instead of introducing the heroine, the simile follows on her heels. Atalanta's entry on the scene mid-flight, not as static beauty but as deadly missile, mocks the literary convention that fixes the beloved in an artistic pose.[96] The litotes *non setius* and the concessive *quamquam* show the inherent contradiction in admiring a moving target, while the familiar phrase *visa est* captures in its double meaning ("was seen" and "seemed") the uncertainty of her fleeting vision. The text now slows down with a description of her body, or rather her hair and feet, the two parts that

[93] Pliny *HN* 36.20–21 tells how Praxiteles made two copies, one clothed and one naked. Stewart sums up the watershed moment that this statue represents for Greek art, s.v. Praxiteles OCD (3rd edn): "In the Cnidia he simply took the final, logical step: the essence of the love goddess was her body, so it must be revealed." The simile is a pointed rejoinder to Diana's prudishness who is the only other goddess seen in the nude (*Met.* 3.192).

[94] Hardie (2004), 101–2.

[95] In a Homeric simile Hera's movement is as swift as human thought (*Il.* 15.82). It appears that Atalanta is even quicker!

[96] See Hardie (2002), 185 on *Aen.* 1.494–5 (Dido's entrance).

illustrate her movement (590–3) before another simile gallantly illustrates the absence of clothes (*Met.* 10.594–6):

> inque puellari corpus candore ruborem
> traxerat, haud aliter quam cum super atria uelum
> candida purpureum simulatas inficit umbras.

Her body with its maidenly whiteness took on redness, not unlike when the purple cloth over the white atria dyes them with artificial shade.

The color that the marble takes on covers Atalanta's naked body both in the literal and figurative sense. Despite the attention that Hippomenes pays, the glance of the reader is deflected from her body to the abstract play of light in the auditorium.[97] The simile thus adds to the ironic play with the role of spectator that Rosati had pointed out earlier: "così come Ippomene è spectator della gara di corsa tra Atalanta e i suoi pretendenti, (10.575), in tutta la lora *icastica* teatralità."[98] Atalanta's body becomes a cross-textual symbol, both a reminder that she is the spectacle and that her naked running corresponds to the custom of picking up girls in the theater. The simile centers on the color and thus draws out an abstraction that goes beyond the physical description to draw attention to the reader's own involved spectatorship.

At the same time, Atalanta's body, reddened from physical exertion, unwittingly gives away her innocence and sexual attraction in the codified red/white contrast that indicates erotic responsiveness.[99] Her complete naturalness contrasts with the artificial elements of the simile, both in the purple dye of the awning and the manufactured shade it gives (*simulatas inficit umbras*, 596). The interplay between the natural and the artificial also refers to the simile's function in illustrating the naked body by covering it up in the process.

The simile's anachronistic image, meaningless and redundant for Venus and Orpheus' audience,[100] singles out Ovid's contemporary reader as the intended audience as it comments on the obfuscation of the immediate image that is relayed from the innermost audience to the eavesdropping

97 Cf. the similarly evasive simile of Diana's blush (*Met.* 3.181–5) that I discuss in Chapter 2.

98 Rosati (1983), 144 (emphasis mine).

99 Dyson (1999), 282–3 argues for Atalanta as a conflation of Virgil's Lavinia and Camilla. Atalanta, however, is still more innocent than Lavinia, as her body does *not* betray her emotions. See Fabre-Serris (1995), 225. Compare also the pseudo-naive wounding of Venus by Cupid: *Namque pharetratus dum dat puer oscula matri/ inscius exstanti destrinxit harundine pectus* (*Met.* 10.525–6) as opposed to Atalanta's ignorance of what love is: *Dixerat utque rudis primoque cupidine tacta/ quid facit ignorans, amat et non sentit amorem* (*Met.* 10.636–7).

100 Adonis may look at Venus for illustration, Orpheus' audience is made up of animals and trees.

reader in the fourth degree (Hippomenes as focalizing character, Venus, Orpheus, narrator).

Both similes play with two aspects of time in relation to the manufacturing of the fictional illusion. First, both are anachronistic and thus openly refer to the reader's need to have the scene illustrated not only by a simile but by a contemporary one that illustrates the beauty and speed of Atalanta in terms that are still impressive for Ovid's reader, rather than have them match the archaic setting with an old-fashioned image. The second aspect of time is the slowdown of narrative time in the simile, acknowledging the presence of the reader in the text. Both times, Hippomenes is made out as distracted by the simile (*dum secum exigit*, *dum notat*). In marking the narrative time it takes for the simile to be noted down,[101] written, reimagined, it displays the interference of the need for comparison to render the immediate experience of seeing Atalanta.

Salzman-Mitchell argues that the similes focalized by Hippomenes aim to immobilize Atalanta.[102] In fact, it is the opposite: Atalanta trips Hippomenes' power of observation as on two occasions she moves faster than he can look – *ut vidit* ... [simile] *obstipuit* (10.578–80); *dum talia secum/ exigit...volat...virgo* (10.586–7); [simile] *Aonio visa est iuveni*, ... *miratur magis* (10.589–90); [simile] *dum notat haec hospes* (10.597). Hippomenes sees only her back (*tergaque*, 592) not because she resembles a statue but because he looks after her. The race is over by the time Hippomenes awakens from his contemplative trance. This tripping up is mutual: Hippomenes is able to outstrip Atalanta because he has taken his fill looking while she is tempted by the sight of the golden apples (*obstipuit*, 580 (Hippomenes); *obstipuit virgo* ... */ declinat cursum* ... */ praeterit Hippomenes*, 666–68). The simile thus manipulates the awareness of time for the audience slowing down in contemplation of Atalanta's beauty while the effect of the race continuing in the meantime makes her appear to run even faster.

As Klein has argued, Venus aims at matching the speed of her discourse to that of her subject, revealing a Callimachean preference for concision. Yet the point is not just the race for the finishing line but rather a toying with what Genette has termed *vitesse narrative*, the experience of tempo,

101 Both verbs connote reflexivity; see OLD s.v. *noto*: (2) to mark (a passage is a manuscript, etc.) as important, (9) to represent, delineate, (13) to be conscious of seeing, to observe; OLD s.v. *exigo*: (10c) to turn over in one's mind, to ponder. The permeability of the text as it is being written is pointed out by Sharrock (1994) in the case of *Ars am.* 2.77–8 (Icarus) where the internal character, a fisherman, and the poet both drop their *harundo* in amazement.

102 Salzman-Mitchell (2005b).

of fast and slow in the narrative. Thus Atalanta is a model for Venus' Callimachean poetics that coincides also with the art of seduction.[103]

Venus attempts to recreate the dynamics of the race in her own 'performance' as storyteller, on which the reader is allowed to eavesdrop. The layering of narrators and readers is an aspect that Klein neglects as she talks about *Venus'* poetics and her *reader*. The anachronism in the simile, however, calls such a direct relationship into question. Venus as narrator is well aware of the conventions of the divine in poetry as she relates how she interceded in the outcome of the game, invisible to anyone but Hippomenes (*Met.* 10.650–1). By contrast, the simile is invisible to everybody but the contemporary reader. Thus the slowdown of the narrative turns out to be a paradox that results from the layering of narrators, performing a function in Venus' narrative that Venus herself cannot control. The anachronistic simile contradicts the fiction of her viva-voce performance as it is fixed in time, clearly marked as belonging to the reality of the written book.[104] Thus the simile's anachronism adds another dimension to the interplay of the two concepts of narrative versus narrated time, taking into account the time outside fiction which contradicts the spontaneity of the dynamic race and competitive storytelling. The focalization of the anachronistic simile through Hippomenes slows the race down and communicates suspense to the reader. Paradoxically, this same effect is invisible to the focalizer himself who has an unobstructed view of Atalanta's naked body.

Rather than reinforcing the immersion in the innermost ring of narration by having the reader share a timeless simile with the multiple audiences, the temporal rigidity of the anachronistic simile reminds the reader at this point of the distance from the primary narrative, and alerts him to the approaching end of the book that coincides with Orpheus' song and the suspension of time through song in the outer narrative frame. In having the viewpoints of primary narrator and innermost focalizer touch, the anachronistic simile would suggest that the deeper one digs, the more one returns to the surface. But the simile of Atalanta's body can also be shown to have meaning for the intermediary narrator Venus, and finally

103 Klein (2005), 161: "sa [sc.Venus'] définition de la brièveté ne consiste pas à courir la poste, plantant là son lecteur frustré par un ouvrage trop rapide et trop succinct, mais à attendre ce lecteur, en jouant avec lui, confiante dans sa capacité à faire preuve, dès qu'il le faudra, de brièveté et d'accélération suffisantes pour ne jamais sembler être un ouvrage long et lent." In the same context (162) she quotes Ovid's *Ars am.* 2.717–18: *Crede mihi, non est Veneris properanda voluptas,/ sed sensim tarda prolicienda mora.*

104 On the opposition of singing and writing see Wheeler (1999), 58–65.

for Orpheus. Why does Orpheus put the words in Venus' mouth, why does the narrator put them in Orpheus'?

A central irony of the description of Atalanta is that because of her nakedness (*posito corpus velamine*, 578) there is not much left to describe.[105] The simile has to lend a hand in conjuring up her beauty through reference to another piece of cloth (*velum/ ... purpureum*, 595–6).[106] Thus the customary ekphrasis is virtually impossible. The absence of formal ekphrasis is even more telling when one considers that Atalanta's name double from book 8 (8.323–8) receives hers in a prominent position at the end of the hunters' catalogue.[107] Orpheus' choice of an Atalanta for Venus' song is ripe with intratextual allusion to the famous boar-killer. Even when she plays huntress, Venus is no Atalanta, as she avoids wild boars (*a fortibus abstinet apris, Met.* 10.539) and counsels Adonis against hunting them, calling them contrary to her nature (10.548–51). They are singled out (along with lions) as being the animals most hateful to her; a boar causes Adonis' death later (10.710–16). The doubling of Atalanta in the *Metamorphoses* is thus explained by Venus' own exigencies in making Atalanta more like her, and Orpheus' characterization of Venus as a failed Diana look-alike.

An additional irony is the internal contradiction of the two similes that illustrate Atalanta's body. The first, that of Atalanta looking like Venus or a woman Adonis, is theoretically restricted to the immediate audience of the story, Adonis. The second, referring to the theater setting outside the mythical reality, is only available to the reader. Thus Atalanta's body may be read as a symbol for the inability to cross fictional barriers, her nakedness standing for the gap in direct communication from internal narrator to reader.

While Venus positions herself in the narrative as both narrator and divine participant, the contradiction of the two similes suggests that she is ultimately another narrating character in a bigger frame and cannot control all of her discourse. As the anachronistic simile is located at the

[105] Without becoming indiscreet. Cf. Ovid *Am.* 1.5.17–23 where the *puella* is described *posito velamine*. Anderson (1966), 4 comments on his predecessors' contortions on the meaning of *talaria*: "There Hippomenes is, raptly surveying the nude loveliness of the speeding girl, and what choice detail does Ovid use to enhance the moment and Hippomenes' raptures? Her shoe laces! Surely Ovid deserves better from his commentators."

[106] Cf. also the personification of Sun in book 2. Phoebus covers his nakedness with a purple gown: *purpurea velatus veste sedebat/ in solio Phoebus claris lucente smaragdis* (*Met.* 2.23–4).

[107] The two Atalantas are also linked through a triangulating allusion to Camilla (*Met.* 10.654–5 ~ Virgil *Aen.* 7.808–9; *Met.* 8.318–21 ~ Virgil *Aen.* 7.815–17 but 7.814–815 ~ *Met.* 10.594–6) and to Parthenopaeus, son of Hippomenes and Atalanta, in *Met.* 8.322–3 (about Atalanta) *talis erat cultu, facies quam dicere vere/ virgineam in puero, puerilem in virgine possis*; *Met.* 10.631 (about Hippomenes) *a! quam virgineus puerili vultus in ore est!*

deepest point of immersion, it shows how far the reader has followed in building up the fictionality of the text. Its anachronism grows with each narrative instance from Orpheus as mythical, bucolic narrator to Venus to her focalizing character Hippomenes. The similes thus show up the heightened immediacy of performance, the dynamics of both the race and Venus' attempt to match it in her storytelling, with the artificial quality of the text that recreates it.

The Atalanta story provides closure for both Orpheus' song and book 10. At the beginning of the next book, the primary narrator reasserts himself as Orpheus returns to being a character in the narrative. In an ironic allusion to the anachronistic simile in Orpheus' own song with which the narrator pointed to his presence in that text, he now picks up the imagery and applies it in an amphitheater simile to Orpheus (*Met.* 11.25–7). Thus the tragic irony of the singer's incongruous performance is turned on himself as the Thracian women, acting out their pseudo-tragic roles as maenads, attack to dismember him. Reality and fiction are inverted in the staged quality of Orpheus' end that contrasts with the bucolic escape from reality in his inset tales.[108] Once his own spell is released, the singer is unable to control the fictional reality around him which is governed by the primary narrator.

Yet another twist is added when one considers that Calliope uses a version of the awning simile in telling the rape of Proserpina to Minerva in book 5 (*silva coronat aquas cingens latus omne, suisque/ frondibus ut velo Phoebeos submovet ictus, Met.* 5.388–9). Calliope is Orpheus' mother, his *musa parens,* whom he invokes at the beginning of book 10 as inspiring his song (*Met.* 10.148), and whose own performance becomes an intratextual source for the simile. Hinds has shown how the evocation of the amphitheater at *Met.* 5.388–9 is used to undermine the staging of the *locus amoenus,* a cautionary note on the bucolic remoteness in which both Proserpina and Orpheus find themselves.[109] Yet the extraordinary length and complexity of the inset tale makes the reader forget that Orpheus exists outside his singing as a character in a fictional landscape himself. The simile of the tinged marble in Orpheus' tale renders erotic attraction as a fascination with beauty as an end in itself, while the simile that is used on Orpheus by the primary narrator (*Met.* 11.25–7) forcefully returns the gaze on the spectacle and breaks the spell of the self-absorbed aesthetics of the audience in his bucolic utopia.

[108] Miller (1990), 146–7. [109] Hinds (1987), 34–5.

The incongruous note of anachronism in the simile thus affirms the narrator's primary control of the poem by making visible how far the reader has immersed himself in the fictional illusion. Ovid uses the exception of the anachronistic simile pointedly at times of the narrative in which he alludes to the fabric of fiction itself and the manipulation of the reader's perception, believing even the most remote myths plausible. The break with verisimilitude is a reminder of the paper-thin division of real and fictional, and of the depth created by the multiple narrators in the poem, a depth that confuses the reader's sense of temporal orientation. The anachronistic simile, as direct communication between reader and author, is a way to tell the reader that he is complicit with the author in allowing the mythical past to become real in fiction.

Conclusion: The protean nature of the simile

> And as imagination bodies forth
> The forms of things unknown, the poet's pen
> Turns them to shapes and gives to airy nothing
> A local habitation and a name.
>
> Shakespeare, *Midsummer Night's Dream* v.i.14–17[1]

When Peleus fails to capture the goddess Thetis who eludes him in the form of a bird, a tree, and a tigress, the hero seeks the advice of the many-figured Proteus. The latter counsels perseverance and warns not to be deceived by the frightening spectacle of Thetis' many shapes (*ne te decipiat centum mentita figuras,/ sed preme quicquid erit, dum, quod fuit ante, reformet!*, *Met.* 11.243–4). Peleus is lucky and wins Thetis – even though the larger conflict of their respective spheres, land versus sea, mortal versus immortal, looms ahead.

The parade of the many faces of the simile and the varied strategies for which it is employed has shown the immense adaptability of the figure. It remains now to ask how the simile itself, as a figure, changes in this context. Its nature is as irreducible as that of Proteus or Thetis; its attraction lies in the ability to generate likenesses which mirror and refract the figures of the narrative. Ovid's similes draw attention to themselves; they do not fit into a superstructure of imagery but work against the grain as hermeneutical puzzles that open up new complexities. Sameness and difference are the two poles between which the simile vacillates. This radical focus on the functioning of the simile itself reveals the fault lines between truth and illusion, seeming and being, and the constraints of categorization.

The simile works as the catalyst to the problem of identity at the heart of the *Metamorphoses*. Its reaction with the context makes it predestined to express the interaction of appearance and identity central to the meaning of the poem. It is precisely the fact that the simile is not capable of

[1] Wells, S. and Taylor, G. (eds.) *William Shakespeare: The Complete Works*, 2nd edn, Oxford, 2005.

effecting permanent change that makes it such a powerful antidote to the iconic power of the *Metamorphoses*. As human beings turn into mute animals, stars, or rocks and are thus reduced to their physical shape, the simile points at the more complex and unresolved problems of the transformation.

Throughout this book, the focus has been on the way in which the simile configures form; it is now time to turn towards its own form and the qualities of its nature.

STATES OF BEING

Metamorphosis involves a transfer of identity. A human being turns into or is transformed into a non-human being, sometimes even into something inanimate. How to tell where and when one ends and the other begins? While metamorphosis is presented as neatly divided by the before and after of the physical transformation, the continuity of the mind, in memory and consciousness, connects the two states. The simile captures this ambiguity of being "neither fish nor fowl."

Similes mark major moments of transition, entrances, and metamorphoses. Thus the simile opens up a character's identity beyond positive description; in stating a likeness, the edges of the discrete state of an individual are frayed. At the same time, insofar as the likeness only connects and approximates, it shows the distance between the *comparans* and the *comparandum*. In this negotiation of similarity and difference the simile develops its destabilizing force. To use a term from the visual arts, what results is a "negative space" delineated on either side by the real object and the object in the comparison, but with its focus on the undefined, "empty" middle. The simile makes a positive identification less certain, and the notion of identity gets expanded as something potentially fluid and diffusive.

The step from literal to figurative thus becomes also a step across the boundary from one level of being to another. The simile marks the transcendence from the defined actual identity to the ambivalent level of figurative identity. The copula "like" introduces a vagueness that expresses the difficulty of interpretation. This is amplified particularly in Ovid's preference for simile chains. Not only does this style draw attention to the varying degree of likeness, the simile sequence develops an internal dynamic, as if the image of the comparison would not hold steady. The best example of this is Polyphemus' love song for Galatea in book 13 in which an interminable simile list only proves the Cyclops' failure to capture her elusiveness. The more he tries, the more he fails. Similes may then be said not so much to capture as to create ambivalent states, holding identity in suspension.

This state of suspension does not necessarily imply balance but rather an underlying tension. The sense of unrest is especially palpable at the stage of coming into being and disappearing, capturing such concepts as "losing oneself," "growing into oneself," "being beside oneself." A particular specialty of the *Metamorphoses* is the quasi-tautological simile which suggests a likeness that mimics reality almost to the point of doubling. In this kind of simile contrast is downplayed to such a degree that it strains the relation between literal and figurative states. This pull towards certain, discrete identity also shows in such formulations as *et primo similis volucri/ mox vera volucris (at first like a bird, soon a real bird)* (*Met.* 13.607) in which the existential doubt is erased by simplifying repetition. Ovid's overt experimentation with the basic function of the simile affects form in a way that affects substance. By drawing a line that both connects and divides the simile makes visible the interstices of discrete identity.

MATERIALITY AND EKPHRASIS

The simile is a verbal image, that is, it produces a mental image with the help of words. This process replicates in miniature the production of mental images in the narrative. The simile is in a sense supernumerate insofar as it adds yet another image to an already rich visual landscape. Yet there is nothing given about this landscape and the actors in it. Even a formulaic introduction of a grotto ponders the visual authenticity of nature imitating art: *est specus in medio, natura factus an arte,/ ambiguum magis arte tamen (a grotto lies in the middle; perhaps created by nature, perhaps by art; art seems more likely)* (*Met.* 11.235–6). Since the simile image exists on a different plane from the images in the narrative, it presents an additional layer, concealing or revealing the truth by concentrating on surfaces and the visual logic of appearances. The poem stages the act of looking and reminds the reader about the artistic creation of its scenes. This insistence on surfaces creates a sense of impenetrability, a kind of painterly "flatness" in which form rules absolute. Yet it is this illusionist perfection that gives room for doubt and allows for questioning the relation between form and essence, looking and being alike. In being "painterly" the poem uses the wrong mode of narration, the mimetic world of painting versus the complex world of narration.

Ovid's ekphrastic similes in particular examine the prominent inherited function of illustration. The ekphrastic simile seems to pass the task to the "ready-mades" of sculpture and painting but it also challenges them insofar as it diminishes the power of their visual perfection. Their status is approximate; the comparison with the visual arts suggests an ideal which the character, like a regular being, can only aspire to: the vision is only ever "like," not a complete illustration. What the simile extracts from the artifact turns out to be its aura of stillness and beauty while its perfection becomes heightened because its visual impact cannot be reproduced.

The exact opposite are similes which focus on visual impressions that are impossible to paint because they lack form – such as the yellow mud of Adonis or the pure color that screens the naked body of Diana. These similes win over painting because they depict formlessness and divide what is indivisible in art: color and line. The simile's hybrid nature, both verbal and visual, draws on and challenges the strategies of the visual arts, in sketching and copying, in foregrounding and playing with dimensions, and not least in the challenge to the senses as a source of truth.

There is a second aspect to the nature of the simile as a verbal image. The simile is an extraneous image insofar as it has no material substance of its own but is the product of a mental association. Like the grin of the Cheshire cat, the simile produces a mental image only in order to abstract some quality from it – it is not the material presence of the cat that is important but the emotional effect of its trace. In contrast to the narrative landscape and its figures, which are assumed as real, the simile is a mental image of the second degree, provoked by a reaction to what is "seen" on the primary plane. The simile has the potential to attach to anything like a parasite; its free-floating ephemerality bestows the illusion of depth and substance on something precisely through contrast with its own lack of those qualities.

It is a striking contradiction that the subject of the simile is the physical world; in fact the world of the simile bears more resemblance to the physical world than to that of the fantastic narrative. Its persuasive force derives from the simplicity of its subjects – natural phenomena that can be observed by anyone. However, the effect of connecting object and subject can range from the outrageous (the curd-like Centaur's brain) to the insidiously appropriate (the flower-like head of Hyacinthus). Why should this matter?

The simile uses the material world not just for purposes of illustration but even more for emotional impact. It uses the "pathetic fallacy" that ascribes to nature and its phenomena feelings, meaning, and patterns which exist only in the mind of the beholder. Yet in using a mental image of a material substance, the simile also exposes the circularity of "reading" the material world. In the context of the poem, the physical consequences of metamorphosis present a barrier which cannot be overcome except for interpreting the new form in anthropomorphizing fashion. The simile thus captures in its form the central contradiction between immateriality and materiality. It seeks to transmit something immaterial through the mental image of something material. In communicating this mode of seeing rather than an actual sight, it shows the human mind as capable of looking through the physical world with the aid of its visual memory that forms random associations and exposes layers of meaning.

The unique position of the simile in the context of the *Metamorphoses* comes out of Ovid's experimentation with the form and convention of this highly traditional figure. The simile couples rather than unites different subjects and thus preserves the inherent tension. The figure itself contains these contradictions: it disavows positive statements in favor of ambiguity; it plays with the verbal and visual aspects of its hybrid nature; and it draws out the immaterial from the physical world. It is the poetic figure most concerned with appearances, while leaving a critical distance open to reflection. Considering the simile among other prominent poetical figures in the poem, such as metaphor, syllepsis, allegory, one detects a general tendency towards entropy that mirrors that of metamorphosis, a merging of word and reality. The simile resists through the barrier of its formulaic "like," and thus enables a reading against the grain. Despite its traditional credentials, in the *Metamorphoses* the simile undergoes the most radical reinterpretation which tests its limits and resonates with the great themes of the poem. The protean nature of the simile eludes the grasp of categorization; the appeal lies in following through its many permutations without getting deceived by its many forms – its essence is alterity.

Bibliography

Abbreviations follow those used in *L'Année Philologique.*

Adams, J. (1982) *The Latin Sexual Vocabulary*. Baltimore, MD.

Ahl, F. (1985) *Metaformations: Soundplay and Wordplay in Ovid and Other Classical Poets*. Ithaca, NY.

Albrecht, M. von (1977) "'Epische' und 'Elegische' Erzählung: Ovids zwei Daedalusfassungen" in *Römische Poesie: Texte und Interpretationen*, 63–79. Heidelberg.

Anderson, W. (1966) "Talaria and Ovid *Met.* 10.591" *TAPhA* **97**, 1–13.

(1972) *Ovid's* Metamorphoses: *Books 6–10*. Norman, OK.

(1989) "Lycaon: Ovid's deceptive paradigm in *Metamorphoses* I" *ICS* **14**, 91–101.

(1997) *Ovid's* Metamorphoses: *Books 1–5*. Norman, OK.

Austin, N. (1975) *Archery at the Dark of the Moon*. Berkeley, CA.

Baldo, G. (1995) *Dall'*Eneide *alle* Metamorfosi: *Il codice epico di Ovidio*. Padua.

(1997) " Una battaglia virgiliana (*Metamorfosi* 5.1–235)" in Papponetti (ed.), 143–65.

Bannert, H. (1978) "Zur Vogelgestalt der Götter bei Homer" *WS* N.S. **12**, 29–42.

Barchiesi, A. (1989) "Voci e istanze narrativi nelle *Metamorfosi* di Ovidio" *MD* **23**, 55–97.

(1997) "Poeti epici e narratori" in Papponetti (ed.), 121–41.

(2005a) "Learned eyes: poets, viewers, image makers" in Galinsky, K. (ed.) *The Cambridge Companion to the Age of Augustus*, 281–305. Cambridge.

(ed.) (2005b) *Ovidio:* Metamorfosi, vol. I, *Libri I–II*. Milan.

(ed.) (2007) *Ovidio:* Metamorfosi, vol. II, *Libri III–IV*. Milan.

Barkan, L. (1986) *The Gods Made Flesh: Metamorphosis and the Pursuit of Paganism*. New Haven, CT.

Ben-Porat, Z. (1992) "Poetics of the Homeric simile and the theory of (poetic) simile" in Shen, Y. (ed.) *Aspects of Metaphor Comprehension*, Special Issue, *Poetics Today* **13**(4).

Bernbeck, E. (1967) *Beobachtungen zur Darstellungsart in Ovids* Metamorphosen. Munich.

Bethlehem, L. (1996) "Simile and figurative language" *Poetics Today* **17**, 203–6.

Bettini, M. (1991) "Sosia e il suo sosia: pensare il doppio a Roma" in R. Oniga (ed.) *Plauto.* Anfitrione: *traduzione e commento*, 9–51. Padua.

(1999) *Portrait of the Lover*. Berkeley, CA.
Bömer, F. (1958) *P. Ovidius Naso: Die* Fasten, vols. 1–2. Heidelberg.
(1969–86) *P. Ovidius Naso:* Metamorphosen – *Kommentar*, vols. 1–7. Heidelberg.
Bongie, E. (1977) "Heroic elements in the *Medea* of Euripides" *TAPhA* **107**, 27–56.
Boyd, B. W. (1997) *Ovid's Literary Loves: Influence and Innovation in the* Amores. Ann Arbor, MI.
Brenkman, J. (1976) "Narcissus in the text", *Georgia Review* **30**, 293–327.
Brogan, J. (1986) *Stevens and Simile*. Princeton, NJ.
Brooke-Rose, C. (1958) *A Grammar of Metaphor*. London.
Brown, R. (1987) "The Palace of the Sun in Ovid's *Metamorphoses*" in M. Whitby, P. Hardie, and M. Whitby (eds.) Homo viator*: Classical Essays for John Bramble*, 211–20. Oak Park, IL.
Brunner, T. (1966) "The function of the simile in Ovid's *Metamorphoses*", *CJ* **61,** 354–63.
(1971) "Deinon vs. eleeinon: Heinze revisited" *AJPh* **92**, 275–84.
Burgess, A. (2001) "Coronis aflame: the gender of mortality" *CPh* **96**, 214–27.
Bushnell, R. (1982) "Reading 'winged words': Homeric bird signs, similes and epiphanies" *Helios* **9**(1), 1–13.
Conte, G. B. (1986) *The Rhetoric of Imitation:. Genre and Poetic Memory in Virgil and Other Latin Poets*. Ithaca, NY.
(1994) *Genres and Readers: Lucretius,* Love Elegy, *Pliny's* Encyclopedia, transl. G. W. Most. Ithaca, NY.
Davis, G. (1983) *The Death of Procris*. Rome.
Davisson, M. (1997) "The observers of Daedalus and Icarus in Ovid" *CW* **90**(4), 263–78.
de Jong, I. (2004) *Narrators and Focalizers: The Presentation of the Story in the* Iliad, 2nd edn. London.
Detienne, M. (1972) *Les jardins d'Adonis*. Paris.
Dirlmeier, F. (1967) *Die Vogelgestalt homerischer Götter*. Heidelberg.
Due, O. (1974) *Changing Forms: Studies in the* Metamorphoses *of Ovid*. Copenhagen.
Dyson, J. (1999) "Lilies and violence: Lavinia's blush in the song of Orpheus" *CPh* **94**, 281–8.
Easterling, P. (1985) "Anachronism in Greek tragedy" *JHS* **105**, 1–10.
Edmunds, L. (2001) *Intertextuality and the Reading of Roman Poetry*. Baltimore, MD.
Edwards, M. (1991) *The* Iliad: *A Commentary*, vol. v, *Books 17–20*. Cambridge.
Effe, B. (2001) "The simile of Apollonius Rhodius: Intertextuality and epic innovation" in T. Papanghelis (ed.) *A Companion to Apollonius Rhodius*, 147–69. Leiden.
Ellsworth, J. (1980) "Ovid's *Iliad* (*Metamorphoses* 12.1–13.622" *Prudentia* **12**, 23–9.
Elsner, J. (1996) "Naturalism and the erotics of the gaze: intimations of Narcissus" in N. B. Kampen (ed.) *Sexuality in Ancient Art: Near East, Egypt, Greece, Italy*, 247–61. Cambridge.

(2000) "Visualising Narcissus in the Roman world" in L. Spaas, (ed.) *Echoes of Narcissus*, 89–110. Oxford.

Erbse, H. (1971) *Scholia Graeca in Homeri Iliadem*, vol. 2. Berlin.

(1980) " Homerische Götter in Vogelgestalt" *Hermes* **108**, 259–74.

Fabre-Serris, J. (1995) *Mythe et poésie dans les* Métamorphoses. Paris.

Fantham, E. (1979) "Ovid's Ceyx and Alcyone: metamorphosis of a myth", *Phoenix* **33**(4), 330–45.

(1993) "Sunt quibus in plures ius est transire figuras: Ovid's self-transformers in the *Metamorphoses*" *CW* **87**, 21–36.

Farrell, J. (1992) "Dialogue of genres in Ovid's 'Lovesong of Polyphemus' (*Metamorphoses* 13.719–897)" *AJPh* **113**, 235–68.

(1994) "Review of David Quint, *Epic and Empire: Politics and Generic Form from Virgil to Milton*, Princeton, 1993, and Susanne Lindgren Wofford, *The Choice of Achilles: The Ideology of Figure in the Epic*, Stanford, 1992" *BMCRev* 94.02.06. http://ccat.sas.upenn.edu/bmcr/1994/94.02.06.html.

Feeney, D. (1991) *The Gods in Epic: Poets and Critics of the Classical Tradition*. Oxford.

(1992) " 'Shall I compare thee…?' Catullus 68 and the limits of analogy" in A. J. Woodman and J. Powell (eds.) *Authors and Audience in Latin Literature*, 33–44. Cambridge.

(1993) "Towards an account of the ancient world's concepts of fictive belief" in C. Gill C. and T. Wiseman (eds.) *Lies and Fiction in the Ancient World*, 230–44. Austin, TX.

(1999a) "Epic violence, epic order: killings, catalogues and the role of the reader in *Aeneid* 10" in C. Perkell (ed.) *Reading Virgil's* Aeneid: *An Interpretative Guide*, 178–94. Norman, OK.

(1999b) "Mea tempora: patterning of time in Ovid's *Metamorphoses*" in P. Hardie, A. Barchiesi, and S. Hinds (eds.) *Ovidian Transformations*, 13–30. Cambridge.

(1999c) *Literature and Religion at Rome*. Cambridge.

(2004) "Interpreting sacrificial ritual in Roman poetry: disciplines and their models" in A. Barchiesi, J. Rüpke, and S. Stephens, (eds.) *Rituals in Ink: A Conference on Religion and Literary Production in Ancient Rome*, 1–21. Stuttgart.

Feldherr, A. (1997) "Metamorphosis and sacrifice in Ovid's Theban narrative" *MD* **38**, 25–55.

(2002) "Metamorphosis in the *Metamorphoses*" in P. Hardie (eds.) *The Cambridge Companion to Ovid*, 163–79. Cambridge.

(2004–5) "Reconciling Niobe" *Hermathena* **177–8** (double issue), 125–44.

Feldherr, A. and James, P. (2004) "Making the most of Marsyas" *Arethusa* **37**(1), 77–103.

Fludernik, M., Freeman, D. C., and Freeman, M. H. (1997) "Metaphor and beyond: an introduction" *Poetics Today* **20**, 383–96.

Fowler, D. (1991) "Narrate and describe: the problem of ekphrasis" *JRS* **81**, 25–35.

Fränkel, H. (1945) *Ovid: A Poet between Two Worlds*. Berkeley, CA.

Freese, J. (1994) *Aristotle: The "Art" of Rhetoric.* Cambridge, MA.
Frontisi-Ducroux, F. and Vernant, J.-P. (1997) *Dans l'oeil du miroir.* Paris.
Galinsky, K. (1975) *Ovid's* Metamorphoses: *An Introduction to the Basic Aspects.* Berkeley, CA.
Gentilcore, R. (1995) "The landscape of desire: the tale of Pomona and Vertumnus in Ovid's *Metamorphoses*" *Phoenix* **49**, 110–20.
Gildenhard, I. and Zissos, A. (1999) "Problems of time in Ovid's *Metamorphoses* 2", in P. Hardie, A. Barchiesi, and S. Hinds (eds.) *Ovidian Transformations: Essays on Ovid's* Metamorphoses *and Its Reception*, 31–47. Cambridge.
Ginsberg, W. (1989) "Ovid's *Metamorphoses* and the politics of interpretation" *CJ* **84**, 222–31.
Griffin, J. (1977) "The epic cycle and the uniqueness of Homer", *JHS* **97**, 39–53.
Gross, N. (1979) "Rhetorical wit and amatory persuasion in Ovid" *CJ* **74**, 305–18.
Haege, H. (1976) *Terminologie und Typologie des Verwandlungsvorgangs in den* Metamorphosen *Ovids.* Göppingen.
Hainsworth, J. B., Heubeck, A., and West, S. (1988) *A Commentary on Homer's* Odyssey, vol. 1, *Introduction and Books I–VIII.* Oxford.
Hardie, P. (1988) "Lucretius and the delusions of Narcissus". *MD* **20/21**, 71–89.
(1990) "Ovid's Theban history: the first Anti-Aeneid?", *CQ* **40**(1), 224–35.
(1993) "Review of Schmidt (1991)" *CR* **43**(2), 264.
(1999) "Metamorphosis, metaphor and allegory in Latin epic" in M. Beissinger, J. Tylus, and S. Wofford (eds.) *Epic Traditions in the Contemporary World: The Poetics of Community*, 89–107. Berkeley, CA.
(2002) *Ovid's Poetics of Illusion.* Cambridge.
(2004) "Approximative similes in Ovid: incest and doubling" *Dictynna* **1**, 83–112. http://dictynna.revues.org/166.
Harrison, S. (2002) "Ovid and genre: evolutions of an elegist", in P. Hardie (ed.) *The Cambridge Companion to Ovid*, 79–94. Cambridge.
Heath, J. (1991) "Diana's understanding of Ovid's *Metamorphoses*" *CJ* **86**, 233–43.
Henderson, A. A. R (1979) *Ovid* Metamorphoses *III: A Commentary.* Bristol.
Hinds, S. (1987) *The Metamorphosis of Persephone: Ovid and the Self-Conscious Muse.* Cambridge.
(1993) "Ovid's Medea: scenes from the life of an intertextual heroine" *MD* **30**, 9–47.
(2000) "Essential epic: genre and gender from Macer to Statius" in M. Depew and D. Obbink (eds.) *Matrices of Genre: Authors, Canons and Society*, 221–44. Cambridge, MA.
Hoefmans, M. (1998) "Myth into reality: the metamorphosis of Daedalus and Icarus (Ovid, *Metamorphoses*, VIII, 183–235)" *Hermes* **126**(1), 80–160.
Holoka, J. (1985) "The point of the simile in Aeschylus' *Agamemnon* 241" *CPh* **80**, 228–9.
Holzberg, N. (2002) *Ovid: The Poet and His Work.* Ithaca, NY.
Hopkinson, N. (ed.) (2000) *Ovid:* Metamorphoses *XIII.* Cambridge.

Hornsby, R. (1970) *Patterns of Action in the* Aeneid: *An Interpretation of Virgil's Epic Similes*. Iowa City, IO.
Humphries, R. (1955) *Metamorphoses*. Bloomington, IN.
Hunter, R. (2006) *The Shadow of Callimachus: Studies in the Reception of Hellenistic Poetry at Rome*. Cambridge.
James, P. (1986) "Crises of identity in Ovid's *Metamorphoses*" *BICS* **33**, 17–25.
(1991–3) "Pentheus Anguigena: sins of the father" *BICS* **38**, 81–93.
Janan, M. (1988) "The book of good love? Design versus desire in *Metamorphoses* 10" *Ramus* **17**, 110–37.
Janko, R. (1986) "The shield of Heracles and the legend of Cycnus" *CQ* **36**, 38–59.
(1992) *The* Iliad: *A Commentary* vol. IV, *Books 13–16*. Cambridge.
Johnson, W. R. (1997) "Vertumnus in Love" *CPh* **92**(4), 367–75.
Kaufhold, D. (1993) "The reification of figurative language in Ovid's *Metamorphoses*", PhD dissertation, Cornell University.
(1997) "Ovid's Tereus: fire, birds, and the reification of figurative language" *CPh* **92**(1), 66–71.
Keith, A. (1999) "Versions of epic masculinity in Ovid's *Metamorphoses*"in P. Hardie, A. Barchiesi, and S. Hinds (eds.) *Ovidian Transformations: Essays on Ovid's* Metamorphoses *and Its Reception*, 214–39. Cambridge.
(2000) *Engendering Rome: Women in Latin Epic*. Cambridge.
(2002a) "Sources and genres in Ovid's *Metamorphoses* 1–5" in B. Boyd (ed.) *Brill's Companion to Ovid*, 235–69. Leiden.
(2002b) "Ovid on Virgilian war narrative" *Vergilius* **48**, 105–22.
Kerrigan, J. (1996) *Revenge Tragedy: Aeschylus to Armageddon*. Oxford.
Kirby, J. (1997) "Aristotle on metaphor" *AJPh* **118**, 517–54.
Klein, F. (2005) "Rursus pomi jactu remorata secundi (*Mét.* x, 671): La mora et la poétique ovidienne de la brièveté" *Dictynna* **2**, 135–64. http://dictynna.revues.org/133.
Knox, P. (1986) *Ovid's* Metamorphoses *and The Traditions of Augustan Poetry*. Cambridge.
Labate, M. (1997) "Un altro Omero: scene di battaglia nelle *Metamorfosi* di Ovidio" in Papponetti (ed.), 143–65.
Lane Fox, R. (1986) *Pagans and Christians*. New York.
Lateiner, D. (1984) "Mythic and non-mythic artists in Ovid's *Metamorphoses*" *Ramus* **13**, 1–30.
Lausberg, M. (1989) "Iliadisches im ersten Buch der *Aeneis*" *Gymnasium* **90**, 203–39.
Leach, E. (1974) "Ecphrasis and the theme of artistic failure in Ovid's Metamorphoses" *Ramus* **3**, 102–42.
Lindheim, S. (1998) "I am dressed, therefore I am?: Vertumnus in Propertius 4.2 and in *Metamorphoses* 14.622–771" *Ramus* **27**, 27–38.
Lonsdale, S. (1990) *Creatures of Speech: Lion, Herding and Hunting Similes in the* Iliad. Stuttgart.
Lyne, R. O. A. M. (1989) *Words and The Poet*. Oxford.

Mandelbaum, A. (1993). *The* Metamorphoses *of Ovid: A New Verse Translation.* New York.
McCall, M. (1969) *Ancient Rhetorical Theories of Simile and Comparison.* Cambridge, MA.
McKeown, J. (1979) "Ovid, *Amores* 3.12" *Papers of the Liverpool Seminar* **2**, 163–77.
(1987) *Ovid* Amores: *Text, Prolegomena, and Commentary*, 4 vols. Liverpool.
Mencacci, F. (1996) *I fratelli amici: La rappresentazione dei gemelli nella cultura romana*. Venice.
Miller, J. (1990) "Orpheus as owl and stag: Ovid *Met.* 11.24–27" *Phoenix* **44**(2), 140–7.
(1999) "The Lamentations of Apollo" in W. Schubert, (eds.) *Ovid Werk und Wirkung: Festgabe für Michael von Albrecht zum 65. Geburtstag*, vol. 1, 413–22. Frankfurt am/Main.
Miller, P. (1994) *Dreams in Late Antiquity: Studies in the Imagination of a Culture.* Princeton, NJ.
Mossman, J. (1995) *Wild Justice: A study of Euripides'* Hecuba. Oxford.
Moulton, C. (1977) *Similes in the Homeric Poems.* Göttingen.
Musgrove, M. (1998) "Nestor's centauromachy and the deceptive voice of poetic memory (Ovid, *Met.* 12.182–535)" *CPh* **93**(3), 223–31.
Myers, K. (1994) *Ovid's Causes: Cosmogony and Aetiology in the* Metamorphoses. Ann Arbor, MI.
Näf, B. (2004) *Traum und Traumdeutung im Altertum*. Darmstadt.
Newlands, C. (1986) "The simile of the fractured pipe in Ovid *Metamorphoses* 4" *Ramus* **15**, 143–53.
(2005) "Ovid" in J. Foley (ed.) *A Companion to Ancient Epic*, 476–91. Oxford.
Nicoll, W. S. (1980) "Cupid, Apollo and Daphne (Ovid, *Met.* 1.452ff.)" *CQ* **30**, 174–82.
Olmsted, W. (1997) "The uses of rhetoric: indeterminacy in legal reasoning, practical thinking, and the interpretation of literary figures" in W. Jost and M. Hyde (eds.) *Rhetoric and Hermeneutics in Our Time: A Reader*, 235–53. New Haven, CT.
Otis, B. (1970) *Ovid as an Epic Poet*, 2nd edn. London.
Owen, S. G. (1931) "Ovid's use of the simile" *CR* **45**, 97–106.
Papathomopoulos, M. (ed.) (1968) *Antoninus Liberalis: Les* Métamorphoses. Paris.
Papponetti, G. (ed.) (1997) Metamorfosi: *Atti del convegno Internazionale di Studi, Sulmona 20–22 Novembre 1994*. Sulmona.
Parry, H. (1965) "Ovid's *Metamorphoses*: violence in a pastoral landscape". *TAPhA* **95**, 268–82.
Pfister, F. (1924) "Epiphanie" *RE* Suppl. **4**, 277–323.
Pianezzola, E. (1979) "La *Metamorfosi* ovidiana come metafora narrativa" in *Retorica e poetica, Atti del III Covegno Italo-Tedesco*. Padua.

Porter, D. (1972) "Violent juxtaposition in the similes of the *Iliad*" *CJ* **68**(1), 11–21.

Pucci, P. (1997) *The Song of the Sirens: Essays on Homer*. Lanham, MA.

Quint, D. (1993) *Epic and Empire: Politics and Generic form from Virgil to Milton*. Princeton, NJ.

Raeburn, D. (2004) *Ovid* Metamorphoses: *A New Verse Translation*. London.

Reed, D. (1997) *Bion of Smyrna: The Fragments and the* Adonis. Cambridge.

Richards, I. A. (1936) *The Philosophy of Rhetoric*. Oxford.

Richardson, J. (1964) "The function of formal imagery in Ovid's Metamorphoses" *CJ* **59**, 161–9.

Richlin, A. (1992) "Reading Ovid's rapes" in A. Richlin (ed.) *Pornography and Representation in Greece and Rome*, 158–79. Oxford.

Ronen, R. (1988) "Completing the incompleteness of fictional entities" *Poetics Today* **9**(3), 497–514.

Rosati, G. (1983) *Narciso e Pigmalione: illusione e spettacolo nelle* Metamorfosi *di Ovidio*. Florence.

Rossi, A. (2003) *Contexts of War: Manipulation of Genre in Virgilian Battle Narrative*. Ann Arbor, MI.

Rudd, N. (1988) "Daedalus and Icarus (ii): from the Renaissance to the present day " in C. Martindale (ed.) *Ovid Renewed*, 37–53. Cambridge.

Russo, J. (1985) *Omero:* Odissea. vol. v, *Libri XVII–XX*. Milan.

Ryan, M.-L. (1995) "Allegories of immersion: virtual narration in postmodern fiction" *Style* **29**(2), 262–86.

Salzman-Mitchell, P. (2005a) "The fixing gaze: movement, image, and gender in Ovid's *Metamorphoses*" in R. Ancona and E. Greene (eds.) *Gendered Dynamics in Latin Love Poetry*, 159–76. Baltimore, MD.

(2005b) *A Web of Fantasies: Gaze, Image, and Gender in Ovid's* Metamorphoses. Columbus, OH.

Sandbach, F. (1990) "Anti-antiquarianism in the *Aeneid*" in S. Harrison (ed.) *Oxford Readings in Virgil's* Aeneid, 449–65. Oxford.

Schiesaro, A. (1990) *Simulacrum et imago: gli argomenti analogici nel* De rerum natura. Pisa.

Schlunk, R. (1974) *The Homeric Scholia and the* Aeneid: *A Study of the Influence of Ancient Literary Criticism on Virgil*. Ann Arbor, MI.

Schmidt, E. (1991) *Ovids Poetische Menschenwelt: Die* Metamorphosen *als Metapher und Symphonie*. Heidelberg.

Schmit-Neuerberg, T. (1999) *Vergils* Aeneis *und die antike Homerexegese*. Berlin.

Scodel, R. (1999) *Credible Impossibilities: Conventions and Strategies of Verisimilitude in Homer and Greek Tragedy*. Stuttgart.

Seaford, R. (1989). "Epic and tragic sacrifice" *TAPhA* **119**, 87–95.

Segal, C. (1998) "Ovid's metamorphic bodies: art, gender, and violence in the *Metamorphoses*" *Arion*, 3 ser. **5**(3), 9–41.

Sharrock, A. (1991) "Womanufacture" *JRS* **81**, 36–49.

(1994) *Seduction and Repetition in Ovid's* Ars Amatoria *II*. Oxford.

(1996) "Representing metamorphosis" in J. Elsner (ed.) *Art and Text in Roman Culture*, 103–30. Cambridge.

(2002a) "Looking at looking: can you resist a reading?" in D. Fredrick (ed.) *The Roman Gaze*, 265–95. Baltimore, MD.

(2002b) "Gender and sexuality" in P. Hardie (ed.) *The Cambridge Companion to Ovid*, 95–107. Cambridge.

Silk, M. S. (1974) *Interaction in Greek Poetry with Special Reference to Early Greek Poetry*. Cambridge.

Skulsky, H. (1981) *The Mind in Exile*. Cambridge, MA.

Solodow, J. (1988) *The World of Ovid's* Metamorphoses. Chapel Hill, NC.

Stevens, W. (1974) *The Collected Poems of Wallace Stevens*. New York.

Tarrant, R. (2002) "Ovid and ancient literary history" in P. Hardie (ed.) *The Cambridge Companion to Ovid*, 13–33. Cambridge.

(2004) *P. Ovidi Nasonis* Metamorphoses. Oxford.

Thomas, R. (1998) "Voice, poetics and Virgil's Sixth Eclogue" in J. Jasonoff, H. Melcher, and L. Oliver (eds.) *Mír Curad: Studies in Honor of Calvert Watkins*, 669–76. Innsbruck.

Tissol, G. (1997) *The Face of Nature: Wit, Narrative, and Cosmic Origins in Ovid's* Metamorphoses. Princeton, NJ.

Versnel, H. (1987) "What did Ancient Man see when he saw a god? Some reflections on Graeco-Roman antiquity", in D. van der Plas (ed.) *Effigies Dei*, 42–55. Leiden.

(1999) *Roman Epic: An Interpretative Introduction*. Leiden.

Washietl, J. (1883) *De similitudinibus imaginibusque Ovidianis*. Vienna.

West, S. (1988) *A Commentary on Homer's* Odyssey, vol. 2. New York.

Wheeler, S. (1995) "Imago mundi: another view of the Creation in Ovid's *Metamorphoses*" *AJPh* **116**(1), 95–121.

(1999) *A Discourse of Wonders: Audience and Performance in Ovid's* Metamorphoses. Philadelphia, PA.

(2000) *Narrative Dynamics in Ovid's* Metamorphoses. Tübingen

Wilkins, E. G. (1932) "A classification of the similes of Ovid" *CW* **25**, 73–8 and 81–6.

Zgoll, C. (2004) *Phänomenologie der Metamorphose: Verwandlungen und Verwandtes in der augusteischen Dichtung*. Tübingen.

Zumwalt, N. (1978) "*Fama subversa*: theme and structure in Ovid *Metamorphoses* 12" *California Studies in Classical Antiquity* **10**, 209–22.

Index locorum

General index

Printed in Great Britain
by Amazon

44067493R00108